DIGITAL ARTS

Bloomsbury *New Media* Series

ISSN 1753-724X

Edited by Leslie Haddon, Department of Media and Communications, London School of Economics and Political Sciences, and Nicola Green, Department of Sociology, University of Surrey.

The series aims to provide students with historically grounded and theoretically informed studies of significant aspects of new media. The volumes take a broad approach to the subject, assessing how technologies and issues related to them are located in their social, cultural, political and economic contexts.

Titles in this series will include:

Mobile Communications: An Introduction to New Media

The Internet: An Introduction to New Media

Games and Gaming: An Introduction to New Media

Digital Broadcasting: An Introduction to New Media

Digital Arts: An Introduction to New Media

DIGITAL ARTS

An Introduction to New Media

Cat Hope and John Ryan

Bloomsbury Academic
An imprint of Bloomsbury Publishing Plc

B L O O M S B U R Y
NEW YORK • LONDON • NEW DELHI • SYDNEY

Bloomsbury Academic
An imprint of Bloomsbury Publishing Inc

1385 Broadway	50 Bedford Square
New York	London
NY 10018	WC1B 3DP
USA	UK

www.bloomsbury.com

BLOOMSBURY and the Diana logo are trademarks of Bloomsbury Publishing Plc

First published 2014
Reprinted 2014

Library of Congress Cataloging-in-Publication Data
A catalog record for this book is available from the Library of Congress.

ISBN:	HB:	978-1-7809-3320-7
	PB:	978-1-7809-3323-8
	ePub:	978-1-7809-3321-4
	ePDF:	978-1-7809-3329-0

Typeset by Fakenham Prepress Solutions, Fakenham, Norfolk NR21 8NN
Printed and bound in the United States of America

CONTENTS

ACKNOWLEDGEMENTS

We thank the series editors, Leslie Haddon and Nicola Green, for their editorial advice and detailed input on chapter drafts. Our appreciation goes to the School of Communications and Arts (SCA), Western Australian Academy of Performing Arts (WAAPA), CREATEC Research Centre and Debbie Rodan at Edith Cowan University for sustained practical support on many levels. Also to Sally Knowles and the Faculty of Education and Arts (FEA) at ECU for the opportunities they provided to complete early drafts of individual chapters during writing retreats. We are particularly grateful for the wonderful contribution made to the final copy by Linda Jaunzems.

Our sincere thanks goes to Lelia Green for her ongoing mentorship and collegial support, without which this book would not have been possible. Lelia has continuously and generously supported the authors through thick and thin. We are very grateful.

We acknowledge Malcolm Riddoch and Jonathan W. Marshall as valuable early contributors to the project. Cat Hope personally thanks Karl Ockelford, Luke, Jazmine, Helen Hope and Lisa MacKinney for their ongoing support and listening. And finally we thank the artists themselves, and in particular those who have allowed us to include images of their works.

1 INTRODUCTION

From online information searches and e-commerce transactions to mobile phone messaging and flash drives, we are immersed in the digital realm on an everyday basis. Information about the world, encoded in the form of digital data, expands exponentially. Consider a yottabyte (YB). It is equivalent to all the books ever written in every language, 62 billion iPhones or one septillion bytes. The American states of Delaware and Rhode Island, divided into city block-sized data warehouses, would currently be what is needed to store a single yottabyte using the average capacity of PC hard drives today. Yet, in the not-so-distant future, a yottabyte could be contained in a miniscule area no larger than a pinhead. Technologies and data rapidly evolve and spread out. Through this kind of futuristic perspective, it could be argued that everything in the natural, material world will soon have a digital, virtual counterpart, of one form or another, or even be replaced by it. These counterparts – as digital data – offer not only unprecedented possibilities for science and technology but also for cultural identity, creative practice and interdisciplinary thinking.

The proliferation of technologies has greatly impacted the arts, leading to what artists and critics now call 'the digital arts'. Artists love to experiment with new technologies, and they have done so throughout history. In Chapter 1 we explore existing theoretical perspectives on the digital arts and discuss the spectrum of artistic approaches that have appeared as digital technology and data continue to progress. The explosion of new media has revolutionized the production of art – redefining the nature of arts criticism, creating more complex markets for art and enhancing public access to the arts. We suggest that an essential first step towards understanding the digital arts is distinguishing the term from discrete but related art forms, including new media, electronic, computer, internet, behaviourist, telematic, virtual and unstable media art. The principal perspectives and contexts explored throughout the volume are democratization, globalization and interdisciplinarity. Towards the end of this chapter, we introduce subsequent chapters in the book and explain key student-focused components, including case studies, reflections, questions and group exercises. Central to this introductory chapter and others is the idea of digital art as part of the ongoing continuum of technology that artists have been fascinated with throughout history – a theme further developed in Chapter 2. But first, we will talk about how to define digitality – the technological foundation of digital art.

WHAT IS DIGITALITY?

The term 'digital' is a ubiquitous part of our vernacular in today's ever more globalized world. The digital revolution of the 1990s introduced computer power to the public at an unparalleled rate (Lovejoy et al. 2011: 2). This period entailed a significant transfer in the production, storage and distribution of data to digital technologies. Multimedia or hypertext documents combining text, images, sound and video have become standard. Living in the 'digital age' now, we frequently come across 'digital technology', 'digital information' and of course, 'digital art', but what does it mean for something – including creative work – to be digital? Indeed, to understand digital art as a movement, we need to start from the ground floor and examine briefly the mechanics of digitality. Typically, the digital is defined as new technology in contrast to older, pre-digital or analogue forms. In digital media, input data – as light (images), sound (audio) or spatial configurations (text, graphs, diagrams) – is converted to numerical patterns, which are then processed and manipulated in various ways by a computer's hardware and software (Lister et al. 2003: 14). Through digital processing, the physical properties of phenomena become numbers or abstract symbols.

In this sense, 'digital' simply means the 'assignation of numerical values to phenomena' (Lister et al. 2003: 15–16). Hence, 'digital' is a mathematical format and process for storing, transferring and modifying information. Algorithms in computer software subject the data to numerical processing. For example, digital image files consist of discrete modular components; assembling these modules into an image requires a series of mathematical executions (see Chapter 3). The numerical system behind digitality is binary, employing variations of 0s and 1s to produce alternating states that underlie how devices function: for example, off or on, current or no current. The conversion of data to a binary schema enables the transfer and storage of information to memory technology (hard drives), digital disks (CDs or DVDs) or online repositories (file hosting and storage services). The modern mathematical processes behind digital technology were founded in the work of German mathematician Gottfried Wilhelm Leibniz (1646–1716), English inventor Charles Babbage (1791–1871) and in the 1930s, English mathematician Alan Turing (1912–54) (see Chapters 2 and 6).

When traditional media (e.g. newspapers, video, records) are digitized, they become dematerialized at the same time. The process of digitization involves the shift from the physical domain described by physics, chemistry, biology and engineering to the symbolic domain explored by computer science (Lister et al. 2003: 16). In other words, the materiality of the original (i.e. paper, magnetic tape, vinyl) is super-seded by an immaterial binary pattern and, therefore, the original medium becomes largely redundant. Requiring specialized technology, such as specific software, digital data (released from their physical media) can be compressed, accessed at high speeds and readily manipulated (Lister et al. 2003: 16).

Whereas digital media exist in a state of flux, analogue media are comparatively fixed. Analogue media, including newspapers, photographs, tapes and films, tend to be associated with technologies of mass production. Yet analogue processes transfer data to another physical object (an 'analogue'), such as light, sound or handwriting, where it is encoded and stored to a physical medium (i.e. grooves on a vinyl record, magnetic particles on a tape or ink on a sheet of paper). An *analogous* relationship is thus forged between the original data and the tangible medium. For instance, the analogue reproduction of a book employs movable type and ink to produce a physical imprint of the original on paper (Lister et al. 2003: 15). In contrast, a book written on a computer undergoes a different process; every letter of the manuscript generates a binary value in response to the touching of the author's fingers to the keyboard. The resulting digital document can be exported in various ways (e.g. as an email attachment, PDF or ZIP file) and eventually published as an e-book without ever being printed to the traditional, material medium. Electronic broadcasting media were also historically analogue. For example, the physical properties of images and sounds were converted to wave forms of differing lengths and intensities, corre-sponding to the voltage of transmission signals.

Reflection

What are some of the ways that digital technologies have revolutionized your life and the society you live in? How often and for what reasons do you use digital devices? Can you think of any disadvantages to using 'the digital' over 'the analogue'? We will return to these sorts of questions in Chapter 2.

WHAT IS DIGITAL ART?

'Digital art' is a name that shifts in the sands of digitality, culture, history, science and art. Impossible to define as a single phenomenon, it represents instead a fluid set of artistic techniques, technologies and concepts – often associated with the history of the computer. There are a great many names for digital art, some of which are more current or useful than others. An important first push for students is to become familiar with the terms in circulation and how they overlap and differ. Indeed, it is difficult to find an academic commentator who will commit to a straight-forward definition, but Beryl Graham has come the closest. She defines digital art simply as 'art made with, and for, digital media including the internet, digital imaging, or computer-controlled installations' (Graham 2007: 93). However, what we now think of as 'digital art' has undergone a multitude of name changes, from 'computer art' in the 1970s to 'multimedia art' in the early 1990s to 'new media art' more recently. In many ways, 'digital art' is outdated language, subsumed within the category of new media art by the end of the 1990s.

Nevertheless, the variety of related words in currency demonstrates that digital art and its naming are 'characteristically in a state of flux' (Graham 2007: 106) – reflecting, in part, the mutability and constant evolution of the technologies used by artists. The bevy of names (often erroneously used as synonyms for digital art) includes – in addition to new media, multimedia and computer art – software art, hypermedia art, emergent media art, unstable media art, electronic art, internet art, net art, browser art, behaviourist art, cybernetic art, telepresence art, virtual art, interactive art and participatory art, among others. The meaning of each term should be considered variable and highly contingent on the historical time frame, the commentator's background (e.g. artist, programmer, curator, archivist or critic) and the technology explored as a medium by the artist. Furthermore, certain terms are subsets of the broader practice of digital art; for example, internet art is based on the internet, browser art makes use of internet browsers and software art involves computer software in some manner. Other terms, such as behaviourist, interactive and sound art are more inclusive than 'digital art' and encompass a continuum of analogue and digital art practices, from site-based installation works to internet-based telerobotics projects. Still, others are period-specific and seem like anachronisms to us now; for example, 'net art' designates the internet art of practitioners working in the 1990s (see Chapter 6).

Despite the name-game, the tendency to hybridize across media boundaries is characteristic of digital art, as we will see in Chapter 2. Thus, by shifting between media and employing a range of techniques, digital artworks eschew categorization according to their genre or form. Installation, film, video, animation, photography, internet art, software art, virtual reality projects and musical compositions can fall under its umbrella (Paul 2003: 70). Rather than venturing definitions, critics tend to foreground the attributes of digital artworks. For example, Bruce Wands points to the new forms that emerge out of digital art practices: 'intricate images that could not be created by hand; sculptures formed in three-dimensional databases rather than in stone or metal; interactive installations that involve internet participation from around the globe; and virtual worlds within which artificial life forms live and die' (Wands 2006: 8). As Christiane Paul (2003: 7) argues, digital art comprises a broad array of practices but lacks a single, unifying aesthetic approach. She makes the critical distinction between digital technologies as tools and technologies as media (see Chapter 2). In this book, we use 'digital art' to refer to the artistic movement encompassing a variety of digital practices. In many instances, we also use the pluralized term 'the digital arts' to stress the diversity of art forms and media (e.g. internet art, software art, telematic art, etc.) included within the singular term. As we see in the next section, an introduction to digital art is very much an exploration of terminology in relation to the history of art and technology.

Reflection

Describe a few examples of digital art that you have seen or experienced in the last week, either online, in public or in a gallery or museum setting. What is distinctive about these digital artworks?

DIGITAL ART AND ITS RELATIVES: UNDERSTANDING THE TYPOLOGIES

New Media Art

Although 'new media art' is often used synonymously with 'digital art', 'computer art', 'multimedia art' and 'interactive art', there are some key differences between these terms to consider. Understanding what constitutes digital art entails understanding the way everyday language changes in the context of technology. For instance, the terms 'digital media' and 'digital new media' have been used to refer to 'new media' (Lister et al. 2003: 14). In the early 1990s, with the release of the first commercial internet browser and the beginning of the digital revolution, the term 'new media art' began to be used by artists, critics and curators working with emerging technologies (Tribe and Jana 2006). Indeed, the appearance of new media art paralleled the proliferation of information technologies. Early new media artworks included interactive installations exploiting a variety of media, virtual reality experiments, telerobotics pieces and web browser-based projects, all using the latest digital technologies of the time. Mark Tribe and Reena Jana define new media art as 'projects that make use of emerging media technologies and are concerned with the cultural, political, and aesthetic possibilities of these tools' (2006: 'Defining New Media Art').

In situating new media art as a distinct movement, Tribe and Jana (2006) distinguish between the categories 'art and technology' (in reference to the collective Experiments in Art and Technology founded in 1967) and 'media art'. On the one hand, 'art and technology' encompasses computer, electronic, robotic, genomic and biological art involving up-and-coming technologies, but not intrinsically media-related. On the other, 'media art' includes television, video and satellite art, as well as experimental film and other forms of art that make use of media technologies that were no longer considered new or emerging by the 1990s. For

Tribe and Jana, new media art represents the intersection of both movements, but with an emphasis on 'new' media technologies: the internet, social media, video and computer gaming, surveillance systems, mobile telephony, wearable technology and GPS (Global Positioning Systems) devices. New media artists critically or experimentally engage with new technologies. However, there are many art-historical precedents that have shaped new media art, including other art movements that questioned the relationships between art, culture and technology. In particular, Dadaism (see Chapter 6), pop art, conceptualism (Chapter 2) and the video art of the late 1960s, exemplified by the work of Nam June Paik (Case Study 2.3), have influenced the trajectory of new media art since its inception. Common themes in new media works include collaboration, participation, appropriation, hacktivism, telepresence and surveillance (Tribe and Jana 2006: 'Themes/ Tendencies') (see Chapter 2).

Electronic Art

The typology 'electronic art' is perhaps the most inclusive for our discussion, aside from the broad category of 'art' itself. It is also the term that has evolved the most since its initial historical emergence. Often interactive and participatory, electronic art incorporates electronic components in the production or display of a work. The range of electronic technologies is vast, and comprises the internet, computing, robotics, mobile devices and virtual reality platforms, as well as the 'old' media of radio, teleconferencing, video, television and film. Moreover, dance, music, performance, writing and installation pieces can be classified as electronic art if they incorporate electronic dimensions. Encompassing both old and new media, electronic art should not, by default, be classified as digital art. However, the adjective 'electronic' is often invoked interchangeably by critics in referring to digital, computer, internet or information-based art. We suggest that it is most instructive to think of the term 'electronic art' as denoting a particular period in the history of Western art, culture and technology. Indeed, the origins of electronic art can be traced back to the early to mid-twentieth century when innovators, notably Marcel Duchamp and, later, Ben Laposky, began to encounter and incorporate technologies in their works (Lovejoy 2004: 1). Electronic media, such as tape, projections and the computer, allowed artists to devise new modes of aesthetic representation and creative possibility. Within electronic art, video art is a central subgenre, especially as the medium melded over time with television, film and music (Rogers 2013; Rush 2003). Beginning in 1965 with the release of the Sony Portapak, video art demonstrates how progress in electronic and, later in the twentieth century, digital art has paralleled developments in technology and science (see Chapter 2 for art-historical precedents). The practices included within electronic and video art have developed rapidly since one of the first video artists, Nam June Paik, placed a magnet on top of a television set to distort the imagery, as discussed in detail in Chapter 2. Named after the analogue video tape, contemporary video art uses the digital media of CD-ROMs, DVDs and real-time streaming.

Computer Art

'Computer art' is another wide-ranging classification with shifting boundaries. It encompasses most forms of software, database, internet, browser and game art, as well as computer music. Broadly defined, computer art takes advantage of computing technology to create or display an artwork. As a subset of computer art, computer music refers to compositions that involve computer technologies at any point in their life cycles, although other definitions are more restrictive (Collins 2009: 2) (also see Chapter 5). According to Dominic Lopes, the two defining characteristics of computer art – interactivity and computing – distinguish it from other interactive performances and some forms of digital art (Lopes 2010: 52). As Lopes (2010: 52) further argues, 'the realms of computer art and digital art overlap. Not all digital art is computer art – most of it's not interactive – but typical computer art is either made digitally or made for digital display'. For other critics, interactivity is not a necessary component of computer art. Within the umbrella term is included a range of subgenres, such as software, database and game art, that evolved when artists began to involve computers in their practices in the mid-twentieth century (Wands 2006: 164).

Briefly, software art can be defined as 'creative work that finds its origins in programmes written by the artist' (Wands 2006: 164). For some critics, implicit within this definition is the notion of authorship; the artist-programmer tends to write the software code, although this is not always the case, as Chapter 3 explains. In slight contrast, database art often 'relies on pre-existing, created or real-time collections of information' while game art uses 'commercial gaming software or incorporates elements of play and role-playing' (Wands 2006: 164). Rather than creating code as part of an artwork, database art tends to reinterpret data collections or engage participants or viewers in the creation of datasets. Hybridity between aesthetics and technology is characteristic of most computer artworks. In particular, computer artists are competent with the use and development of software, including gaming platforms, database programs and computer languages such as C++, Java and Visual Basic. A prominent example of a computer artwork is Lynn Hershman Leeson's *Synthia* (2000–2), a sculpture using three-dimensional animation to represent streaming stock market data. The character Synthia responds according to market trends, for example, dancing when the stocks are up or chain-smoking when they drop (Wands 2006: 167).

Reflection

What do you think it means for an artwork to be interactive? Have you ever experienced an interactive artwork? If so, what were some of its characteristics?

Internet Art

As the typologies (i.e. new media, computer, behaviourist, cybernetic, telematic, virtual, unstable media) explored in this section reveal, there are different ways to classify and analyse digital artworks. Inevitably, the categories overlap and – as individual terms – are incomplete descriptions in themselves. A single work (such as the work *Dialogue with the Knowbotic South* explored under the heading 'virtual art' later in this section) may exhibit aspects of all categories, depending on which of its components is emphasized. Like 'computer art', 'internet art' is another example of an umbrella term for various interrelated digital arts practices. Within internet art falls a variety of practices (Lovejoy et al. 2011: 7). For example, some software art is coded by artist-programmers and made publicly available over networks. Internet browser-based artworks use software such as Netscape Navigator. Telerobotics works connect remote places and participants via webcams. Participatory performance works are created by online visitors. Hypertext poetry projects experiment with new forms of digital storytelling. Netactivism initiatives exploit the capabilities of digital networks to question commercial interests in the digital era. Social media artworks make use of Twitter or Facebook (see Chapter 9). A telling example is Mark Napier's *net.flag* (2002–present), which cuts across several of these categories. The classification of the work depends on who is interested: artist, audience, technician, conservator or critic. It is an interactive, browser-based, performance work with overtones of netactivism. As with most browser-based digital artworks, *net.flag* entailed the development of software to accommodate the specific needs of the project and its long-term conservation (see Chapter 8 for more detail on the project). Finally, *net.flag* is an unstable media work necessitating an individualized conservation plan.

Post-Media Aesthetics

Rather than adopting the typologies of new, old or multi- media art, theorist Lev Manovich proposes a 'post-media aesthetics' (Manovich 2001b). The 1960s and subsequent decades were marked by the rapid development of novel art forms – for example, happenings, installations, public works, performances and conceptual art – all of which called into question the predominance of the traditional medium-based 'spatial' arts of painting, illustration, sculpture and architecture as well as the 'temporal arts' of music and dance. The emerging art forms of this period either combined a range of media (e.g. installation works using painting, sculpture, video and audience participation) or 'dematerialized' artworks altogether through a focus on the primacy of concepts (see the discussion of conceptual art in Chapter 2). Post-media art forms interrogated the practices of mass culture and mass distribution, normally associated with old media. Manovich asserts that, with post-media art, the criteria for discerning between media depends not on the materiality of the work but rather the manner in which an audience is involved and the space (i.e. public or private) in which the interaction takes place. Post-media artworks rupture the conventional linkages between an artwork's identity and its medium (e.g. a sculpture in stone, a painting on canvas or a novel on paper). Since the digital revolution, new art genres – such as net art or computer art – arose from this long-standing tendency to define an artwork through its medium (Manovich 2001b: 5). For Manovich, this correlation is a mistake that limits a broader comprehension of art in the digital era. A post-media aesthetics points to the need for new typologies to characterize how artworks organize information and human experience of that information. An aesthetics concerned with user behaviour and data organization over materiality is not limited through exclusive focus on an artwork's medium.

Behaviourist Art

An example of Manovich's notion of post-media aesthetics is the category of 'behaviourist art' or 'cybernetic art'. Proposed in 1966 by artist and theorist Roy Ascott, these interrelated categories of art draw 'the spectator into active participation in the act of creation' and in which 'the evolution of the artwork/experience is governed by the intimate involvement of the spectator' (Ascott 2001: 97–8). For Ascott, who is discussed again in Chapter 9, mid-twentieth-century art is characterized by open-endedness, uncertainty, flux, transition and dialogue with the spectator, user or participant – irrespective of the particular medium employed by the artist. Behaviourist art involves the spectator in unprecedented ways, producing artworks that can be said to exhibit some form of behaviour. Ascott points to a 'fundamental behavioural quality' that distinguishes art of this period from its predecessors (Ascott 2001: 102). He further argues that 'the vision of art has shifted from the field of objects to the field of behaviour and its function has become less descriptive and more purposive' (Ascott 2001: 97). To be sure, such artworks trigger in spectators new ways of being and interacting with art and, reciprocally, the spectators instigate unpredictable behaviours in the artwork. Rather than a fixed object emanating preconceived ideas, attitudes and values, the work became a 'matrix' and 'catalyst' for creative experiences and spontaneous modes of participation.

The mechanism of 'feedback' between all constituents of the artwork is essential to making the 'artist/artwork/observer' triad 'an integral whole' (Ascott 2001: 98).

Within the dynamic feedback loop of behaviourist works, the experiences of artists and viewers are no longer clearly demarcated. Ascott's vision of behaviourist art was influenced ostensibly by the science of cybernetics, founded in the 1940s by American mathematician Norbert Wiener (Shanken 2002) (also see Chapter 2). Wiener defined cybernetics as a method of regulating the behaviour of communication systems through the control of information feedback or interactivity. Early cybernetic principles identified commonalities between the ways machines and the human brain process information. In 1956, French-Hungarian artist Nicolas Schöffer created the 'cybernetic sculptures' *CYSP 0* and *CYSP 1* in collaboration with engineers from the Philips company. The titles combined the first two letters of the words 'cybernetic' and 'spatio-dynamique' (Shanken 2009: 62). Regarded as the first cybernetic sculpture, *CYSP 1* comprised a microphone, photoelectric cells, a base mounted on four rollers and 16 motor-controlled polychrome plates. The kinetic sculpture had an electronic brain connected to sensors, allowing the work to change its overall form in response to variations in light, sound, colour and audience movement (Shanken 2009: 62). This early interactive robotic sculpture is an example of Ascott's notion of behaviourist art and demonstrates the use of feedback loops by artists.

Telematic Art

An extension of behaviourist and cybernetic art, telematic art is regarded as an evolution of Ascott's experiments in science, technology, art and consciousness from the 1960s onward. Telematics is defined as the science integrating telecommunications and computer technologies, resulting in familiar and commonplace modern technologies, such as email and ATMs (automatic teller machines) (Shanken 2003: 1). Much digital art since the 1990s exhibits features of telematic art, especially the interdisciplinary synthesis of science, technology and art. Moreover, telematic artworks frequently take the form of interactive, non-linear, online projects exploring the fundamental nature of communication through networks (see Chapter 2). French economists Simon Nora and Alain Minc coined the word 'telematics' (or *telematique* in French) in their book *The Computerization of Society*, initially published in 1978 as a policy document presented to the French president at the time. They maintained that the increasing interconnections between computers and telecommunications would transform data processing, information science and human experience more generally (Nora and Minc 1981).

In 1978, around the time of Nora and Minc's report, Ascott first used the term 'telematic art' as part of *Terminal Art* (1980), a computer conferencing project connecting eight artists physically based in the United States and United Kingdom, including Ascott (Shanken 2003: 62). The teleconferencing project used the Infomedia Notepad System to allow participants to download and upload information to a central computer through portable terminals. Although emerging fully under the banner of telematic art in the early 1980s, the use of communications technologies by artists can be traced back to Hungarian artist László Moholy-Nagy (1895–1946) and his work *Telephone Pictures* (1922) (see Chapter 6). Like behaviourist art, telematic art calls into question the conventional relationship between a human viewer and an artistic object by creating 'interactive, behavioural contexts for remote aesthetic encounters' (Shanken 2003: 1). As the *Terminal Art* project demonstrates, telematic artworks often occur within a global space where participants in dispersed locations collaborate via electronic networks. Another example of telematic art is Ascott's *Ten Wings* (1982). The project used ARTBOX computer conferencing to organize the first global throwing of the *I Ching* or *The Book of Changes*, the ancient Chinese divination system dating from the sixth century BCE. Ascott conducted *Ten Wings* as part of artist Robert Adrian's *The World in 24 Hours* (1982), a telecommunications project connecting artists across the globe. Ten different participants contributed to a 'master hexagram', demonstrating the linkages between networked communication systems and esoteric divination, in Ascott's view (Ascott 2003: 184–5).

Virtual Art

Art historian Oliver Grau (2003: 3) contends that digital art 'exists in a state of limbo'. Grau navigates his way through the limbo by investing in the category 'virtual art' as a way of speaking broadly about media art (video, animation and computer graphics), new media art (internet, virtual reality), interactive art, telepresence art and genetic art (a form of bioart; see Chapter 4). The hallmarks of virtual art are interface, interaction, immersion and image evolution (Grau 2003: 10). Immersion involves the sensation of being inside a constructed image or reality which appears to surround and engulf the viewer. In some technological environments, human subjects lose the sense of separation between themselves and the simulation (Lister et al. 2003: 387). Like telematic art, virtual art also integrates art and technology through the use of virtual reality (VR), augmented reality (AR) or mixed reality (MR) environments. Grigore Burdea and Philippe Coiffet (2003: 3) define virtual reality as 'a high-end user-computer interface that involves real-time simulation and interactions through multiple sensorial channels'. VR environments have no real counterparts and are distinguished by human immersion, interaction and imagination (Burdea and Coiffet 2003: 3). Augmented reality, also known as enhanced reality (ER) or mediated reality (MeR), incorporates elements that exist in the material world, thus hybridizing the real and the virtual. Related to augmented reality is mixed reality (MR), in which digital and physical objects intermingle in real time and within a shared space. For Grau, the computer has created the foundation for the emergence of virtual reality as the chief creative medium of our societies.

Computer technologies produce the impression of 'immersing oneself in the image space, moving and interacting there in "real time," and intervening creatively' (Grau 2003: 3). An example of a virtual artwork is the installation *Dialogue with the Knowbotic South* (*DWTKS*) (1994–7) by the Knowbotic Research group, consisting of Yvonne Wilhelm, Christian Hübler and Alexander Tuchacek. The work entailed the visualization of scientific data uploaded every three hours from field research stations in Antarctica to create an abstract, interactive representation of the icy continent. Visitors could manipulate the data fields by using hand-held electronic wands in the installation space. An immersive mixed reality environment included air cooled to the Antarctic readings and pumped into the installation. *DWTKS* necessitated computer programming in C++ and Java languages, showing the synthesis of art and technology that is at the core of Grau's concept of virtual art. In particular, the work pointed to questions about representation, simulation and scientific knowledge.

Reflection

Virtual and telematic art integrate art and technology by creating immersive environments for viewers. What are some other aspects of immersive environments? How might a virtual environment appeal to all the human senses (sight, hearing, touch, taste and sound)?

Unstable Media Art

The multi-disciplinary V2 Institute for Unstable Media in The Netherlands was established in 1981 to stimulate research into experimental technology-driven arts practices. Capturing Unstable Media (2003) was a project spearheaded by V2 on archiving and preserving unstable media (Fauconnier and Frommé 2004). Mostly used by V2 and other digital arts conservation organizations, the term 'unstable media art' reflects, in particular, the perspectives of conservators and curators. This category (although straying from Manovich's notion of post-media aesthetics) under-scores the ephemeral and fragile nature of media art and the unique strategies, such as scoring and notation, that must be implemented to ensure the future survival of digital artworks (see Chapter 8). V2 uses the metaphor of the electron to convey the instability of these works. However, the electron metaphor also expresses the trans-formative power of digital art to cross categories and to catalyse change within the arts and society more generally. According to V2, unstable media artworks consist of:

> electron streams and frequencies, such as motors, light, sound, video, computers and so forth. The word unstable is, according to us, more adequate than electronic, because it refers to one of the most important

properties of these media, to wit, the rendering unstable of all things social, political and cultural within our society—the unstable electron as a basic concept for our society. (cited in S. Wilson 2002: 862)

The emphasis on instability in this category further underscores the difference between digital works and traditional objects of art (e.g. paintings, illustrations, sculptures), which are relatively unchanging over time. Exposed to harsh light, high temperatures or rough handling, a painting will unquestionably deteriorate; but with proper conservation its form can remain comparatively intact and identifiable through the ages. In contrast, unstable media works – often based on audience participation, one-off events and critical concepts – are in states of perpetual flux and, hence, resist the notion that all artworks are unchanging objects. The ever-changing nature of some digital artworks poses challenges to conservators who, instead of conceptualizing works as objects, must think in terms of processes, happenings and the pervasive importance of novelty.

PERSPECTIVES ON TECHNOLOGY, CULTURE AND THE DIGITAL ARTS

Digital art includes the principle of change as an artistic idea. However, in addition to the analysis of the nature of artworks, we can also examine the broader contexts in which art evolves and in which artists work. In this section, we explore three themes – democratization, globalization and interdisciplinarity – that can help us situate digital artworks in a variety of cultural, social, political and intellectual areas.

Democratization

One of the conceptual strands we explore throughout *Digital Arts* is the perspective that digital technologies can democratize the arts. The ethos of democratization includes the belief that every person has the right to engage in the arts. A democratic view of the arts argues that all individuals should be able to explore their creativity and appreciate the artistic works of others. Thus, the democratization of art increases public access and involvement in artworks through a form of 'regime change' (e.g. the development of new platforms for interactive art outside of 'sanctioned' gallery or museum spaces). There are, however, a number of interpretations of what democratization means for the arts and a variety of factors that influence the process. Art historians and sociologists of art measure democratization in terms of access, participation, interactivity, reciprocity and decentralization. For example, Paul DiMaggio and Michael Useem point to the 'increasing representation of nonelites among visitors to museums and performing arts events' as an indication of a growing democratic environment (DiMaggio and Useem 1989: 166). Improved participation in the arts counterbalances the historical trend in which involvement in the arts was primarily the domain of the middle and upper classes. Hence, democratization is a political and social process that aims to remove barriers to access among rural communities, the working classes, the disadvantaged and those without university educations, fostering an 'elite experience for everyone' (Zolberg 2003). Enhanced access to an artistic resource (e.g. a gallery, museum, exhibition, installation, object of art, creative process, medium or material), along with the right to experiment and create, are the essential ideals of democratization. One's involvement in an arts community (online or virtual, either as an artist or spectator) thus becomes more central than one's social, political or economic status.

The democratization of the arts through technology relates to the development of critical theory to interrogate the social value of old and new media. In the late 1960s and early 1970s, a call for public participation in democratic processes was based on the belief that social progress could be fostered through lateral, non-hierarchical and two-way forms of communication. A radical critique of mainstream media channels (e.g. television, radio and newspapers) entailed growing support for a new, democratic media that would involve a broader social and community base. The critique of mass media was by no means unique to the revolutionary atmosphere of the 1960s. The Frankfurt School in the 1920s criticized mass media and wanted social and political communications to operate in a more transparent and accessible manner (Lister et al. 2003: 43–4). The Frankfurt School was a group of scholars and critics based in Germany, including seminal philosophers and critics Theodor Adorno, Herbert Marcuse, Max Horkheimer, Walter Benjamin and Jürgen Habermas. In particular, we will explore the ideas of Adorno and Benjamin in subsequent chapters. In the context of World War II and the social upheaval triggered by Fascism, the Frankfurt School developed 'critical theory' through Marxist principles that advocated fundamental change of the world (activism), as well as critical analysis (scholarship). Frankfurt scholars argued that the 'culture industry' produced passive consumers rather than engaged, participating and independent citizens (Lister et al. 2003: 386–7). With this basis in critical theory, throughout the twentieth century, the call to democratize the media consisted of three aims: (a) the revival of community structures and the creation of a free public sphere of debate; (b) the liberation of communication from authoritarian control and threats of censorship; and (c) the experimentation with new forms of virtual community and the construction of identity as an active and ongoing process involving the input of the public (Lister et al. 2003: 70).

The democratization of the arts through digital technologies can occur on multiple levels. Increased public attendance at physical gallery and museum spaces is but one dimension of a larger and more complex process. The advent of online platforms, especially evident in browser-based projects such as Olia Lialina's *Anna Karenin Goes to Paradise* (1994–6) (see Chapter 7), means that art can be available to anyone with an internet connection anywhere in the world and at any time, 24 hours a day. Here, democratization takes shape through the interpretation of the internet as an artistic medium; artists exploit the inherent possibilities of new media for increased public involvement. However, new media has made it possible to transform viewership and spectatorship into engagement and participation, thereby taking the process of democratization one step further. The public can play an active and central part in generating form and content. For example, the installation piece *Fractal Flesh* (1995) by performance artist Stelarc empowered the audience to affect the artist's muscle movements remotely through electrodes connected to the internet (see Chapters 2 and 4). Audience presence in the artwork becomes integral and indispensable rather than optional or intermittent; the work *is* the dynamic interaction between artist, audience, technology and concept. Other digital artworks necessitate ongoing user input over many years, thus posing certain challenges for the conservation of digital art (see Chapter 8). Furthermore, the digital revolution has granted users, who would not necessarily consider themselves artists, the tools to explore creativity on an everyday basis through new technologies. In the world of photography, for example, the democratization of art takes place with every digital camera click, followed by the use of photo touch-up software to fine-tune the composition before the posting of images to social media websites such as Facebook and Flickr.

Reflection

What conditions might limit the democratization of the arts through digital technologies, as just defined? Is democratization the same for everyone around the world? How might the process differ from country to country, city to city, neighbourhood to neighbourhood, person to person, project to project? Can you think of some specific examples?

Globalization

In addition to democratization as a perspective on technology, culture and the arts in the digital era, we also refer to globalization as a context in which many arts practices have evolved in relation to their relevant media (e.g. the internet, teleconferencing, mobile telephony, social media). Moreover, polycentrism and decentralization present countervailing perspectives to that of globalization. Both of these concepts contribute to the dispersion of power and the creation of new forms of community. In his essay 'Globalization and (Contemporary) Art', art historian T. J. Demos poses a pertinent question for our introduction to the digital arts: 'How does artistic practice…define, negotiate, and challenge the cultural, economic and political forms of globalisation?' (Demos 2010: 211). If digital art is 'made with, and for, digital media including the internet, digital imaging, or computer-controlled installations' (Graham 2007: 93), then what is the relationship between art and the processes of globalization to which such media are inextricably connected? Classically a contentious theme within political science, economics and communications theory, globalization can be defined as 'a dissolving of national states and boundaries in terms of trade, corporate organization, customs and cultures, identities and beliefs' (Lister et al. 2003: 10). One outcome of globalization is an international economy produced by the activities of multi national businesses, the emergence of global financial markets and the increasing homogeneity of goods and services around the world (Lister et al. 2003: 194). Moreover, the emergence of 'global culture' is attributed to globalization and, specifically, the world-wide influence of the American mass media (e.g. reality television shows, conservative online news programmes and Hollywood cinema motifs).

New media has contributed to the processes of globalization by facilitating instantaneous digital communication that transcends regional or national boundaries. To conceptualize globalization as the product of digital media, however, invites the idea of 'technological determinism' into the debate (Lister et al. 2003: 201). This position takes a variety of forms and strengths, all of which broadly maintain that technology underpins the shape of human culture, society, values and practices. The issue of determinism points to the dynamics between humans and the devices we produce through our innovation and scientific experimentation. Most of us would agree that technological conditions affect everyday life and the construction of culture, to some extent (Lovejoy 2004: 311). On the one hand, 'weak technological determinism' concedes that we ultimately control technology, even though technology always shapes our culture (Feist et al. 2010: 5). On the other hand, a stronger version of determinism – or what is called 'autonomous technological determinism' – asserts that there is the potential for humans to lose our grip on technology; that is, for our digital devices to take on an almost Frankensteinian form of liberation from us and to impact the world in unprecedented and, possibly, harmful ways (Feist et al. 2010: 5). Therefore, one of the organizing themes for students to consider throughout this book is the relationship between new media, globalization and the digital arts. We encourage students to think about the following questions and others that come to mind: How do digital artists negotiate 'global culture' as a progressively more powerful and homogenizing phenomenon? How are new media tools utilized by artists in ways that call attention to and invite critiques of globalization? To what extent are the shapes of digital artefacts (e.g. browser-based artworks or photographic images) determined by technology? Do the artist and audience ultimately decide the nature of a digital artwork, despite the important and inescapable influences of technology? And, finally, do artists and their artworks reflect affirmative, neutral or negative attitudes towards new media?

Globalization brings to the fore the issue of cultural production in the context of mass culture and mass media. Just as digital artists probe the intrinsic democratic possibilities of new media, so too do they engage with the global interactive potential of internet technologies. An alternative way to think about globalization and its homogenizing effects is through the concepts of polycentrism and decentralization. Polycentrism argues that the dynamics between the global and the local, the centre and the periphery, the north and the south, are as vital to consider as the broad-scale impacts of globalization and the traditional geographical centres of economic and cultural power (Western Europe, the United States and, more recently, parts of Asia). The concept foregrounds the dynamics between multiple, interrelated 'sites', including physical locations, cultural positions, philosophical orientations or aesthetic ideas (Scholte 2005). Ella Shohat and Robert Stam propose a 'polycentric aesthetic' to encompass a diversity of 'sites' and to call attention to artists and artworks existing at the thresholds between concepts, discourses and identities (cited in Jones 2011: 169). A polycentric perspective of a digital artwork examines the multiple positions that constitute a work – from the physical locations where collaborators are located to the theoretical, ethical and aesthetic values and modes of the participants. The 'local' dimensions of the work (i.e. the contribution of each geographical site to the artwork as a whole or the technological innovations forwarded by artist–engineer collectives with specific affiliations) figure into a polycentric interpretation of a digital artwork. Decentralization involves the decentring of established regimes (e.g. political, economic and, we argue, aesthetic) and the weakening of the control mechanisms of authority hubs. The networks spawned by new media have facilitated the process of decentring by democratizing access to information (Lister et al. 2003: 10). In terms of digital art, decentralization provides an illuminating perspective for analysing works. How does an artwork distribute authorship and creative authority across a widely based network of anonymous participants? How does virtual or internet art decentralize the activities of artists, contributors and institutions in a myriad of ways?

Interdisciplinarity

The third context of the digital arts that we explore, along with democratization and globalization, is interdisciplinarity. Is a digital practitioner an artist, poet, scientist, engineer, conservator, or all of the above? This question points to the hybrid identities of artists and artworks. A term coined by social scientists in the mid-1920s, 'interdisciplinarity' is the convergence of knowledge disciplines. The perspective reflects a broader momentum during the twentieth century to resolve the 'two cultures' (i.e. art vs science) dilemma in which the disciplines (e.g. the arts, humanities, biological sciences, engineering, etc.) were thought to limit the possibility of knowledge integration. Addressing concerns over specialization, interdisciplinarity entails the use of more than one discipline in an artistic practice. Its premise is that the disciplines collectively form the foundations of creativity and that, while individual disciplines maintain discrete identities within theory and practice, there is a degree of interplay that is important to foster. We distinguish between 'interdisciplinarity', in which disciplines collaborate to produce knowledge forms, and 'transdisciplinarity', in which there is a deeper degree of integration and greater loss of disciplinary identity. Transdisciplinary artistic practice requires the methods and theories established in disciplines, and, conversely, disciplines need thought that is transdisciplinary in nature to go beyond the inherent limits of the discipline. Many of the artists and artworks featured in *Digital Arts* are interdisciplinary or transdisciplinary in character insofar as they cross between art, science, engineering and specific sub-disciplines (e.g. studio practice, biology, robotics, optics, etc.).

Interdisciplinarity is defined according to the degree of intermeshing between disciplines. Joe Moran (2010: 14) defines interdisciplinarity as 'any form of dialogue or interaction between two or more disciplines'. What is most essential to inter-disciplinarity, according to Julie Klein (1990: 13), is a 'dispersion of discourse' characterized by the placing of creative activities within a broader (i.e. not discipline-specific) framework. Allen Repko (2008: 6) describes the space between disciplines as 'contested terrain'. Other scholars stress the reality of engaged formal and informal interactions between disciplines (Soulé and Press 1998: 399). These theorists point to the fact that interdisciplinary artists should understand the languages of other disciplines before, during and after cooperative projects.

Roland Barthes (1977) asserts that interdisciplinarity is more than disciplinary knowledge streams converging to produce new epistemological forms. It is rather the dissolving of disciplinary strictures altogether:

> It is indeed as though the *interdisciplinarity* which is today held up as a prime value in research cannot be accomplished by the simple confrontation of specialist branches of knowledge. Interdisciplinarity is not the calm of an easy security; it begins *effectively* (as opposed to the mere expression of a pious wish) when the solidarity of the old disciplines breaks down. (155, italics in original)

Expanding interdisciplinarity beyond its disciplinary allegiances, the neologism 'transdisciplinarity' appeared in the 1970s in the works of psychologist Jean Piaget, sociologist Edgar Morin and astrophysicist Erich Jantsch to indicate the transcendence of knowledge boundaries (Nicolescu 2002). In the nineteenth century, English polymath William Whewell's concept of consilience signified the interpenetration of knowledge 'where disciplines are not juxtaposed additively but integrated into a new synthesis' (Walls 1995: 11). Borrowing from Whewell's work, *Consilience: The Unity of Knowledge* by biologist Edward O. Wilson (1998), offers a contemporary interpretation of the interplay between the sciences, arts and humanities. Wilson defines consilience as 'literally a "jumping together" of knowledge by the linking of facts and fact-based theory across disciplines to create a common groundwork of explanation' (1998: 8). As we will see in subsequent chapters, transdisciplinarity is applicable to a wide spectrum of research areas and creative practices in the digital era.

Reflection

Consider your academic studies. As an arts, humanities, social sciences or cultural studies student, what would it be like to sit in on an engineering, chemistry or genetics lecture? To what extent does language affect our ability to comprehend other disciplines? What could be some of the challenges of interdisciplinary and transdisciplinary artistic practice that crosses between the arts and sciences?

AN OUTLINE OF THE FOLLOWING CHAPTERS

Each chapter of *Digital Arts: An Introduction to New Media* consists of several case studies and reflections. The case studies are designed to provide detailed examples of key artists, artworks, artistic movements and theoretical positions that help to illuminate the chapter themes. The reflections, in the form of prompting questions, offer opportunities for you to think critically about the arts in relation to the digital revolution, the new media era, postmodernity, globalization and your personal experiences. Each chapter situates the digital arts in conceptual, art-historical and technological contexts. Group exercises and questions at the back of the book present additional springboards for reflection on the content of chapters. As an introduction to the digital arts, the book aims to cover seminal practitioners, works, technologies and ideas. It is, however, only a partial account of the field. We encourage students to refer to the 'Annotated Guide to Further Reading' for supplementary readings on the digital arts, including theoretical texts that you can apply to the analysis of artworks. Importantly, in order to appreciate the nature of digital creativity, it is vital to interact with some of the works or projects we discuss by visiting the URLs provided or by locating digital arts installations in your local areas. Participation is crucial to your learning. As an active participant in an artwork or long-term initiative, you will gradually become more knowledgeable about the digital arts as a whole. In closing Chapter 1, we now offer a brief overview of each chapter to give you a sense of the trajectory of the book, from historical contexts to the arts of the future.

Chapter 2 explores the principal vocabularies, themes, ideas, artistic movements and technological innovations contributing to the development of the digital arts over time. New media theorists have argued that one of the defining features of the digital arts is interdisciplinarity. The digital arts dissolve the boundaries between art forms and between art, science and culture. The critical frameworks of materiality, embodiment, hybridity, interactivity and narrativity that we outline in Chapter 2 form the basis of our discussions of art forms and practices in subsequent chapters. By examining Dadaism, Fluxus, Conceptualism, public art and other influential movements of the twentieth century, we consider the claim that digital art did not develop in a historical vacuum. These movements spurred the emergence of kinetic, sound, video and performance art, and the techniques of montage, collage and appropriation adopted by digital artists later in the twentieth century and today. In Chapter 2 we foreground the relationship between traditional, analogue art forms and their digital arts counterparts vis-à-vis the internet and social media in particular.

Photography could be the most familiar of the digital arts to you. Chapter 3 examines the digitization of photography and the moving image in contemporary arts. Terms such as 'post-photography' and 'soft cinema' have led to the reclassification of photography and cinema through notions of 'lens-based media' and 'media arts'. Some of the formal theoretical challenges that the digital manipulation of images has prompted are discussed following a brief historical overview of the area. Initially, the uptake of digital photography was hampered by the fact that silver gelatine and other analogue media had a significantly longer lifespan than digital prints, but as these issues were addressed, so too did arts institutions and artists become increasingly willing to adopt digital methods. Digital artists regard themselves as artists in a sense that is broader than the category 'photographers' allows. They move across media by reconfiguring existing works of art in media representations through techniques such as morphing, shaping and re-crafting imagery, as well as experimenting with identity.

How does digital technology affect performance? Chapter 4 explores 'live' art and its various permutations, such as dance and theatre, with respect to digital forms. The performative qualities of the digital arts are explored in relation to the unexpected aspects of performativity across the artistic spectrum. The arguments of Philip Auslander in *Liveness: Performance in a Mediatized Culture* (2008) address these issues. The chapter goes on to engage with the role of contemporary digital media in 'live art'. Examples of how multiple media have been integrated in theatre and dance since World War II are derived from RoseLee Goldberg (*Performance Art: From Futurism to the Present* [2011]) and Marvin Carlson (*Performance: A Critical Introduction* [2004]), who claim that the advent of performance art changed the performing arts as a whole, particularly in relation to narrative, character and audience. Trends such as telepresence or networked performance are outlined, as are the possibilities of interdisciplinarity, transcription and replay. Digital media demonstrate that digital aesthetics cannot be broken down into a simple binary between technology and humanity. Through the performative arts, it becomes apparent that humans too are a technology – a soft or 'wetware' form, as some theorists maintain (Rucker 2013).

What is the role of sound in the digital arts? The manipulation of sound is a significant area of practice that crosses into almost every other digital art form and has revolutionized, yet also fragmented, music practice. Chapter 5 focuses on the effect that digital technologies have had on the creation and performance of new music. Digital approaches integrate sound installation and related experimental practices within the canon of music, extending the effect of digital technologies beyond basic audio functions to creative processes and experiences. The synthesis of sound and digital recording processes has offered up unlimited materials with which to compose. Digital audio works with an immaterial stream of data. As with the moving image, digitization has taken recording out of expensive studios and into people's homes, providing yet another example of the democratization of the arts through digital technologies. Digitality has offered a platform for reinterpretation through basic editing, sampling, mixing and remixing tools. Glitch culture and noise music, where the detritus of digital processes are used as the primary creative material, are examined, and a history of the computer outlines the development of computer music through to digital music. Performative approaches, such as live coding, laptop and networked performance, will demonstrate the fragmentation of electronic music as a genre, as it continues to evolve.

Chapter 6 argues that the development of internet art reflects the hybridization of the arts through digital media. Responding to the increasing ease of use and accessibility of computer hardware and software, internet art is a continually growing area of the digital arts that incorporates most of the art forms covered in previous chapters. The impact of social networking, open source software and operating systems, as well as the influence of artists and art movements on these developments, will be discussed. The possibilities for different forms of internet art are examined, including email art, software projects and telematic online and offline works. The democratization of internet production, distribution and marketing communities connects artists to massive audiences worldwide, and also enables the circumvention of mainstream distribution channels, such as museums and galleries. Internet art has had a significant influence on the art world by augmenting the capacity of the public to participate in artworks. Chapter 6 concludes with a consideration of the future of internet art. What was once a form of 'new media' art is becoming an accepted part of mainstream arts practices, reflecting the evolution and maturation of internet technologies in mainstream society and the further dismantling of boundaries between arts practices.

Chapter 7 addresses the evolution of internet technologies for arts distribution, and the manner in which digital technologies have reconfigured the dynamics between production and consumption. The chapter considers the impact that the internet has had on global audiences for digital arts of all kinds, and how that development is driving the evolution of digital copyright. Discussing some of the technological aspects of user access and the erosion of conventional, pre-digital forms of distribution, we consider 'Web 2.0' social networks and the emergence of new mechanisms for digital data exchange. The mainstream adoption and development of internet-based technologies include the exemplary case of audio file sharing, revolutionizing the ways artists and listeners interact. The chapter touches on how consumers consistently push the limits of technology towards novel forms of access to and distribution of digital materials. Illegal file-sharing platforms have enabled relatively unfettered exchange between artists and their global online audiences. Discussing the digital formats for music, image and video compression, including two-dimentional and three-dimentional, the chapter emphasizes the role of the internet as an audiovisual medium in its own right, triggering new markets and radical forms of distribution.

How will we remember and preserve the digital arts? How do we safeguard our digital heritage for future artists and audiences? The heritage of the digital arts is linked to impermanent, mutable and intrinsically fragile technologies. Chapter 8 explores how the digital arts have precipitated changes in the arts market that impact the preservation of art. The chapter discusses how creators, conservators and archivists negotiate the preservation of digital artworks as file sharing and participatory media increasingly inform their production. The challenges of conservation are related to the constantly changing technological landscape in which contemporary culture across the world is becoming constantly more digitized and, as we argued earlier in this chapter, homogenized and globalized. The multiplicity of file formats and complications derived from fragile and obsolete media are examined. Issues of interoperability between archives, the classification of metadata, the cost and rapid upgrading of digital infrastructure and the difficulties involved in enabling access to media over networks are considered. The digital arts have revolutionized traditional modes of interacting with and conserving art through acquisition and collection. Different models of collection and archiving are presented in reference to the changing character of art production and technological landscapes. Chapter 8 considers the shifting role of libraries, museums, galleries and other institutions that house art collections. The development and application of digital copyright present further issues for the long-term conservation of works.

The conclusion, Chapter 9, draws together the themes and case studies of the book to argue that, while contemporary cultural and aesthetic practice has deep roots in the history of modernity, the rise of digital culture and its ever-greater penetration into all aspects of life – even in relatively underdeveloped nations – reflects both a new state of the arts and several possibilities. In Chapter 9, we consider the future of the digital arts as technology continues to grow and impact our everyday lives. The digital arts offer different means for addressing the major issues of today's world, including social, cultural and environmental fragmentation.

Chapter Summary

This chapter introduced *Digital Arts* as part of a new media series. It prefaced the book through a discussion of theorists, artists and artworks. The first two sections explained the nature of digitality and forwarded key definitions of digital art, encouraging students to begin to think of the interrelationship between art, culture, science and technology.

■ In order to provide a foundation for subsequent chapters, we discussed the primary typologies used alongside and in relation to digital art, including new media art, electronic art, computer art and internet art. The notion of a 'post-media' aesthetic is evident in the typologies 'behaviourist', 'telematic' and 'virtual' art, which go beyond a focus on an artwork's medium. The classification of art depends on the perspective of the artist, critic, audience or conservator. For example, the typology 'unstable media art' reflects the concerns of conservators and archivists over the fragile and mutable nature of digital media.

■ We then examined three perspectives on technology, culture and the digital arts: democratization, globalization and interdisciplinarity. Democratization is the argument that digital technologies increase public access to the arts through the inherently interactive virtues of new media. Globalization is the larger context out of which (and sometimes against which) many digital arts practices assert creative identity. Countervailing perspectives to globalization are polycentrism and decentralization. Furthermore, interdisciplinarity and transdisciplinarity also help to describe the digital arts and the works of many practitioners.

■ The final section provided a chapter-by-chapter overview, ranging from Chapter 2 (contexts) to Chapter 9 (the future of digital art). We suggest that the evolution of digital art depends on the course of technologies in the future and that digital art will continue to impact the art world in unforeseen ways.

2 KEY CONCEPTS, ARTISTIC INFLUENCES AND TECHNOLOGICAL ORIGINS OF THE DIGITAL ARTS

This chapter explores the vocabularies, themes, ideas, artistic movements and techno-logical innovations contributing to the development of the digital arts over time. As new media theorists have argued, one of the defining features of the digital arts is the breakdown of divisions between art forms and between art and society, effecting a hybridization of the arts, culture and technology (for example, Manovich 2001a and 2005). The chapter outlines how digital processes intersect with aesthetic and conceptual forms. Relevant frameworks, such as materiality, embodiment, hybridity, interactivity and narrativity, create the basis for the discussions of digitization and art pursued in subsequent chapters. Digital artworks, like digital media, are interactive, participatory, dynamic and customizable, incorporating shifting data flows and real-time user inputs (Paul 2003: 67). The customization of content and technology, as well as the recontextualization of information, characterize the digital arts.

We consider the characteristics of the digital arts as a whole in relation to hybrid, avant-garde (or neo-avant-garde) art movements of the twentieth century, including Dadaism, Fluxus, Conceptualism and public art. The emergence of kinetic, sound, video and performance art, as well as the techniques of montage, collage and appro-priation, are presented. We sketch the genealogy between traditional, pre-digital art forms and their contemporary digital arts counterparts – especially with respect to the introduction of late twentieth-century technologies, such as the internet and social media. The predominant themes and characteristics of the digital arts are situated in four case studies that consider the materiality and abstraction of various art forms in the broad context of poststructuralism and postmodernism. Case studies include Roland Barthes and his notion of 'the death of the author' (2.1), the pioneering computer art of Ben Laposky (2.2), the innovative video art of Nam June Paik (2.3) and Stelarc's interactive performances on embodiment and technology (2.4). The democratization of art through digital practices is the principal argument we develop in this chapter and throughout the book (see Chapter 1 for a definition of 'democratization').

INTERACTION, IMMERSION AND INTERFACE: KEY IDEAS FOR THE DIGITAL ARTS

In this section we introduce readers to key theoretical terms used in discussing the digital art forms, projects and practitioners referenced in later chapters. The terms we briefly outline include *materiality, embodiment, the cyborg, hybridity, interactivity, narrative* and *interface*. Between these terms, there are considerable interconnections and commonalities. For instance, materiality necessarily involves the notion of embodiment; the cyborg reflects the concept of hybridity; an interface makes interactivity possible. We also probe the essential conceptual distinction between digital art as a 'tool' and a 'medium' (Paul 2003), as well as the difference between 'digital' and 'analogue' art, expanding the discussion of the digital arts begun in Chapter 1. Case Study 2.1 highlights the work of French literary theorist and philosopher Roland Barthes (1915–80) whose early use of the terms 'link', 'node' and 'network' is a precedent for the language we commonly use now to speak about contemporary digital practices and technologies. Artists referenced in this chapter include Luc Courchesne, Joey Holder, Kate Steciw, Stelarc, David Rokeby and Victoria Vesna.

To begin with, throughout this chapter and elsewhere, we contrast the digital arts to analogue, traditional or pre-digital art forms, broadly including painting, sculpture, film-based photography, ink-based printmaking, sound recordings on vinyl records and writing done on a typewriter rather than a computer. Within the category of analogue art, most writers differentiate between the fine arts and the fibre arts (Janson 2004: 17). Both kinds of art make use of tangible, physical materials (e.g. canvas, paint, film, ink, vinyl, steel, wood and stone) and are created by hand or with non-computerized instruments. As indicated by the range of analogue practices recognized as art, historians over time have expanded the field of art to accommodate emerging forms and mediums. (Note that 'analogue' also refers to an early form of technology, explored later in this chapter.) The label 'fine arts' typically refers to sculpture and architecture, as well as painting, illustration, drawing, printmaking, silk-screen printing, bindery and other graphic art forms printed on paper. Additionally, throughout the history of art, stained glass and illuminated manuscripts have been considered forms of painting and, therefore, classified as fine art, whereas photography has been more recently admitted. In contrast, the term 'fibre arts' includes textiles, metal-smithing, ceramics, glasswork, beadwork and other productions in mixed mediums (Janson 2004: 17).

It is important here to consider the various ways that the terms 'medium' and 'media' are used. In the context of fine and fibre arts, a medium refers to the material from which the artwork is made. However, in terms of the digital arts, we use 'media' to refer to 'new' and 'social' media, such as the internet, Facebook, YouTube, mobile phones and other technologies that allow immediate access and contribution of content in the form of digital images, video and text. Moreover, 'multimedia' usually describes works mixing text, audio (music or voice), static images (scanned images or computer graphics) and moving images (video, cinema or computer animation) (Wilson 1993). Historically, the term 'multimedia' referred to slide shows accompanied by audio (Wilson 1993). More recently, the term 'hypermedia' points to an interactive, non-linear structure enabling viewers to select unique trajectories through information (Wilson 1993).

Reflection

An article in the British newspaper *The Observer* discusses a growing number of contemporary artists who are committed to analogue practices. The writer states that 'the work of these artists is born of a dissatisfaction with digital culture's obsession with the new, the next, the instant' (O'Hagan 2011). Is the use of analogue techniques merely nostalgic, or do older mediums offer unique creative possibilities to practising artists? Can you think of examples from your daily life — artistic or otherwise — which show your preference for the analogue (old) over the digital (new)?

As many examples in this book demonstrate, there are different ways an artwork comes to be categorized as digital. Consider a photograph of a mountain taken with an analogue camera, developed in a lab using traditional film development processes, and then scanned and manipulated with digital software tools. In contrast, think about a photograph of the same mountain taken in a digital medium, then printed to paper and appearing identical to the analogue version of the work. Referring to this difference, theorists of media art distinguish between a 'tool' and a 'medium' in characterizing the use of digital technologies by artists (Lovejoy et al. 2011: 7). As a tool, a technology facilitates the creation of a traditional artwork — a sculpture, painting or dance — or makes possible the conversion of an analogue work to digital format to enhance its distribution, storage or long-term preservation. Digital technologies applied as tools in the production of art may include, for example, digital photography and imaging. Indeed, artists working in different media — including painting, drawing, sculpture, photography and video — make use of digital technologies as a tool (Paul 2003: 27).

Digital tools make possible an array of techniques for manipulating an artwork, resulting in the synthesis of art forms and the integration of media as separate as photography, film and video (Paul 2003: 27). Other outcomes of the use of digital tools include the recontextualization of an original artwork through the techniques of collage or appropriation, as well as the general blurring of the relationship between a copy and the original (Paul 2003: 27). For example, a painting is digitized and uploaded to a gallery's website for online distribution or a dance is recorded digitally and burned to a DVD or broadcast on YouTube. In contrast, as a medium, a technology intrinsically underlies an artwork's production, preservation and distribution. As a result, the work engages in a significant way with the medium's interactive, dynamic, participatory and customizable possibilities (Lovejoy et al. 2011: 7). Digital technologies applied as mediums may include installation three-dimentional artworks (usually created for indoor spaces), music, sound, film, video, animation, internet art, software art and works based on virtual reality. Works that employ digital technologies as a medium vary from browser-based internet projects to interactive installations combining telerobotics and webcams.

Materiality is a core theoretical term for the digital arts and, in many ways, relates to the above discussion of the differences between analogue and digital, and between tools and mediums. Broadly defined, 'materiality' connotes the physical qualities of an object, artefact, substance, living body or artistic work. For instance, a common tool, such as a modern hammer, can be defined by a set of properties: the hard steel of the head, the fibreglass of the handle and the pliant rubber covering the fibreglass and providing a surface for the human hand to grip (Leonardi 2012: 28). In traditional (that is, analogue) art terms, materiality is a property of the medium of an artwork. Mediums such as stone, wood or paint all possess a suite of specific material qualities – hardness, malleability or viscosity, among others – that make them appealing to artists and appropriate for creating particular kinds of works. On a broader level, materiality signifies the larger physical world with which an artist engages or from which the artwork is generated. For example, site-specific productions, such as Andy Goldsworthy's *Sheepfolds* (1996–2003), intrinsically reflect the materiality of places – a field, mountain or riverine environment, as well as the interplay of flora, fauna, elements, weather and seasons that constitute the place.

While the materiality of an artwork is definable, it is not fixed. Instead, materiality consists of the ever-changing matter (material) and form (structure) of a physical or digital work. While the physical properties of the tangible world are obviously vital for artists and their works, the term 'materiality' is neither synonymous with 'physicality' nor does it merely designate the materials employed to produce an artwork. The interpretation of materiality as both matter and form is significant for artists and writers attempting to describe digital artworks – such as internet browser art

– which can be extremely variable over time, often consisting of little or no physical matter (e.g. no stone, wood or paint, but rather electrons on a screen manipulated by the user's mouse and keyboard). Moreover, materiality is the lasting aspect of a work. As theorist Paul Leonardi reminds us, 'when we say that we are focusing on a technology's materiality, we are referring to the ways that its physical and/or digital materials are arranged into particular forms that endure across differences in place and time' (2012: 29).

Furthermore, art historians refer to materialization as a process whereby a concept becomes matter and takes form. For example, the artistic skill of a craftsperson brings the hammer into existence. The idea of a hammer becomes a tangible object in the world; the concept of the hammer is materialized. In the same way, the participation of a viewer in a browser-based artwork materializes the work's form before that form is transformed by another user (see, for example, Mark Napier's *net.flag* in Chapter 8). Indeed, the materialization in the artwork of a participant's intention can increase and sustain viewer involvement over time (Stiles and Shanken 2011: 45) – a condition of central importance to many open-ended, interactive artworks without fixed conclusions or physical parameters. On a comparable note, numerous digital artworks confront the material conditions of the human body in relation to the digital interfaces (e.g. screens, browsers and email portals) through which our bodies connect to technologies and, thus, interact with the works, leading to considerations of the role of the human body in an exponentially more technological world (Paul 2011: 111) (see Case Study 2.3).

The term 'embodiment' describes a condition of being in the world in which the mind and the body are not constructed as separate or independent entities. In contrast, the mind/body split is attributed to the French philosopher René Descartes (1596–1650) whose famous assertion 'Cogito ergo sum' or 'I think therefore I am' paved the way for Cartesianism as the doctrine of logic and reason (the mind) over intuition and the senses (the body). The philosophy of embodiment contends that the mind and the body intertwine – reciprocally modifying one another as human beings experience, affect and are shaped by the world around us. In close relation to the notions of materiality explained previously, embodiment points to the vital interactions between a subject and an environment (living or non-living), leading to certain human behavioural patterns and mental states (Scott and Bisig 2011: 306). In other words, rather than 'I think therefore I am', the philosophy of embodiment revises Descartes' famous yet problematic aphorism to 'I am immersed in the world therefore I am'.

The Australian performance artist Stelarc, whose works deal at length with notions of embodiment, comments that 'when I talk about the body, I mean this cerebral, phenomenological, aware, and operational entity immersed in the world. Not only should we not split mind and body; we should not split the agent from its environment' (Stelarc and Smith 2005: 216). For digital artists, artworks and 'agents' (e.g. viewers, users, participants, technologies or other living or non-living objects immersed in the work and contributing to its development), the notion of embodiment also calls attention to the incorporation of technological devices into human bodies. This intimate role of technology relates to concepts of the cyborg (a 'cybernetic organism' possessing natural and artificial parts) and human-machine interdependence in the digital era. In fact, the theme of embodiment across various forms of digital art encompasses questions about broader human relationships to virtual and physical spaces (Paul 2003: 165), particularly those associated with emerging technologies like computer-simulated virtual reality (VR) (see Chapter 9).

Reflection

Think of the last time you used the internet, a mobile phone or a social networking tool. How was your body (e.g. your posture, movements, physical reactions and senses) involved when you used the technologies to manage, locate or erase information? What were different parts of your body doing during this process? To what extent is it possible to be 'disembodied' (i.e. to have no bodily involvement) when surfing the internet, sending an SMS, tweeting a message or friending someone on Facebook?

The cyborg as a cybernetic organism is a metaphor for human-machine hybridity. In the 1940s, American mathematician Norbert Wiener (1894–1964) proposed the science of cybernetics as the comparative study of communication systems between humans, other organisms and machines. His book *Cybernetics, or Control and Communication in the Animal and the Machine* (originally published in 1948) argued that 'feedback' provides a crucial way to understand how humans and other living beings adjust to their surroundings (Wiener 1961). Weiner used the analogy of a steersman controlling a rudder to navigate a turbulent river in order to demonstrate the link between control and communication. His writings imparted a new technical significance to communication and language through a mathematical basis, creating a different perspective from the Newtonian model of the universe based on energy and matter, to one based on information flows and embodiment (Mitra and Bokil 2008: 7–8). The cyborgian metaphor of 'man–machine symbiosis' is explored by a number of contemporary digital artists (Paul 2003: 9), including Stelarc and bioartist Eduardo Kac (see Chapters 4 and 6). Moreover, the concept of the cyborg – as a modern form of human embodiment that integrates machines into the body – underscores the relationship between identity and digital technologies. How should we understand ourselves and our globalized world in reference to a number of opposing contexts: real and virtual, animate and inanimate, human and machine (Lovejoy 2004: 241)?

Californian media artist Victoria Vesna's work interrogates notions of information flows and embodiment in digital environments. Developed in conjunction with musicians and programmers, *Bodies INCorporated* (1996) (http://www.bodiesinc.ucla.edu) is a website that enables users to create a 'cyberbody' (Paul 2003: 168). The project's avatar – a spinning golden head with a copyright symbol emblazoned on its forehead – welcomes visitors to the website. Indeed, web viewers become immersed in a parody of a corporate structure (Kac 2005: 94). Clicking on the logo, you find the conditions of use and, before proceeding, must agree to the 'legalese' embedded in 'restrictions on use of materials', 'termination', 'disclaimer' and 'limitation of liability'. Further inside the artwork, you are invited to build bodies – which 'become your personal property, operating in and circulating through public space, free to be downloaded into your private hard drive/communication system at any time' (Bodies INCorporated n.d.). You choose a body to wander in through different spaces including the 'gated community' known as 'home', 'limbo' where 'immaterialized thought-forms are detained until final judgment' and the 'dark and foreboding, yet oddly inviting Necropolis'. More disturbingly, you can decide to kill off your body and replace it with another. The spinning avatar head reminds us of the rejection of the human body's central role in the world by the Cartesian philosophy of knowledge, in which the mind continually transcends the body – just as an aircraft overcomes the Earth through the sophistication of technology. The *Bodies INCorporated* spoof calls attention to the Western cultural fixation on property ownership and its protection through cumbersome legal mechanisms. Another theme evident in the artwork is the issue of maintaining personal privacy despite the skilful data-gathering techniques of internet companies (see Chapter 9).

Besides materiality and embodiment, digital art is also recognized on many levels by hybridity, making the classification of digital art into specific categories challenging and, in some ways, superfluous. Borrowed from the biological sciences, 'hybridity' refers broadly to the combination of separate, seemingly unmatched elements into a new, unified form. Although there are many applications of the term, we explore three dimensions pertinent to the digital arts: (a) the blurring of the material and virtual worlds, creating unique hybrid realities in which a work is performed, experienced and preserved; (b) the cross-cutting of categories of artistic practice, dismantling traditional definitions of a creative work of art; and (c) the combining of different media, such as video, animation and graphic art, into new digital artworks.

In the first sense of the term, hybridity points to our immersion in the physical and virtual worlds through an artwork (Knight 2013). We are, at an ever increasing rate, experiencing digital/virtual and material/embodied realities at the same time, all the time. In fact, our perceptions and understandings of the physical world (and our bodily or sensory experiences of it) are gradually transformed through the more and more commonplace use of technologies in our daily lives. For example, camera phones make it possible for us to take photos and easily upload them to social media websites, such as Facebook, creating instant opportunities for dialogue about our day-to-day experiences. In relation to this type of hybridity, British artist Joey Holder draws attention to the problematic separation between the organic and the artificial in her exhibition *Digital Baroque* (2012). A series of abstract images includes analogue paintings alongside digital renderings from biology, natural history and nanotechnology. For example, the framed digital prints *Tunicate* and *Running Ants* juxtapose the natural, rounded forms of sea and land organisms to the geometrical patterns of hard-edged computer-generated abstractions, calling into question the conceptual divisions we accept as normal and use to classify the world around us (Holder 2012).

In the second sense of hybridity, the distinction between the real and virtual worlds is dismantled when the very format of an exhibition shifts between a conventional gallery space and an online platform. Digital artists interrogate the geographical and temporal constraints of galleries and other exhibition venues; that a viewer must travel to a gallery in a physical location open during set hours limits access to artworks and could be said to promote an elitist viewership. In contrast, many web-based works are available globally, at any time and free of charge, fundamentally transforming the conventions of artistic practice and expanding the criteria used to define artworks. For example, installation artist Kate Steciw's *Popular Options (Yellow Diamonds in the Night)* (2012) employs Adobe Flash animation to display graphically the most popular Google search terms of 2011. Launched on the website of Klaus Gallery in London, the artwork mirrors the human desire for information and fulfilment in the digital era. Steciw randomized the sequence of Google search terms as an artistic response to the somewhat anarchic flow of imagery and information on the internet. In its use of an online exhibition space affiliated with a physical gallery, the work demonstrates the hybridity of the digital and the material, in parallel to the hybridity of information flows in online environments (Steciw 2012). That digital artists are often computer programmers or designers suggests a related dimension of hybridity (Lovejoy 2004: 173). Indeed, the pioneers of the digital arts, including mathematician Frieder Nake (b. 1938), software developer Georg Nees (b. 1926) and engineer A. Michael Noll (b. 1939), were trained initially as scientists (Rush 2003: 172).

The fusion of different media (e.g. video, sound and text) into a single work marks the third level of hybridity. As the next section goes on to explain, in the 1990s, new computer technologies instigated a desire for hybrid art forms. Technological experimentation challenged longstanding divisions between artistic genres. Out of necessity, formal definitions of a creative work began to shift. Art theorist Darren Tofts attributes this shift to what he calls the 'mediascape' and identifies four interrelated fields of practice that came to be hybridized by digital artists working during this period. These fields are video art, performance art, installation and animation, all linked by their capacity for hybridity (Tofts 2005: 33). Seminal works from 1990s media art reveal a tendency towards creating hybrid forms. For example, Canadian artist Luc Courchesne's *Landscape One* (1997) was an interactive video installation producing an immersive virtual environment for participants. Microphones, videodisc players, video projectors, screens and body detectors were networked together by four computers with touch-plates. A maximum of 12 participants could enter the work at the same time. Video projectors 'painted' a single, photo-realistic 360-degree image of the garden landscape of Mount Royal Park in Montreal, Canada, engulfing the participants. Four rear-view projection screens displayed panoramic views of the garden during different times of day over a 24-hour period (Lovejoy 2004: 172). Installation participants interacted with virtual human guides in these projected parkland spaces, with each guide possessing speciality knowledge of an area of the virtual garden. People in the park became virtual characters with whom the participants engaged (Gagnon 2000). *Landscape One* combines elements of video, performance, installation and animation, demonstrating the signature concepts of 1990s art: interaction, interface and immersion (Tofts 2005: 33).

Figure 2.1 Luc Courchesne, *Landscape One* (1997). Photograph of artwork. Image courtesy of the artist.

Like hybridity and other terms outlined thus far, the exact definition of 'interactive' has been rendered confusing and, to some extent, meaningless because of its application in a number of seemingly unrelated contexts (Paul 2003: 67). Indeed, digital arts theorists define the term in various ways. In general, 'interactive' suggests an audience's ability to manipulate events or to alter the artwork. For most theorists, participation and choice are central to the notion. Simply put, interactive artworks necessitate that viewers or spectators become users or participants. Margot Lovejoy defines an artwork as interactive when 'the viewer has the power to be an active participant in the unfolding of a work's flow of events, influencing or modifying its form' and in which the viewer makes 'choices in moving along different paths through the work' (Lovejoy 2004: 167). She offers a lucid explanation of this quite challenging and problematic term:

> Interactivity deeply entwines the functions of viewer and artist. In the process, the artist's role changes. This convergence transforms what had been two very different identities of artist and viewer. What interactive art now solicits from the viewer is not simply reception but an independent construction of meaning. In interactively participating, the viewer derives power somewhat parallel with that of the artist: to choose one's own path and discover one's own insights through the interactive work. (Lovejoy 2004: 167)

Crucially, 'interactive viewing is completely different from linear activity' (Lovejoy 2004: 165) because interactive works forego the linear narratives of novels or films and instead empower the audience to make choices. Moreover, interactive digital artworks depend on the participation and input of multiple users (Paul 2003: 68), who affect the form or meaning of the work not determined or dictated by the artist. Other theorists of digital art define 'interactive' according to the varieties of meaning that result from the work, or as the 'complex interplay between contexts and productions of meaning' from the multiple inputs of the artist, viewer and participant in the work (Lovejoy et al. 2011: 5). The loosely defined genre 'interactive art' requires the viewer to take an active part in the artistic process, influencing the creation and manifestation of time- or process-based works (Simanowski 2011: 120–3).

Case Study 2.1
Roland Barthes and the Death of the Author

French theorist Roland Barthes (1915–80) greatly influenced modern literary and cultural studies (Allen 2003). His concepts of 'intertextuality' and the 'death of the author' are fundamental to the continued evolution and application of the principles of poststructuralism and postmodernism in today's world. Although problematic to define as a single or unified intellectual movement, poststructuralism refers loosely to a group of theories and theorists attending to the relationship between the world, human beings, language and the production of meaning (Belsey 2002: 5). The term principally encompasses the French philosophers and critics most active in the 1960s and 1970s, such as Jean Baudrillard, Gilles Deleuze, Jacques Derrida, Michel Foucault, Julia Kristeva and Jacques Lacan. Poststructural theorists maintain that the distinctions recognized in the world are not fixed but rather are perpetually created by the symbols and systems of meaning that we use, rather than predetermined structures (Belsey 2002: 7). Poststructuralism is often defined as a reaction to Structuralism, the early to mid-twentieth-century paradigm originating in the writings of linguist Ferdinand de Saussure, philosopher Louis Althusser and anthropologist Claude Lévi-Strauss — all of whom argued that structures are the unchanging principles determining human behaviours, perceptions and understandings (Kurzweil 1996). Barthes, Foucault, Lyotard and other poststructuralists critiqued the possibility of objectivity and unchanging meaning that was central to structuralist philosophy (Lovejoy 2004: 65). Similarly, postmodernism has been defined as an intellectual and cultural response to modernism, associated with the modern period between the end of the Enlightenment in the late 1700s and the middle of the twentieth century (Lovejoy 2004: 4). As a varied historical period, Modernism corresponded to the Machine Age of the early 1900s (especially, in Walter Benjamin's terms, marked by new technologies of photography and cinematography) in which there was a profound belief in technological progress. Modernism in art (approximately 1930–45) was expressed as an aesthetics of pure form, shown in the geometrical, grid-like paintings of Piet Mondrian and others. Mondrian's non-representational paintings were based on arrangements of black lines, primary colour fields (e.g. reds, blues and yellows) and a white background rather than realistic images of people or scenes.

Whereas modernists subscribed to the linear trajectory of progress, postmodernists questioned the possibility of progress in the first place. Postmodernism in art emerged in the 1950s as Western architectural approaches embraced the vernacular or 'folk' styles that reflected different social and cultural influences (Lovejoy 2004: 6). In this context, Barthes discusses the interactive possibilities of new kinds of networks that lack the hierarchies of modernism. Although much of Barthes' work concerns literary texts, we suggest that his ideas can be usefully applied to understanding artworks of all kinds, including digital works. In his short book *S/Z* (first published in 1974), Barthes writes that 'the goal of literary work (of literature as work) is to make the reader no longer a consumer, but a producer of the text' (Barthes 1990: 4). This blurring of the difference between producer and consumer is an essential tenet of the digital arts, as we discover in Chapter 7 in our discussion of access to digital artworks. Moreover, intertextuality collapses distinctions between text and user, owner and customer, author and reader, making possible 'the opening of networks' (Barthes 1990: 5) with each network having 'a thousand entrances' (12). Many digital artworks demonstrate (at least in their conceptual design) how access occurs not through a single, restricted or privileged mode but through several entrances, offering numerous possibilities for public engagement (Lovejoy 2004: 227).

Furthermore, the kind of interdisciplinary knowledge described by Barthes is not confined to paradigms or disciplines, but exists within networks between individuals and groups (see Chapter 1). This is particularly important to the digital arts where artists collaborate with scientists, programmers, curators and others with different backgrounds. In a truly poststructuralist sense, language shapes our interpretations of the world. Most importantly for a poststructuralist theory of audience engagement, there can be multiple interpretations of the same material and numerous pathways facilitating interaction. Barthes' writings enable us to think about an interactive work as 'one which uses branching systems and networks for creating connective links and nodes' (Lovejoy 2004: 8). In *S/Z* and elsewhere, he makes reference to the concepts 'link', 'node' and 'network' — familiar language, having now become commonplace vernacular in talking about new media. Furthermore, the notion of networks and links that never close prefigures internet-based artworks — such as Steciw's *Popular Options*

(Yellow Diamonds in the Night) (2012) mentioned previously in this section — that are always freely accessible via an online connection. Barthes' famous essay 'The Death of the Author' (1968) is evidence of his refinement of a poststructuralist approach to reading, writing and texts (cited in Allen 2003: 73). The decentring of the author (artist or creator) — the reduction of their control over how the artwork is experienced — invites a level of interactivity in which the audience contributes in an ongoing way to the shape of the work. In other words, the death of the author for the digital arts happens interactively through the technological tools (operating systems, multimedia functions, browsers, digital archive platforms, etc.) available to the user/participant.

For the digital arts, the quality of interactivity is the outcome of an ongoing dialogue between the work, artist and audience members – whether physically present in an exhibition space or virtually present in an online environment. Interactive installations, such as *Landscape One*, call for the audience to become physically involved – to shape the work – thus transforming the idle spectator or viewer into an engaged participant who makes choices. Therefore, one of the intentions of interactive projects is to provide spaces for creative dialogues to transpire and for works to go forward in unanticipated ways. Pivotal to the notion of interactivity is the likelihood of sudden or remote interventions by audience members. As the artist takes a less prominent role, the audience assumes a more significant part in the execution of the work, shifting the traditional balance of power in which an artwork is gazed upon at a distance, its form more or less determined by the creator. The digital artist provides the framework or context for the work to emerge through the processes of 'exchange, learning and adaptation' that characterize interactive approaches (Lovejoy 2004: 168). And, while interactive systems are usually participatory, they are infrequently collaborative. The artist nevertheless dictates, to some degree, the form or forum in which the interaction takes place and the meaning which subsequently emerges.

In contrast to interactive media, 'non-interactive media' include paintings, photographs, novels, movies, theatre performances, symphonies and other musical events (Wilson 1993). Critics of interactive media argue that these non-interactive forms of media, in fact, can also be interpreted as participatory. Although the media are fixed (e.g. a novel is recognized as a novel for its specific plot structure and characters), the process of engaging with them can actually be intensively interactive. The 'choices' of audience members influence their experiences of reading, viewing or appreciating. The different emotional responses, personal memories and other associations that the audience draws upon when interpreting and reacting to a text or performance vary enormously. Therefore the narrative sequence is not as predetermined as some theorists argue. For example, a book can be started at any page or the flow of a movie can be changed easily by pressing fast forward (Wilson 1993). Another critique of interactivity argues that the degree of interactivity may in fact be a property of the technology rather than of the art form. New media theorists, such as Lev Manovich, problematize interactivity specifically in reference to computer art, stating that 'a modern computer is an interactive device by definition, so the word does not say anything more than simply that an artwork is using a computer' (Manovich 1996).

Reflection

What do you think are the differences between these three terms? Is an interactive experience always participatory? Why should an experience be thought of as collaborative? Provide examples from your everyday life. Imagine yourself as a digital artist: which of the three qualities would you prioritize in your own creative work?

Another concept explored extensively by digital artists is the narrative. In its simplest form, a narrative is a story with a relatively linear progression of events – when one element, for example one part of the story, is meant to follow another in a fixed order – experienced when you read a novel, watch a film or see a play in its entirety. It is suggested that many forms of art make use of narratives, but some do so in more obvious or dramatic ways. A traditional narrative develops according to the structure of a work (e.g. a novel, photography series or video installation), producing a plot or cohesive sequence of occurrences over time. The author or artist puts characters in a variety of situations, building experience, knowledge and memory of the narrative in the minds of the audience (e.g. readers, viewers or participants). Through the believability or compellingness of the subject matter, an audience becomes immersed in the story, gaining an overall understanding of events and imagining a variety of possible conclusions or outcomes. Narrative awareness takes hold when the audience reflects on recollections of previous occurrences while continuing to follow the events of the story. Hence, every narrative functions according to an 'agreement' between the author and the audience (Colson 2007: 84–7).

In understanding the relationship between the digital arts and narratives, we should be aware of how some artistic practices invert the conventional definition of the narrative. Digital artworks – specifically those of the 1990s net art movement described in Chapter 6 – tend to reconfigure narrative structures, resulting in a 'non-linear', randomized, parodic or open-ended narrative where there is little sense of resolution or closure (Lovejoy 2004: 192–3). As Lovejoy further argues, new media have created a multitude of traditional narrative and non-linear narrative possibilities. 'Stories can move front to back, sideways or up and down, incorporating radically different points in time as the story develops' as multiple threads of a story occur all at once or 'embedded features' make it possible for the audience to access other stories (Lovejoy 2004: 192). A 'non-linear' narrative in a work requires Tofts' characteristics of interaction, interface and immersion.

Importantly, rather than narrative being the strongest 'pull', symbols and concepts compel an audience to navigate a work, become immersed and participate as subjects in the production of meaning (Lovejoy 2004: 165). Consider the avatar of Victoria Vesna's *Bodies INCorporated*, discussed earlier in this section. Its design demonstrates how the aesthetics of a digital artwork relate intimately to the artist's use of inter-active technologies. Non-linear information retrieval systems impact the sequence in which information is conveyed and, thus, disrupt conventional, sequential forms of narrative. For example, hypertext, defined in the 1960s as 'non-sequential writing as a text that branches and allows choices to the reader' (Nelson cited in Lovejoy 2004: 165), led to the evolution of hypermedia involving images, sound, animation and other forms of information. Interactive CD-ROMs and DVDs enable users to manipulate images, video, sound and animations, further showing the impacts of technologies on user choices and the formation of open-ended data networks over fixed narrative structures (Lovejoy 2004: 166).

Last, in this section, the concept of the 'interface' is key to the emergence of digital art. A range of artists exploit the technical design and cultural meanings of interfaces, as well as their possibilities and inherent limitations (see Chapter 9 for a discussion of living interfaces). Familiar interfaces include, for example, television control panels, audio remote controls, telephones, fax machines and internet browsers. We are surrounded by interfaces in our everyday lives. Christiane Paul defines an interface as a technology that allows a user or viewer to experience an artwork (Paul 2003: 70). She further characterizes an interface, in cybernetic terms, as the point of intersection between humans and machines:

> The word interface has become almost synonymous with the navigational methods and devices that allow users to interact with the virtual three-dimensional space of a computer program. Yet, the term has existed for over a century, describing the place at which independent "systems" (such as human/machine) meet and the navigational tool that allows one system to communicate with the other. The interface serves as a navigational device and translator between two parties, making each of them perceptible to the other. (Paul 2003: 70)

In a comparable way, Brenda Laurel defines an interface as 'a contact surface', whereas Donald Norman defines the term in less optimistic language as 'an obstacle: it stands between a person and the system being used' (cited in Munster 2006: 117). Lev Manovich argues that a digital artwork typically uses interfaces to connect to databases containing multimedia material (Paul 2003: 70). For digital artists, an interface proffers a space for improvisation and, as such, is a shifting topography in itself, as Canadian electronic, video and installation artist David Rokeby (b. 1960) explains: 'The interface becomes a zone of experience, of multi-dimensional encounter. The language of encounter is initially unclear, but evolves as one explores and experiences' (cited in Munster 2006: 119). The interfaces of various digital artworks 'reflect a constantly shifting context that is dependent on the navigational choices we make' (Lovejoy et al. 2011: 6), further underscoring the notions of interaction and immersion that are key to the digital arts. For example, Rokeby's *Very Nervous System* (*VNS*) (1986) employed video cameras, computers, image processors and audio equipment to create an interface with an ambient environment. Participants produced a suite of sounds through their physical interaction with the work (Munster 2006: 118). The focus on bodily experience, sound and technology in *VNS* is characteristic of an early new media aesthetics. Likewise, Rokeby's *Giver of Names* (1990) uses a computer connected to a video camera and small projection system to assign names – either meaningful or ridiculous – to objects. When something is placed on the empty pedestal, the computer processes an image of the object – the results of which are linked to words and ideas, producing a sentence in English spoken by the computer. Through the concept and structure of the interface, Rokeby's installation is a commentary on the logic of new technologies, virtual spaces and artificial intelligence (Graham 2007: 98).

THE DIGITAL ARTS IN PERSPECTIVE: INFLUENTIAL ART-HISTORICAL CONTEXTS

This section continues our contextual discussion of the digital arts through key art-historical influences. Specifically, the digital arts are indebted to Dada, Fluxus, Conceptualism and public art (Paul 2003: 11) – all of which triggered new forms of performance, theatre and installation. These early to mid-twentieth-century art movements explored concepts, processes, events and audience involvement, rather than traditional, material objects of art exclusively. In foregrounding the three movements, we refer to other significant art forms including kinetic, sound, video and performance art, as well as the techniques of montage, collage and appropriation. Although outside the scope of this section, the digital arts also reflect some of the ideals of the avant-garde movements Constructivism, Futurism and Bauhaus, including a fascination with technologies and the aesthetics of machines. In particular, the questioning of the relationship between human societies and technologies is acutely evident in Russian Constructivism's focus on the social function of art and architecture. Moreover, the interconnection between art, technology, culture and society is a characteristic of the digital arts. Satellite and laser art, to be elaborated later in the chapter, are precursors to the digital arts that demonstrate this interconnection. In this context, the digital arts have developed out of the interdisciplinary initiatives of the 1960s, prominently Experiments in Art and Technology (EAT), which spanned the fields of art, science and engineering (Graham 2007: 96).

Other writers contend that the digital arts have evolved independently of modernist artistic-historical movements and practices and, instead, have 'roots not so much in academies of art as in military defense systems' (Rush 1999: 171). We investigate these competing notions through two case studies: Case Study 2.2 highlights Ben Laposky, and Case Study 2.3 focuses on Nam June Paik.

Reflection

The avant-garde movements of the early twentieth century produced new ways of seeing the world and of making art. Later in the 1900s, French theorist Guy Debord (1931–94) predicted that 'the arts of the future will entail the shattering of situations, or nothing' (cited in Shaw and Weibel 2003). Interestingly, Debord's comment can also be translated as 'the arts of the future will be radical transformations of situations, or nothing at all'. What do you think it means for art to be radical? How does art transform the world and our understandings of ourselves and society?

The digital arts can be traced particularly to the Dada movement (or Dadaism) – established in New York in 1915 and Zurich, Switzerland in 1916, and active internationally throughout the early twentieth century (see also Chapter 6). Dada artists reacted against the social turmoil of World War I, the global appearance of conservative politics in Europe and elsewhere and the persistence of traditional art practices (Hopkins 2004). Dadaism aimed to dissolve the boundaries between different art forms – and between art and the everyday lives of people – through the approaches of collage, photomontage, assemblage, appropriation and audience participation (Wands 2006: 98). Collage is a technique that was central to Dadaism and a number of other art movements (including Futurism and Pop Art) in which an artwork is created by assembling different media or forms (e.g. photographs, painting, texts, sounds or machines). A related technique is known as montage, used especially in filmmaking to condense a series of scenes in time. (Russian filmmaker Sergei Eisenstein is known as the founder of montage.) Dadaists experimented with performance, sound, mail and telecommunications art, as well as the creation of immersive and interactive environments. Usually regarded as deconstructive and highly conceptual, Dada artworks are also playful, ironic and politically satirical through their use of a variety of non-traditional techniques. Rather than feverishly random, many Dada projects began with formal instructions or rules that became central to the process of creating art, resulting in a distinctive 'interplay of randomness and control' (Paul 2003: 11).

The Dada combination of order and chance – in terms of our discussion of the digital arts – parallels the algorithms (the codes, instructions or rules) that make possible the use of computer software by artists and others. Programming as a series of instructions and coding as the rules governing online environments are both vital concepts that lend shape to many digital arts projects today. Like their contemporary counterparts, Dadaists exploited communications technologies for conceptual, political and social commentary. For example, one of the earliest uses of a telegram for artistic reasons occurred in 1919 when Dada artists Richard Huelsenbeck (1892–1974), Joannes Baader (1875–1955) and George Grosz (1893–1959) sent a telegram from Berlin to Milan. The artists addressed the message to the Italian poet and soldier Gabriele D'Annunzio (1863–1938) in response to his participation in the military invasion of the independent Free State of Fiume in present-day Croatia. The telegram read: 'Please phone the Club Dada, Berlin, if the allies protest. Conquest a great Dadaist action, and will employ all means to ensure its recognition. The Dadaist world atlas Dadaco already recognises Fiume as an Italian city' (cited in Kac 2005: 28).

For digital artists, the most influential Dadaist was the French-American artist Marcel Duchamp (1887–1968), whose work instigated a broader shift in the art world from pictorial representation to conceptual investigation and audience inter-action. Duchamp foregrounded viewer involvement in experimenting with kinetic sculptures producing optical effects. For example, *Rotary Glass Plates (Precision Optics)* (1920) is a kinetic or moving work consisting of a motor connected by an axis to five panels of glass of different sizes (Knowles 2009: 6). Duchamp painted the ends of the glass panels white with black curves to produce an optical illusion of continuous circles when viewed at a distance. Although the work is not interactive or participatory as defined in the previous section, the kinetic machine mesmerizes an audience with its optical configurations. In 1912, the prestigious Parisian exhibition Paris Salon des Indépendants rejected Duchamp's *Nude Descending a Staircase*, a painting which would later be recognized as a classic work of Modernism. Subsequently disenchanted with the very premises of art in modern life, Duchamp began experimenting with 'ready-mades', appropriating ordinary things or 'found objects' (e.g. a rack, wheel or stool) for artistic work. By 1916, Duchamp had produced four ready-mades – *Bicycle Wheel*, *Snow Shovel*, *Trap* and *Hat Rack* – leading in 1917 to his most widely recognized found object, *Fountain*, a porcelain urinal (Cros 2006: 52–3). Ready-mades, such as these, question the possibility of originality in art and call attention to the differences between everyday objects and artworks (Cros 2006: 121). Duchamp's ready-mades exhibit concepts of appro-priation (the objects were taken from everyday settings) and viewer participation (the full impact of the object relates to the irony and humour of its placement in a formal gallery). As the Mexican poet Octavio Paz comments, 'the "ready-mades" are anonymous objects which the gratuitous gesture of the artist, by the simple act of choosing them, converts into "works of art." At the same time, this gesture dissolves the notion of work. Contradiction is the essence of the act' (Paz 2002: 84).

Reflection

Why should objects that have been taken from or are 'found' in everyday life, such as Duchamp's urinal, rack, wheel and shovel, be considered artworks? What is it about an artist's selection of such ordinary objects that 'converts' them into artworks? In his use of ready-mades, what sorts of criticisms might Duchamp have been lodging against modernist art?

The Dada phenomenon greatly influenced Fluxus – an international group of artists, performers and musicians working in the 1960s. The key characteristics of Fluxus include the interplay of chance and structure, the involvement of an audience in the production of a work and the dissolving of boundaries between different forms of art. The American Fluxus movement grew in the late 1950s out of experiments in music and education, specifically related to the work of avant-garde composer and teacher John Cage (1912–92) (see also Chapter 5). His compositions often incorporated elements of 'found' sound (e.g. from household appliances or cars on the street) within an overall, prearranged musical structure. Similarly, the European Fluxus scene developed alongside the work of a composer, Karlheinz Stockhausen (1928–2007), who later collaborated with Korean-American artist Nam June Paik (Case Study 2.3) on early electronic music projects. Reflecting elements of Duchamp's ready-mades in its employment of instructions and chance, Cage's work set the momentum for later precedents in participatory and interactive art (Paul 2003: 13). In New York, Cage and students conducted experiments on chance in music, performance and poetry, crossing the boundaries between the arts in doing so (Higgins 2002: 1).

Indeed, many Fluxus artworks aimed to promote interactions between artists, performers, writers, technicians and audience members – a transcending of the conventions of art and a significant influence on the digital arts today. Attending classes with Cage were conceptual artist George Brecht (1926–2008), performance artist Allan Kaprow (1927–2006) and others who would become seminal Fluxus figures and pivotal to the later digital arts trends. Demonstrating Dada principles and Cage's emphasis on randomness, the Fluxus poet Jackson Mac Low (1922–2004), for example, became known for writing poetry according to random operations. Some of Low's poems could be read in any direction: left to right, right to left, top to bottom. Further developing forms of experimentation in relation to chance, Kaprow went on to coin the term 'happening' in Cage's class to refer broadly to multimedia theatre events with some elements of randomness (Higgins 2002: 1–2). Like the Dadaist use of rules, Fluxus happenings were often based on exact instructions, resulting in the unique combination of chance and predetermination. The Fluxus stress on audience participation during happenings is a precursor to the 'interactive, event-based nature' of some internet artworks (Paul 2003: 13). In addition to the use of randomness as an artistic principle, Fluxus artists foregrounded collaboration, participation and 'open-ended' works over modernist principles of individuality and exclusivity in the production of unified art objects (Smith 2005: 123). The Fluxus notion of creative practice as not limited to only one area of the arts effectively dismantled the divisions between music, performance, poetry and other art forms. (For further discussion of Fluxus and its influence on internet art, see Chapter 6.) Both Dada and Fluxus influenced the growth of installation art throughout the 1960s and 1980s in response to the aesthetic and social constraints involved in 'framing' artworks when locating them in galleries (Rush 2003: 116). In particular, the 'anti-art' of Dada was a reaction to the elitism of galleries, their exclusion of lower social classes and the privileging of objects of art (i.e. paintings and sculptures).

Inspired by the ready-mades of Duchamp and the happenings of Fluxus, conceptual art (also known as Conceptualism) emerged as a neo-avant-garde movement in the 1960s and 1970s, particularly in New York City. Referred to humorously as 'Modernism's nervous breakdown', conceptual art can be defined as art that foregrounds the concepts or ideas in which the work develops over materiality or aesthetic design. Conceptualism opposed the modernist interpretation of art as existing only in painting and sculpture. Instead of art as a commodity, conceptualists regarded art as a common property (Lovejoy 2004: 58). In 1967, the American artist Sol LeWitt (1928–2007) characterized conceptual art as art built upon and reflecting a stable set of ideas:

> In conceptual art the idea or concept is the most important aspect of the work … In other forms of art the concept may be changed in the process of execution … When an artist uses a conceptual form of art, it means that all of the planning and decisions are made beforehand and the execution is a perfunctory affair. The idea becomes the machine that makes the art. (cited in Alberro 2003: 35)

On the whole, conceptual artworks exhibit the qualities of evanescence (i.e. fading from sight), irony, satire and self-reflexiveness. The distinction between an artwork and its contexts (social, cultural, philosophical, political and so forth) and the division between an artwork and the world are wholly questioned. Conceptual artworks critique the materiality of objects of art, along with the visual conventions and assumptions of artistic practices. Alexander Alberro (1999: xvi–xvii) outlines four precursors to the conceptual art movement of the 1960s. The first involves problematizing the traditional object of art in certain modernist practices. Rather than valorizing the aesthetic genius of artists, early conceptualists were interested in all aspects of the work including the technical or manual decisions required to execute the work, as well as the notions or philosophies out of which the work arose.

The second precursor involves a response to 'reductivism' or the limited under-standing of artworks as material objects only. In contrast, conceptual art prioritizes the processes and concepts leading to and underpinning the artwork. Hence, the viewing of the work is dependent on the context and the numerous intangible elements comprising the work. The third precursor, in Alberro's view, is the negation of formal visual aesthetics, especially evident in Marcel Duchamp's ready-mades in which traditional artistic qualities of beauty, symmetry, balance, harmony and colour are replaced with the concept and context of the raw found object placed before the viewer. The fourth influence is a deep consideration, typical of avant-garde art movements, of the traditional roles of the artist, subject and audience, as well as the conventions reflected by artworks. Examples of conceptual artworks include Robert Barry's *Telepathic Piece* (1969) consisting of a chain of thoughts about an artwork communicated to the exhibition by the artist, and Douglas Huebler's exhibition of photographs shot at two-minute intervals while driving (1970).

Another key art-historical influence on the emergence of the digital arts is public art – defined as art with social use value that is conceptualized, is created for and exists in the public domain. Contemporary public art developed out of the Russian Constructivists who combined technology and art in anticipation of a new societal structure (Lovejoy 2004: 38). The Constructivists explored theatre, poetry, film, architecture and other art forms for the social good in the spirit of the Russian Revolution. They employed photo collage as a technique to spread political propaganda. Public art also bears a relationship to Dadaism, Conceptualism and other avant-garde movements of the 1960s, particularly the happenings of Fluxus. Characteristic of public art and its precursors is the subversion of traditional, commercial art forms focused on the production of art objects. In the 1970s, public art gained traction through the postmodernist assertion that meaning results from the numerous contexts (social, political, environmental, theoretical and so on) of the artwork (Lovejoy 2004: 82).

On the whole, public art engages notions of interactivity and audience partici-pation, outlined in the previous section, and, undeniably, electronic and digital technologies of the last 50 years have expanded the possibilities of public art. As with conceptual art, public art often necessitates extensive artist involvement with the news media to promote the work to the public. *The File Room*, initiated in 1994 by Catalan-American artist Antoni Muntadas (b. 1942), is an example of an ongoing public installation about the history of censorship (www.thefileroom.org). Created collaboratively and with a number of physical versions installed in European galleries in the mid-1990s, the work is an online archive of censorship cases dating as far back as the banning of Socrates' books in 387 BCE (Muntadas n.d.). characterizes the project as 'an organic initiative; its shape ultimately determined by the input of participants'. Another example of a public artwork is the billboard-based project

Protect Me from What I Want (1986) by American artist Jenny Holzer (b. 1950). Projected over Times Square, New York City, the work is both poetry and installation art. It used a massive electronic signboard to broadcast the phrase 'protect me from what I want', in the middle of one of the world's major commercial and financial hubs.

Case Study 2.2
Laposky's Oscillons

In the early 1950s, American artist and mathematician Ben Laposky (1914–2000) became a pioneer of computer art and one of the first artists to apply electronic technologies in his creative work (Wands 2006: 24). Laposky's experimentations anticipated the term 'computer graphics', coined in the 1960s by American graphic artist William Fetter (1928–2002) nearly ten years after Laposky's initial work. Laposky used an oscilloscope to produce the first abstract electronic images of mathematical wave forms he called 'oscillons'. An oscilloscope is a device that uses a cathode ray tube to produce an image of an electrical current on a fluorescent screen. An analogue computer managed the visible output on the oscilloscope's display in which the movement of an electron beam produced the lines of an image (Terras 2008: 20). Laposky photographed the elegant, simple and organic images of the oscillons – a series of mathematically based patterns that a human hand could not produce – directly off the oscilloscope's display with high-speed film. Laposky's first named electronic image was *Oscillon Number Four – Electron Abstraction* (1950). His interest in the aesthetic and technical dimensions of the oscillons is considered a legacy for some digital artists who have both artistic and scientific interests (Greenberg 2007: 14). He also described the creation of oscillons as 'analogous to the production of music by an orchestra' (cited in Sito 2013: 21).

As an artist-scientist hybrid, Laposky fused the technologies of his era, represented by analogue computers, with an artistic practice. In the early to mid-1900s, analogue technologies, oscilloscopes and fluorescent interfaces were revolutionizing mathematics and information. The curves of the oscillons mirrored the internal waveforms of analogue computers, used as early as the 1920s to carry out complex mathematical calculations, such as differential equations. In the late 1940s, American companies began manufacturing electronic analogue computers on a commercial scale (Small 2001). In the digital age we live in now, we take for granted that the term 'computer' automatically denotes an electronic PC or Mac desktop or laptop. However, before 1940 all computers were analogue systems that used continuous variations in voltage to make real-time calculations possible. Analogue computers were less precise than their digital counterparts and operated according to the shifting properties of electricity, mechanics or hydraulics as reflected in voltage, temperature or pressure variations. In contrast, digital computers use distinct, finite signals without mechanics or hydraulics.

Another artist known for working with analogue computers was John Whitney (1917–96), widely regarded, arguably along with Laposky, as 'the father of computer graphics' (Paul 2003: 15). In the 1960s, Whitney experimented with computer animation and typography using a 4-metre-high analogue computer he invented. His short, 7-minute film *Catalog* (1961) presented a collection of the computer graphics he had generated over a number of years. Whitney's subsequent films include *Permutations* (1967) and *Arabesque* (1975). Yet, Laposky and Whitney were not the only innovators of computer art active during this period. The computer image *Parcours* (1976), by French artist Vera Molnar, resembled a drawing done by hand (Rush 2003: 178). As early as 1968, Molnar started using an IBM 370 computer with an IBM 2250 CRT monitor and plotter to produce artworks.

By the late 1960s, avant-garde artists began involving computers in the production of artworks. In addition to Dada, Fluxus and conceptual art-historical influences, the digital arts should be understood in relation to the impact of the personal computer (PCs) and other military technologies developed by the West during the Cold War. During this period, research funded by military defence departments demonstrated the potential of the computer as a visual medium (Gere 2002: 98). In 1957, the United States National Bureau of Standards developed the first image-processed photo. Begun in 1961, the American defence project known as SAGE contributed to the technological development of graphical interfaces or what we now know as Graphical User Interfaces (GUIs) in collaboration with major computer companies including IBM. These kinds of technological strides, made possible through defence funding and corporate investment, occurred alongside the neo-avant-garde movements of the era, such as conceptual art. Indeed, most early digital artists were affiliated with scientific research facilities, prominently Bell Labs (Rush 2003: 176). In the late 1950s and early 1960s, Edward Zajac at Bell Labs experimented with the visualization of data through video generated by computers (Gere 2002: 99). A. Michael Noll, also of Bell Labs, created computer-generated replicas of Mondrian's paintings. Noll's *Gaussian Quadratic* (1963) series, using algorithms to produce geometric artworks, was exhibited at the Howard Wise Gallery in New York City. Noll's image *Computer Composition with Lines* (1965) was created on an IBM 7094 digital computer and a General Dynamics SC-4020 microfilm plotter (Gere 2002: 99). By 1965, partly due to the work of Bell Labs artist-scientists, computer replication of visual phenomena reached a significant level (Lovejoy 2004: 173). In 1965, the Wise Gallery and the Galerie Niedlich in Stuttgart, Germany, concurrently hosted the exhibition Computer-Generated Pictures. In 1968, the Museum of Modern Art (MoMA) in New York organized *The Machine as Seen at the End of the Mechanical Age*, a travelling exhibition of computer-generated art (Blecksmith 2011: 526). During this time, Charles Csuri started developing computer-generated artworks using algorithms, leading to the emergence of computer art as a distinct area of the digital arts (see also Chapter 6). Many conceptual artists also became interested in artificial intelligence, cybernetics and other theoretical and practical possibilities emerging through computer science (Lovejoy 2004: 180).

Throughout the 1970s, artists continued to adopt new technologies to create performances, installations and other interactive pieces. Two notable trends that emerged during this timeframe are satellite art (or art that makes use of communications objects put in orbit around the Earth) and laser art (or kinetic art that uses laser technologies). In his essay 'Art and Satellite', Nam June Paik describes satellite art as a 'two-way connection between opposite sides of the earth' that gives 'a conversational structure to the art' based on 'improvisation, in-determinism, echos, feedbacks, and empty spaces in the Cagean sense'. Moreover, Paik argues that 'satellite art must make the most of these elements (for they can become strengths or weaknesses), creating a multitemporal, multispatial symphony' (Paik 1996: 435). Since the early 1970s, artists Kit Galloway and Sherrie Rabinowitz have experimented with the use of interactive communications technologies in art. In 1977, the *Satellite Arts Project: A Space with No Geographical Boundaries* became the first multitemporal, multi-spatial satellite dance performance (Lovejoy 2004: 232). The interactive work was transmitted between artists on the East and West coasts of the United States (Lovejoy et al. 2011: 2), resulting in composite video images of dancers on opposite sides of the country. The virtual performance space afforded by the satellite technology gave the participants the impression they could see, hear and even touch one another as they moved individually in their respective locations (Lovejoy 2004: 232). Like satellite art, laser art brought about an expansion of art forms in the 1960s and 1970s. The term 'laser' is an acronym for 'light amplification by stimulated emission of radiation'. In the late 1960s, expensive lasers containing krypton gave artists access to a palette of colours to use in performances (Hecht and Teresi 1998: 233). Nam June Paik became one of the first artists to use lasers, after a residency with Bell Labs where the technology was extensively advanced. With laser sculptor Norman Ballard (b. 1950), Paik later created *Laser Cone* (2001/10), a large-scale, immersive and kinetic installation of laser light.

During the 1990s, internet art became the next phase in the evolution of artists using technology (see Chapter 6). In many ways, internet art spans art, science, engineering and information in a manner reminiscent of the Experiments in Art and Technology (EAT) group, founded in 1967 by artist Robert Rauschenberg and scientist Billy Klüver. EAT fostered creative interactions between artists, scientists and engineers. Indeed, many early internet artists were also computer programmers who worked across the different spaces of the disciplines, demonstrating the bringing together of the arts and technology. Two of the first exhibitions of internet art were *Beyond Interface: Net Art and Art on the Net* (1998) and *Art Entertainment Network* (2000) (Graham 2007: 94). In 2000, London-based artist Graham Harwood's *Uncomfortable Proximity* became the first internet artwork commissioned by the Tate Gallery for its website (www2.tate.org.uk/netart/mongrel/home/default.htm). The artwork appropriates the design of its host, telling a different story about the British art system through the structure and motifs of the Tate's website (Lovejoy et al. 2011: 6). Through its use of hypertext mark-up language and browser interfaces, *Uncomfortable Proximity* also questions the role of digital media in the curation of art (Graham 2007: 95) (see Chapter 8).

Case Study 2.3
Nam Jun Paik and Video Art

Korean-American artist Nam Jun Paik (1932–2006) is widely considered the founder of video art. However, Paik's work alternates between music, video, television, performance and, as we saw previously, laser art. His first solo exhibition, *Exposition of Music – Electronic Television* (1963), took place at the Galerie Parnass, the private home-based gallery of architect Rolf Jährling in Wuppertal, Germany. In this installation, Paik scattered, in Dadaistic fashion, a number of found objects – for example, pianos, violins, mannequins, the head of an ox and television sets – across the premises of Jährling's home gallery. Paik's provocations were inspired by John Cage, who attempted to free music from its conventions and structures (see Chapter 5). Chance as a creative principle is further evident in Paik's installation *Random Access* (1963) in which he pinned strips of audio tape to a wall and asked audience members to play the segments through a playback head wired to speakers. In connection with the Fluxus group, Paik participated in a residency at Bell Labs where he would have come into contact with artist-engineers such as A. Michael Noll and others. In 1966, as a result of his residency, he produced the work *Digital Experiment*, exploring the differences between digital and analogue technologies.

   One of Paik's first and more famous works to engage television as an artistic medium is the 'machine collage' *Magnet TV* (1965), consisting of a television set and magnets. The application of the magnets distorted the television's scanning components and resulted in visible and audible electronic effects, including 'kaleidoscopic shapes, luminous colours, and electronic noises' (Berger 1990: 128). In the spirit of Dada, Paik disrupted the iconic status of the television in mass culture while creating a technique for elucidating to the human senses the mysterious nature of broadcast technology. In 1974, Paik created the video installation *TV Buddha*. A video camera transmitted images of a Buddha statue to a video monitor, setting up the critical comparison between the 'mindful' stare of the Buddha with the 'mindless' gaze of the television viewer (Lovejoy 2004: 95). While most historians of electronic art recognize the contributions of Paik to video art, others challenge the extent to which Paik invested in a cultural critique of the television. Where does Paik's work leave us? For example, Martha Rosler argues that Paik's role has been greatly mystified and that his mesmerizing television installations merely 'replicate viewer passivity' and aestheticize mass entertainment technologies (Bolognini 2008: 74). For Rosler, Paik's installations neither offer an analysis of television messages nor provide an alternative discourse for coming to terms with a new technological medium storming society (Rosler 2004).

We conclude this section by thinking about the relationship between the arts and technology – a prevalent theme in this book. In his essay 'The Death of Computer Art' (1996), Lev Manovich divides the digital arts into 'Duchamp-land' and 'Turing-land', the latter named after the British mathematician and 'father of computer science' Alan Turing (1912–54). Manovich reflects on what he saw as the impending union between art and computers, evident in many of the movements we have just discussed but reaching a greater intensity during the 1990s. On the one hand, Duchamp-land is the traditional art world of prestigious journals, galleries and museums, as well as artistic concepts and practices endorsed by them. On the other hand, Turing-land refers to the nascent, c. 1995 computer art world associated with the International Symposium on Electronic Art (ISEA), Ars Electronica and other high-profile events. Manovich outlines three characteristics of those works admitted to Duchamp-land: they are oriented towards content; they must be appreciated as 'complicated' objects situated in larger cultural contexts; and, in the postmodernist sense, they exhibit aspects of irony, especially with regard to the materials they use. For Manovich, Paik's work falls into this category because he disrupted the conventions of technology through his ironic subversion of video monitors and laser technology. Some characteristics of works admitted to Turing-land include an attention to the technologies themselves, rather than the content; simplicity and a lack of irony; and a concerted exploration of technology and its limitations. Manovich concludes by stating that 'what we should not expect from Turing-land is art which will be accepted in Duchamp-land. Duchamp-land wants art, not research into new aesthetic possibilities of new media. The convergence will not happen' (Manovich 1996). Furthermore, Manovich's argument could reflect the broader differences between artists and computer programmers, as observed by digital arts theorists (Lovejoy 2004: 173).

Reflection

Arguments like those of Manovich involve setting up a very strong dichotomy in order to predict the non-convergence of art and new media. Thinking about any of the examples cited here or other ones you know, is that dichotomy too strong? Are there examples that do not fit his characterization? Reflect on this as you encounter examples in later chapters.

OLD AND NEW MEDIA: TECHNOLOGICAL CONTEXTS FOR THE DIGITAL ARTS

The development of new technologies influences artistic practices. Early twentieth-century French poet Paul Valéry anticipated the ascendency of the digital arts when he commented that 'we must expect great innovations to transform the entire technique of the arts, thereby affecting artistic invention itself and perhaps even bringing about an amazing change in our very notion of art' (cited in Lovejoy 2004: 1). In this section, we consider Valéry's claim by identifying which key technological trends have influenced the development of the digital arts. New digital devices and software presently enable artists to experiment with the possibilities of art, combining technical proficiency and 'artistic invention' in the process. However, the innovative application of technologies by artists has also catalysed developments in the technologies themselves – a theme we further propound in Chapter 6

(Rush 1999: 178). We briefly sketch the history of television, video, computers, the internet, software and social media. Indeed, during the 'digital revolution' of the 1990s, computer technologies became more and more commonplace (Lovejoy et al. 2011: 2). Case Study 2.4 presents examples of Stelarc's body of work, which draws to great degree from the combination of different electronic and digital mediums, including robotics, teleconferencing, interface technologies and the internet.

Early technological contexts for the digital arts include the prominent telecommunications mediums of television and video. In the 1950s, television became a 'visual cultural phenomenon', exceeding the influence of print media (books, newspapers and magazines), radio and cinema (Lovejoy 2004: 78). Decades earlier, in 1873, the history of television began with the discovery of the 'photoconductive' capacity of selenium. This scientific breakthrough made possible, for the first time, the concepts of 'seeing by electricity' and sending moving images electronically between locations. Late nineteenth-century scientists, such as Alexander Graham Bell, experimented with transmitting pictures through wires. By 1926, the Scottish electrical engineer John Logie Baird demonstrated a simple form of television in London, and in 1927 American inventor Philo Farnsworth produced the first television set. In 1936, the first high-definition broadcasting system was made public in the UK, followed by comparable developments in Japan, the USSR, the USA, France and Germany. In 1939, the cathode ray tube became the main component of television sets (Rush 2003: 14). By 1960, 90 per cent of American households had television. Meanwhile, electronic video for recording, duplicating and broadcasting moving images grew in the 1950s and 1960s, especially with the appearance of the Portapak, the first portable video camera and recorder, released by Sony in 1967. This technological advance allowed artists access to video as a creative medium, leading later to the work of Wolf Vostell and Nam June Paik (Case Study 2.3).

Computers have further revolutionized art. The artist-programmer hybrid is now a common phenomenon. The computer is ever more an instrument for 'high speed visual thinking' in art (Lovejoy 2004: 170). However, computers are part of the broader, intermeshed history of science and technology that has impacted the trajectory of the digital arts (Paul 2003: 8). This history includes technologies developed at military, academic and commercial research centres and eventually exported to consumers around the world. The foundations for the modern computer were put down in 1801 when French merchant Joseph Marie Jacquard (1752–1834) demonstrated the Jacquard loom. His mechanical loom used a chain of punched cards to control the process of textile manufacturing. In 1834, English inventor Charles Babbage (1791–1871) designed the 'analytical engine', a hand-operated device for performing calculations (Wands 2006: 20). Later on, in 1946, the University of Pennsylvania produced the first digital computer, known as ENIAC (Electronic Numerical Integrator and Computer) (Rush 1999: 176). As Case Study

2.2 notes, before the mid-1900s, all computers were analogue. In 1951, UNIVAC was patented as the first computer designed for a commercial market.

In the late 1940s, American mathematician Claude Shannon (1916–2001) discovered that the algebraic logic developed by English mathematician George Boole (1815–64) could be used to construct a data storage device. Boolean logic became the foundation for the digital computer. To appreciate the difference between digital and analogue computers is to understand the practices of counting and measuring or what we refer to as 'calculating' (Youngblood 1970: 183). 'To compute' literally means to calculate. There are two forms of calculating: measuring and counting. On the one hand, a measuring device is based on an analogue process because it makes an 'analogous' comparison between a quantity and a number that represents the quantity. For example, a speedometer measures a speed by assigning a number: 100 kilometres travelled at that rate of travel over an hour. On the other hand, a counting machine is digital because it uses 'two-way switches' to express quantities directly as digits or units of the binary system (Youngblood 1970: 183). The binary system uses the number 2 as its base, just as the decimal system uses 10. The binary code of digital computers is expressed as variations of the numbers 1 and 0, underlying functions such as on or off, yes or no, and voltage or no voltage. A series of binary switches then relays voltages. The 'bit' as the basic unit of digital information is the contraction of 'binary digit' (Youngblood 1970: 183). We will refer more to the technical aspects of computers in subsequent chapters.

However, before the appearance of the PC in the 1980s, computers were expensive, specialist technologies. Hence, except for a few pioneering practitioners affiliated with research centres such as Bell Labs, most artists in the early years of computing were not seriously engaging the creative possibilities of computers as tools or mediums. The situation started to change as computer technology became more accessible through a number of advances. In 1968, American engineer Douglas Engelbart (1925–2013), of the Stanford Research Institute, conceived of bitmapping, windows and the computer mouse. The process of bitmapping enabled the electrical pulses in a computer's processor to be reflected in an image on the display. The 'on' or 'off' state of the electrical pulses corresponds, as mentioned above, to binaries of 1s and 0s (see Chapter 1). Small units of computer memory are assigned to the pixels of a computer screen. These concepts underpin the graphical user interface (GUI), as well as the desktop and windows interfaces pioneered by Apple's Macintosh computers and, later, the Microsoft Windows operating systems of PCs (Paul 2003: 10–11). In 1980 and 1981, manufacturers, such as Hewlett-Packard, began to make PCs commercially available to the public. *Time* magazine selected the PC as the 'Man of the Year' in 1982, a role usually reserved for international leaders (Swedin and Ferro 2005: 96). In 1984 the Apple Macintosh was branded the 'computer for the rest of us', indicating a trend towards the democratization of technology and data (see Chapter 1). Rather than the awkward MS-DOS text commands of the PC, the Mac employed user-friendly and more intuitive icons, menus and a mouse. Reflecting the relationship between embodiment and technology in the computer age, the mouse became an extension of the user's hand.

Hardware advances are not the whole story. Developments in the digital arts also are indebted to advances in computer software, defined as programs that control the processor of a computer, allowing the execution of certain functions. Lev Manovich argues that artists use two kinds of software: 'data searchable structures' and 'algorithms'. The first results in 'hypernarratives' without beginnings and ends in which the artist navigates a pathway through a database (defined as a software program) of items presented non-hierarchically. The second negotiates the 'hidden logic' of algorithms, as evident in the creation of 'gamelike objects' (Lovejoy 2004: 163). In the early 1970s, artists such as German artist Manfred Mohr (b. 1938) and American artist-programmer Duane Palyka (b. 1944) began devising special software to suit their creative imperatives (Lovejoy 2004: 173). Similarly, pioneers of computer music German-American composer Herbert Brün (1918–2000) and American composer Lejaren Hiller (1924–94) developed compositional software specific to their musical aims. Hiller co-authored the program MUSICOMP to automate certain aspects of composition (see Chapter 5). Under the tutelage of Hiller, Brün learnt the programming language FORTRAN, producing the computer-generated works *Infraudibles* (1968) and *Mutatis Mutandis* (1968) (Holmes 2008: 255). Their software anticipated the appearance of the synthesizer (Rush 1999: 178). In the world of digital photography, image manipulation software has also been crucial. While photography has always been marked by some degree of manipulation, software developments have triggered an explosion in the scope and impact of these processes (see Chapter 3). As early as 1987, Thomas Knoll began writing an image processing program called Display, later evolving into the editing software Adobe Photoshop as we know it today. Photoshop and other image applications have transformed the practice of photography.

Reflection

Can you think of any ways in which technological developments – using a very broad definition of technology – might have influenced artistic practice prior to the digital arts?

The internet has played an indispensable role in the genealogy of the digital arts. In 1945, American engineer and inventor Vannevar Bush (1890–1974) proposed the idea of the Memex, an analogue device that would allow users to browse books, serials and images on microfilm. Although it was never constructed, the concept of the Memex prefigured the internet as a universally available database of digitally networked content (Paul 2003: 8–9). A decade later, the United States Department of Defense founded ARPA (Advanced Research Projects Agency) in 1957 to advance the exploration of Cold War technologies. By the late 1960s, ARPANET matured into a data network having no central authority, safeguarding American military information from loss or hacking. In 1963, American sociologist Theodor Holm Nelson (b. 1937) coined the terms 'hypertext' and 'hypermedia' to refer to hyperlinked writing and reading environments in which the dynamic interplay between text, images, video and audio allows the user to select a personal pathway through the data (Paul 2003: 10). Hyperlinks make it possible for users to shift easily between areas of content that, in an analogue context, would be accessed only in the physical domain of books, shelves, cities and countries (Lovejoy et al. 2011: 3).

The dawning of Web 2.0 around the year 2000 called for social media to 'nurture connections, build communities and advance democracy' through technology or, in other words, to create a more social Web (Van Dijck 2013: 4) (also see Chapter 9). The latest technological frontier for the digital arts is the emergence of social media, exemplified by Wikipedia (2001), LinkedIn (2003), Myspace (2003), Facebook (2004), Flickr (2004), YouTube (2005) and Twitter (2006) (Chapters 7 and 9). Social media necessitates a number of internet applications, including podcasting and streaming or 'on-demand' video or audio, developed in the 1990s. A podcast refers to audio, video or textual content downloaded on a subscription basis to a mobile device or computer. British journalist Ben Hammersley proposed the term 'podcasting' in *The Guardian* newspaper in 2004 as a contraction of 'pod' and 'broadcasting'. Also in 2004, Liberated Syndication developed the first podcast hosting service. Internet Transmission Control Protocol (TCP), originating in the work of American computer scientists Vint Cerf and Bob Kahn in the 1970s, facilitates the transfer of content over the internet. Other technologies, such as the serial port microphone allowing users to record audio and the MP3 as the universal standard for audio files, underpin podcasting (Chapter 7). Ideas of interaction, participation and democratization characterize social media as a 'tool' or 'medium' for creating new possibilities in the digital arts. Just how artists will engage with social media technologies is becoming increasingly evident at this very moment (see Chapter 9).

Case Study 2.4
Stelarc and Human Embodiment

Also explored in Chapter 4, Australian performance artist Stelarc (b. 1946) negotiates concepts of identity and embodiment through artificial intelligence, robotics and prosthetics (Allain 2012: 71). Stelarc is known for using prosthetic instruments to wire his body to telecommunications devices and robotics, enabling remote muscle manipulation and expanding the 'power and reach of the human body' (Kac 2005: 180). Critics have referred to his work as body art because it investigates external and internal physical realities. Other writers observe aspects of voyeurism in his performances (Allain 2012: 71). The bodily focus of the majority of Stelarc's work foregrounds questions concerning human evolution in technological environments (Kac 2005: 178–9). Some examples of his work involve the physical connection of his body to the internet. *Muscle Stimulator System* (1994), for example, employed software developed by Stelarc to allow the audience to manipulate his body with electrical impulses, causing involuntary movements through the application of electrical charges to selected muscle groups. The physical manipulations were orchestrated by spectators present physically at the performance or virtually via the internet. A live website relayed Stelarc's image to online spectators, creating a dynamic sense of interaction with a remote audience. In this regard, *Muscle Stimulator System* is a cyborgian composition of human movement. Other works, such as *Parasite: Event for Invaded and Involuntary Body* (1997), performed at the Ars Electronica Festival, further display the themes of embodiment and disembodiment.

Both the public and the machine have power over the body. Stelarc's performances make us aware of the 'great amount of external forces that constantly bear on our embodiment' (Clarke 2005: 202). *Fractal Flesh* (1995) involved audience manipulation of electrical impulses through electrodes linked to the Web (Massumi 2005: 170). Remote participants used PictureTel teleconferencing software to control Stelarc's arms and one leg through the stimulation of electrodes while viewing him through a video monitor (Kac 2005: 81). The touch-screen interface enabled audiences at the Pompidou Centre in Paris, the Media Lab in Helsinki and the Doors of Perception in Amsterdam to affect the involuntary movements of his body according to their own preferences (Clarke 2005: 201–2). Images of Stelarc were then uploaded to the performance's website (Kac 2005: 81). Similarly, *Ping Body/Proto-parasite* (1995) empowered remote participants to determine Stelarc's physical movements through an interface (Goodall 2005: 15). Electrical signals controlled by sensors and transducers converted Stelarc's body into a multimedia mixer. Such works suggest that the human body is becoming obsolete and that we might never again be embodied individually due to the interventions and interconnections of technology (Goodall 2005: 17).

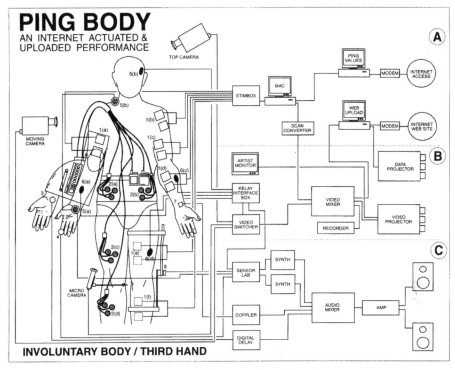

Figure 2.2 Stelarc, *PING BODY*, 1996. Diagram by Stelarc. Image courtesy of the artist.

Chapter Summary

The digital arts cross between the arts, the sciences and technology. This chapter has discussed the key theoretical, art-historical and technological contexts in which the digital arts evolved. Common terms for describing digital art practices, including materiality, embodiment, hybridity, interactivity and narrativity, have been outlined, along with the chief differences between analogue and digital media. The crucial distinction between technology as a tool and medium has been explored in preparation for understanding the artists and artworks discussed in the book.

- The digital arts reflect core tenets of postmodernism and poststructuralism, including the emphasis on context and interpretation.
- Materiality encompasses the physical properties and form of a digital artwork as it changes over time.
- Digital artists, such as Stelarc, probe issues of embodiment, raising questions about human relationships to new technologies and virtual environments.
- Hybridity describes the fusion of the material and virtual worlds, the cross-cutting of conventions of artistic practice and the use of different media (e.g. television, video and satellite) in a single work.
- Dada, Fluxus, Conceptualism and public art are among the prominent influences on the emergence of internet and computer-based art in the 1990s.
- The development of television, video, computer, internet and social media technologies have impacted and will continue to influence the trajectory of the digital arts.

3 DUMB VISIONS AND FABULOUS IMAGES: PHOTOGRAPHIC, DRAWN AND MOVING IMAGE

The previous two chapters discussed a range of influences on and characteristics of broader digital art forms. Many of these are most clearly articulated through the digitization of the image. Static, moving, photographic, drawn – the image saturates contemporary society. The list of different ways in which images are employed in digital art is long, and continues to grow and change. The impact of the digital on imagery is far-reaching.

KEY CONCEPTS

Theoretical concepts help establish an approach for discussing and understanding a digital aesthetic. Early essays that address photography, cinema and conceptual art can be read in conjunction with more recent ideas about media art and the impact of digital technologies on art (see Chapter 2).

One of the key writers who discusses ideas that apply to digital images is the German cultural theorist Walter Benjamin (1892–1940). His seminal 1936 essay 'The Work of Art in the Age of Mechanical Reproduction' (2006) proposes that photography's ability to make images almost infinitely reproducible will change the way we consume art. Against the backdrop of Marxist principles, Benjamin discusses the concept of authenticity as it applies to reproduction, arguing that the act of reproduction changes the context of the original artwork. In philosophy, authenticity refers to the degree in which one is true to one's own personality, or the way the conscious self comes to terms with the material world (Golomb 1995). In his essay, Benjamin introduces the concept of the 'aura' of an original artwork, and claims that it is lost in the kind of reproduction possible with photographs and films (also see Chapters 6 and 7). Benjamin explains his concept of the 'aura' by comparing it with our experience of nature; for example, looking at a mountain range or the shadow of a tree at a certain time of day. The presence of the object confirms its authenticity, giving it an aura, something inaccessible and out of reach. Technical reproduction has changed the way we produce and consume artworks, especially digital images, leading to a desire for authenticity to be replaced with new ways to perceive art. Benjamin foresaw the possibility of mass viewings of artwork, as is now the case with many digital images, a markedly different environment for viewing art than has been experienced in the past. The concepts of aura and authenticity offer frameworks in which to discuss the impact of digital images in art, and have been used by artists to critique historic artworks as well as to create new ones.

Another important concept in regards to digital art is that of the sublime. In eighteenth-century philosophy, the theory of the sublime refers to the grandeur of natural phenomena (Bolognini 2008). When applied to art where new technology plays an important role, the sublime refers to the possibility of reproducing and consuming this grandeur through technology, rather than nature. French philosopher Jean-François Lyotard claims that the sublime was the founding move of the modernist period in art, which, as we saw in Chapter 2, was a movement that rejected the ideology of realism (Lyotard 1994). For Lyotard, the sublime expresses the edge of our conceptual understanding and reveals the multiplicity and instability of the postmodern world. The technological sublime is a term that suggests the machine has replaced nature as the model for the sublime, where the machine demands an almost religious-like reverence (Slack and Wise 2005). The concept of the sublime provides another framework through which the impact of digital technologies on art can be discussed.

Reflection

French philosopher Roland Barthes posited that 'reference is the founding order of photography' (Barthes 1981: 76). In his book *Camera Lucida* (1981), Barthes discusses photographs as a kind of superimposition of reality and the past, not really a memory but something different. Given the discussion about authenticity, aura and the sublime, how do you think the idea of 'reference' applies to the digital image?

HISTORICAL PRECEDENTS FOR DIGITAL IMAGES

Many of the techniques used to manipulate images in digital art were developed in art movements of the early twentieth century. These include the Cubist, Dada and Surrealist movements, which often used the printed page as raw material for collage. In these movements, media were explicitly identified with the creation of fantastic spaces, bodies and desires. They cut and reassembled media not unlike the 'cut and paste' technique that forms the very basis of computer control. The works of French Surrealist photographer Man Ray (1890–1976), for example, used procedures such as double exposure, combination printing, montage and solarization, dramatically evoking a meeting of dream and reality that challenged perceptions of reality. The result was the creation of incomplete, fragmentary, pliable and plastic imagery – features that underpin digital aesthetics. The model of the image as plastic contrasts with the indexical nature of the database, as discussed in Chapters 2 and 8, and this friction forms the basis of many discussions around the digital image. In addition, the visual illusions, magic lantern performance and other similar devices explored in the 1920s can be seen as the origin of similar desire to explore the magical moving world of the not-quite-real.

These practices led to a different approach to the representation of reality. Building upon the fascination artists upheld with objects rather than images in twentieth-century art, the image was no longer fixed in time or materials, and instead came to reflect the fluid and interactive world offered to us on a computer. This fluidity results in the ongoing transformation of images, which while destabilizing them, also creates an enthusiasm for the alteration of reality where the real can seem illusory (Rush 1999: 192). This manipulation of images also means that art is no longer the only 'invented image' in culture, and the role of the viewer has been changed. The viewer is no longer a passive recipient who just 'looks at pictures', but rather transforms, shares and interacts with them. The manipulation so accessible within the digital framework offers a new level of translation and scope available to art. Images may be changed to represent completely different things than originally imagined by the artist, and this scope for change and its subsequent distribution is continually growing.

Terms such as 'post-photography' (Carani 1999) and 'soft cinema' (Manovich 2005) have led to the reclassification of photography and the moving image in terms such as 'lens-based media' or 'media arts'. As discussed in Chapter 2, digital artists see themselves as *artists* in a more general sense than simply photographers, painters or filmmakers. They move across media, reconfiguring existing works of art in media representations. Digital can stand alone or be part of a collection of other elements, existing inside and/or outside computers. Similarly, digital forms have seen the dissolution of art genres, as we will see through many of the following chapters. In the past, photography has been thought of as an evolution of drawing, and films as an evolution of photography – digital imagery erases these kinds of divisions.

THE CHALLENGES AND REWARDS OF TECHNOLOGICAL CHANGE

This chapter will demonstrate how art has significantly contributed to technological developments in the digitization of the image. Many artists have created new tools while creating artworks, demonstrate an enthusiasm to utilize new technological developments, and critique the impact of these tools on society in their work. The pace of technological development in digital tools for image making and repro-duction has been startling (see Chapters 1, 2 and 9). What began as large-scale digital post-production equipment necessary in the 1980s moved to affordable desktop PCs in the 1990s, and on to mobile media such as mobile phones and tablet computers in the 2000s. Similarly, the constant evolution of the media in which data is delivered and stored has sped past – from magnetic tapes, CD-ROMs, DVDs, and computer and projection screens, to hard drives, flash memory and downloads from the internet cloud (see Chapter 7). This has led to the democratization of digital art and, as Walter Benjamin predicted in his writing about photography (1980, 2006), many more people see digital images but also have access to the tools to make them. As discussed in the previous chapter, digital art is characterized by hybridity: every aspect of digital information – sound, image and text – can be fused by the artists and consumers. Electronic image production is immaterial, as it has no physical substance, unless the artist decides he or she wants to turn it into a material object. The ease with which anyone with a computer or mobile phone can add, edit, put in motion, share, upload or print an artwork created by either him/herself or someone else is a demonstration of the democratization of art brought about by digital technologies (see Chapter 7). And this tendency is nowhere more obvious than with the image.

The quality of the digital image has evolved significantly over time. The quantity of data included in a digital image file has seen the need to compress images so they do not take up too much hard drive space, challenging the idea that the digital image is infinitely reproducible. The construction of 'smaller' document versions for emailing or web posting can lead to significant degradation of quality, which has itself been the subject of artworks (see 'glitch art' below). New methodologies and protocols for compression are ongoing. In addition to this loss of quality in many digital prints, countless early works have not been printed on archival paper, often meaning the only remaining evidence of some digital images is documentation of their exhibition. This is despite the endless copying of digital images that has been taken for granted as part of the medium – technically, if not ethically. The challenges digital images have brought to consumers, archivists and preservation will be discussed in detail in Chapter 8.

WHAT IS A DIGITAL PHOTOGRAPH?

The word photograph is taken from Greek: *photo* (light) and *graphein* (writing). Technology has driven the development of photography since its invention in the nineteenth century (Wolf 2010: 31). The ongoing evolution of new cameras, film types, printing techniques and, more recently, software has invited artists to involve their imagination more and more, rather than rely on what is simply represented in front of the camera.

Case Study 3.1
Lev Manovich's 'The Paradox of Digital Photography' (1995)

This essay explores the ramifications of digital photography and film. Manovich examines the difference between traditional, or analogue, photography and digital (also discussed in Chapter 1). As mentioned in Chapter 2, Manovich has made an important contribution to the discussion around digital images. He posited that old photography was being replaced by something different, what he calls 'photo media'. He supports remediation – an idea that suggests new visual media achieve their cultural significance by paying homage to, rivalling and refashioning earlier media (Bolter and Grusin 2000). Even though it has dated somewhat – a common problem when writing about new technology – the article demonstrates the danger of referring to particular software and machines, as technologies change or are replaced over time. However, the essay remains an important early contribution to the debate around the techniques and aesthetics of the digital image.

We are continually exposed to digital images in advertising and the media. We now make and share photographs with our mobile phones and digital cameras, then proceed to look at them on websites and in newspapers. Yet the large degree of manipulation possible on a photograph taken with a digital device has led many to ask if these images are indeed photographs at all (see Chapters 2 and 9). The act of photographing, for example, may be familiar to us all, yet the incredible range of possibilities available to edit these images was unheard of with analogue photography. Now, the 'photographic' appearance of images can be created on a computer with drawing, animation and three-dimentional tools.

Perhaps the most important defining feature of a digital photograph is simply the absence of film. In a digital photograph, there no longer needs to be a 'hard copy' printed from the negative. The photograph exists primarily as data on a hard drive. What was termed 'grain' on photographic film has been replaced by independent squares known as 'pixels' on a screen, each of which can be modified, removed or replaced. Pixels have precise numerical values that determine their location and colour range, and are organized according to a series of algorithms that create the visual form. This encoding process means that the digital image can never be representational, as it no longer records or reproduces physical reality (Paul 2003: 47). An analogue photo must be 'taken', yet a digital photo can be 'made' – implying that reality is changeable and unfixed, and that the distinction between taking and making a photograph has all but collapsed (Wolf 2010: 48).

According to Margot Lovejoy, a computer creates artificial simulations of reality that look like a photograph, but are actually not photographs at all, even if the act of acquiring the image was 'photographic' in nature (Lovejoy 2004: 155). Sylvia Wolf (2010) defines a digital photograph as an image that transforms light into coded data, producing a mathematical model of the real: a new kind of representation. An analogue photograph creates something similar (analogous) to something else by recording changes in light onto film. While any photograph requires light and a subject, what happens after that is radically different for a digital photograph: it can no longer be taken for granted as a representation of a moment in time. Digital photography can be considered as distinct from, yet embedded in, the history of photography (Wolf 2010: 51).

There are other differences between digital and analogue photography. A digital photograph entails a radically different process to build the image, giving an editor – who may not even be the photographer – much more scope for manipulation, a process that may continue after its publication and distribution. As discussed above, this process may even begin with an analogue photo, digitized into pixels the moment it is scanned into the binary world of the computer. This scanning is in itself a kind of photography that has come about as one of an extended range of different possible output options – including printing, projection, screening and/or transmission.

The manipulation of a photograph is performed with different aesthetic and conceptual aims for artists. Wolf claims there are three main motivations for an artist to manipulate a digital photograph: for sociopolitical reasons, the desire to create other dimensions and worlds, or to critique the media itself (Wolf 2010: 45). As an example of sociopolitical art, Chris Jordan's *Plastic Bottles* (2007) is a large digitally constructed image of two million empty plastic beverage bottles, the number the artist claims are used in the USA every minute. As a large image it seems like a beautiful pointillist painting, but on close examination the true content is revealed. In terms of the creation of other worlds (involving the creation, rather than description of an image), the artist is able to distort or create new realities. This can be done in many ways, for example, by challenging perspective. Perspective has been one of the cornerstones in visual art, a concept introduced in the fifteenth century where a view is understood from a single point in space and time that represents subjects and objects in logical relationship to one another relative to scale (Wolf 2010: 43). One of the first artists to produce digital photographs that provide visions of other dimensions was the innovative American photographic and video artist Peter Campus (b. 1937), whose 1988 series of works experiment with the structural characteristics of the digital imaging medium, using photomontage, digital drawing and digital image manipulation. Noriko Furunishi's (b. 1966) vertical landscapes, such as *Untitled (Waterfall)* (2007) look real at first glance, yet closer inspection reveals these photographs to be manipulated through the distortion of perspective, creating a scene that is hyperreal (see Chapter 9). Likewise, the British artist Paul Smith's (b. 1969) *Artists Rifles* series (2011) is a series of self-portraits, often with other men, in army fatigues, where the loss of individuality and anonymity experienced by the artist during his

Figure 3.1 Chris Jordan, *Plastic Bottles* (2007). Detail of photograph. Image courtesy of the artist.

time in the military is offset by a sense of humour. The photographs are composed in a way that reflects classical painting, but dispose of the visceral reality of war, retaining the drama and egocentricity of childhood games. Here we see imaginary heroes usurped by the spectacle and paraphernalia of war in a constructed, virtual world where the viewer adopts a narrator's role.

Finally, artists have created works that critique conceptual issues and questions underlying the very idea of photography itself. Many early examples of digital photography referred to existing works of art, provoking questions about the relationship of painting and photography through digital means, and could be thought of as providing the kind of 'remediation' discussed in Case Study 3.1. In addition to Case Study 3.2 of Yasumasa Morimura included below, American artist Sherrie Levine (b. 1947), one of the original appropriation artists of the postmodernist 1980s, undertook a process of interrogating other artists' works. Her pixel study *After Cézanne: 5* (2007) depicts French painter Paul Cézanne's work as an abstract colour grid, where the pixels are large and more clearly defined than the overall image itself.

Case Study 3.2
Yasumasa Morimura's *An Inner Dialogue with Frida Kahlo (Festive Decorations)* (2001)

Japanese artist Yasumasa Morimura (b. 1951) is often referred to as an 'appropriation artist'. 'Appropriation' in art is the borrowing of existing elements in the creation of a new work. This can be the adoption, borrowing, recycling or sampling of human-made visual culture. Morimura's work borrows images from artists as disparate as the Renaissance painter Rembrandt to contemporary photographer Cindy Sherman, and he inserts his own face and body into the photographs (a process referred to as 'Photoshopping', in reference to one of the early and common software packages that makes the process possible). Through this process, doubt is cast on the realism of even the most classic images. An important role of art is its ability to question its own role in culture, critiquing the tradition of art itself. The combination of Morimura's image with important existing artworks interrogates them and contemporary society, simultaneously. His photographs address identity — of the artist in respect to the past, as well as the past itself. An important early work that uses compositing and collage techniques to critique the history of art is American artist Lillian Schwartz's (b. 1927) *Mona/Leo* (1987) where an artist's face — Leonardo da Vinci — is juxtaposed to one his most important paintings, *Mona Lisa*. The painting can be viewed at:

http://www.luhringaugustine.com/artists/yasumasa-morimura#/images/15/

As pointed out in Chapter 1, it is important to highlight the difference between medium and technique when discussing art. Digital techniques began as replicating and augmenting tools and aesthetics employed in analogue photography, and are still moving along a trajectory towards techniques unique to the digital. The sheer scope and possibility for detail in digital photographs are constantly being redefined and expanded upon. Repetition and detailed composite techniques are used to redefine aspects of human anatomy in the digital photographs of Spanish artist Daniel Canogar's (b. 1964) *Horror Vacui* (1999), an installation where repeated, repositioned and interlocked images of hands seem to wallpaper the gallery with a new being. The photograph reflects upon the body and what it stands for by transcending naturalism and looking to the artificial (Paul 2003: 45).

American artist Nancy Burson (b. 1943) pioneered the technique of morphing by applying changes to photographs of people. In *Mankind* (1983–5), Burson uses digital pixel manipulation to blend facial characteristics of different people, using archival databases of different digital and analogue photographs, while maintaining the aesthetic of old photographs. The techniques she developed would later be used by police to identify crime suspects, an example of how techniques generated by artists would influence the development of certain technologies (see Chapter 1). Burson's work provided an early example of how digital manipulation can mask the authenticity of photographs taken to verify identity. A different and more recent interrogation of identity can be found in the photographs of American artist Anthony Aziz (b. 1961) and Venezuelan artist Sammy Cucher (b. 1958). Their *The Dystopia Series* (1994–5) is a series of large-scale colour portraits where computer manipulations blur over and digitally erase eyes and mouths, dehumanizing the heads, using rendering techniques. The erasure of features hints at a loss of identity and means of communication in, and because of, the technological world.

DIGITAL IMAGERY IN ALL ITS DIMENSIONS

Not all digital images begin as photographs, and the evolution of digital tools and techniques has seen an integration of photography and drawing. Perhaps the most famous example of early digital art could be *Study In Perception* (1967) by American computer programmers Leon Harmon (1922–82) and Ken Knowlton (b. 1931) based at Bell Labs in the USA. The work is a computer-generated print that uses the small electronic symbols that replaced the grey scale in a scanned photograph to depict a reclining nude. The image began as a prank installed in a colleague's office, which could only be seen as a nude if one stepped far enough away. It has now become a classic early digital artwork.

The Key Digital Drawing Tools

Pixel-based tools and images (also known as bitmaps) use the smallest part of a digital image to manipulate it. As we have already seen, each pixel can be modified, removed or replaced. Pixels have precise numerical values that determine their location, colour range and resolution. Resolution is defined as the number of horizontal and vertical pixels in an image, and determines its refinement. For example, 300 dpi (dots per inch) is the current standard for printing.

Vector-based images are defined using geometric rules, and are resolution independent. Images are produced using mathematically defined points, curves and shapes to create the image, rather than to define them through a finite number of pixels. Images can be scaled to any size without losing quality of line.

Drawing was one of the first art techniques to be explored in a digital format. American artist-programmer Charles Csuri (b. 1922) explored drawing to create some of the first works of digital art in 1965 (also see Chapters 2 and 6). His *SineScape* (1967) is an example of the how mathematical functions of repetition and reiteration can be employed in an artwork, creating what seems to be a notation of a computer's own characteristics (Paul 2003: 28). The result is an elegant, beautiful landscape-like image. The ever-growing variety of software packages, refinement of computer graphics (offering over 16 million colours) and the development of programming tools (such as plotters and three-dimensional imaging mechanism) continue to expand the potential for generating images on a computer.

The term 'digital image processing' has been coined to describe the myriad of possibilities with the digital image. Some digital manipulations emphasize the representational image in art, while simultaneously continuing the postmodern trends of appropriation. Freehand drawing on computers, for example, was an early development – beginning with a light pen on a screen, and developing with the use of drawing tablets and touch interfaces that emulate a pencil, pen, or brush. Early works required the computer to be programmed before the drawing process could take place, as the graphic user interface (GUI) had not yet been developed. This process of programming the computer to create an artwork has led to a genre of art known as 'algorithmic art', pioneered by American artist Roman Verostko (b. 1929). Works such as *Cyberflower IV, Gold Version* (2000) involve programming as part of their creative process. Often, computers were even credited with making 'computer-assisted art', as in the works of English artist Paul Brown. His *Untitled Computer Assisted Drawing* (1975) is made through the control of individual elements that evolve or propagate in accordance with a set of simple rules. Many contemporary digital artists still use programming as part of their toolbox.

In more recent examples, developments in digital modelling and simulation software, as well as manufacturing machines, have redefined the forms that traditional sculpture may take. While three-dimensional modelling will often lead to the creation of an object in space, some might only ever live on a screen. As such, digital tools have removed tangibility as a defining element of sculptural practice. The creation and simulation of objects through computer drawings, and the construction of moulds or sculptural objects, can all be outcomes of digital processes. Three-dimensional modelling relies on access to a database that defines all parameters of the image or object in mathematical space. Cameras, lights and objects can be placed in the virtual space to render an image. This is different from two-dimensional works, where the manipulation of colour to change shade, light and shadow is the primary tool. Digital sculptors often use software to experiment with the scale of an object or change proportions of different parts. They are able to view the object from different vantage points, and experiment with blending objects in three dimensions.

The use of computer software to generate three-dimensional images was pioneered by American sculptor Kenneth Snelson (b. 1927), who developed the form often referred to as 'visual sculpture'. His work in the early 1990s integrates sculpture, mathematics and photography, and is epitomized in works such as *Forest Devils' Moon Night* (1991). The work is stereoscopic images (two next to each other) that give the impression of a three-dimensional environment when viewed together. Stereoscopic images are the basis of three-dimensional cinema.

Digital artists have been fast adopters of tools developed for military and manufacturing applications (see Chapters 2 and 6). The automation of machining tools with computer programming has led to the ability to prototype a sculpture with surprising accuracy and speed in a way that is not hampered by factors such as gravity, weight or size. A model generated using CAD (computer automated drawing) techniques can be used alongside CAM (computer aided machining) programming, which manufactures the item in a virtual environment. This programming can then instruct a CNC (computer numerical control) enabled machine to manufacture the object. This machine can be a three-dimensional printer, which uses additive processes, as opposed to more traditional subtractive processes, to build an object. Three-dimensional printers allow for interior voids, nested elements and lattice-like structures, not possible with traditional machining techniques, that build through the removal of materials (Wands 2006: 79). The sculptures of French artist Christian Lavigne (b. 1959) pioneer digital and visual sculpture. Lavigne produced the first rapid prototype sculpture in France in 1994 (Wands 2006: 93). *Cybersaly: Le Secret de l'Être* (2002–3) is a head made up of many other heads, based on scans of Lavigne's wife's face, constructed from synthetic polyamide. As a further example, American artist Dan Collins' *Twister* (2003) is a life-sized self-portrait sculpture, produced by a CNC and milled in urethane. The work is made from a data set gathered by the artist in 1995 using a full-body laser scanner, which scans the artist's body from every vantage point, enabling a very accurate three-dimensional reconstruction when required (Wands 2006: 83).

Figure 3.2 Emilio Gomariz, *Ai Everything* (2012). Screen shot, from the *Macintosh Lab* series (2009, ongoing). Image courtesy of the artist.

Finally, the very basis of computers, electricity, can also become the media for digital artworks. Some of the earliest examples of this are in the computer-programmed light installations of German artist Otto Piene (b. 1928) which he called 'sky art'. His recent installation, *Das Geleucht* (Mining Lamp) (1998–2007), is a 30-metre-high tower featuring steel, glass and LEDs. The interface of a computer's operating system can also be a medium for art making, where the very tools of the medium become the basis of the artwork, as seen in the works such as *Ai Everything* (2012) by Spanish artist Emilio Gomariz. This work uses the presentation modes and 'windows' of a computer desktop as the materials for visual artworks, by overlaying, repeating and manipulating them.

THE MOVING IMAGE: VIDEO ART, ANIMATION AND CINEMA

The replacement of film by digital formats has also impacted the moving image. The change was not a fixed or stable event, and to date there have been 12 different file formats for video data over 16 years, starting with the Digital Video (DV) in 1996, to, most recently, MPEG multiview video coding. The impact of digital technologies on the moving image has been equally as important as it has been to photography. The development of video art in the 1960s highlighted the diversification of the moving image in art. While computer animation proceeded to develop and interlink with developments in computer drawing and sculpture, the tools of the film industry were digitized and gradually made available on every computer desktop. Concurrently, television was seen as 'commercial media' that held a very separate and controlling role in culture when compared to video art and film. Yet, more recent developments in live video streaming and mobile technologies are changing that role.

Reflection

Theorist Marshall McLuhan saw television as a 'mosaic space' which represented similar ideas found in both physics and modern art, requiring the participation and involvement of the whole being (Meigh-Andrews 2006: 106). Can you think of places where art and television come together?

Gene Youngblood, in his influential book *Expanded Cinema* (1970), summarizes and surveys the technological communication tools and aesthetic preoccupations of the late 1960s. He views technological progress as a literal force (Meigh-Andrews 2006: 108). The replacement of film with data storage had an enormous impact on all time-based media. Early video artists, for example, would need to assemble image sequences in order or re-record in 'real time' to make a master tape. The ability to access chunks of data from a hard drive was a very different, non-linear approach from cutting tape. It also opened the way for different kinds of narrative models that do not necessarily involve the sequential unfolding of time – which had been explored in earlier experimental cinema. English writer and artist Malcolm Le Grice, in his influential 1997 essay 'A Non Linear Tradition: Experimental Film and Digital Cinema', proposed two categories of moving image work that break away from the narrative tradition:

- abstract non-representational works of film and video that draw on the musical and painterly elements of the fine art discourse; and
- films that make a conscious break with the narrative tradition.

The separation of artworks and film highlights what Le Grice argues is the inevitability of perceptual linearity, linked to the continuity of consciousness and nature rather than any kind of technological development (Meigh-Andrews 2006: 268). Yet the ubiquity of digital techniques might be challenging the very idea of consciousness itself (see Chapter 9).

VIDEO ART

Video is perhaps the technology most readily associated with electronic art of the 1970s and 1980s – it fused easily with genres of art and signified a break with art-historical traditions. Video art was an important new art form established in the 1960s that has considerably influenced cinema and television, despite developing in opposition to commercial television (Popper 1993: 54). It was an art form born with a piece of equipment, the Sony Portapak, which maintained the recording of real events as part of film and video history. The first work of video art was created in 1965 by Korean-American artist Nam June Paik (1932–2006), with the Portapak, on the very same day he acquired it (Popper 1993; also see Chapter 2). That happened to be the same day the Pope was visiting New York, and Paik filmed the Pope's procession through the streets of the city and played the footage that same night at a café. From then on the ability to generate original content became more affordable and accessible, and the use of webcams continues that trend. As revealed in Paik's work, the realism of the recorded image was video's main appeal, with cameras initially being employed as 'dumb technologies' – tools that simply replicate what the eye can see. Guerrilla video, the act of filming without permission and as a free agent, was a connected development that purported to portray the immediacy of reality to the viewer, something that seemed obscured by the heavy production values associated with cinema and television.

Video art led to developments in multi-screen presentation, interactivity, projection surfaces projectors and automation, and was quick to be adopted in the fine art world. It was a media free from traditional art history hierarchies, and allowed for time-based electronic manipulations, easy duplication, low production costs, and the possibility for artists to work alone or in collectives. Venues for enjoying video art soon expanded beyond art galleries and spread to the internet, DVD and film festivals. Importantly, video art interrogated the role of the spectator through its ongoing development. Closed-circuit cameras make viewers part of the artist's work and vision. A development on the closed-circuit is demonstrated in Dutch artists Bram Snijders and Carolien Teunisse's installation *RE:* (2010), which makes the projector the subject. Using mirrors, it projects onto itself, bringing the projector's role as transmitter and light receiver to the fore, wrapping the digital projectors in light. Mistakes have also made an important contribution to digital discovery across all genres. Glitch art refers to the aestheti-cization of digital errors, often inspired by computer crashes or unwanted data (see Chapter 9). It can be made by corrupting code or data deliberately. British artist Beflix's (a.k.a. Tony Scott) work *GLITCH #01 LIORE* (2001) is an image consisting of lines of different densities across a page, creating a delicate abstract image which he says is made by waiting for – or forcing – something to go wrong on a computer (Scott 2001). Glitch is also a sub-genre of music, discussed in Chapter 5.

Digital video works increasingly focus on the issues of how one gains access to reality, and the degree of mediation which vision generates. Video art and music have long been intertwined, and many music videos provided short commercial showcases for new tools. Emmy-Award-winning animator Rebecca Allen's music video for Kraftwerk's *Musique Non-Stop* (1986), from their album *Electric Café*, explored new facial animation software to create animated versions of the band members (Goodman 1987: 175). Artists' collectives made possible the acquisition of what was initially expensive post-production equipment, and in contrast to the trends in computer art described above, processing techniques used in video artworks were developed and built by artists, rather than scientists or programmers (Goodman 1987: 168). Video art was also a vehicle for experimental research into electronic systems. This included a video synthesizer that would add colour to black and white, developed by British artist Richard Monkhouse, which was intended for musicians as well as visual artists (Goodman 1987: 171). Video art also provided a forum for exploration into video sculptures, installations and theatrical performance.

Paik is credited with putting television into the art world by using it as a medium in his works (see Chapter 2). Some artists saw this as 'anesthetising its domestic function', without any critical analysis of the television's role in everyday life (Rosler cited in Meigh-Andrews 2006: 15). Others, such as the American immigrants Steina and Woody Vasulka, two very important figures in the development of digital imaging and video art, viewed Paik as the one who elevated video to an art form in its own right. Even the proliferation of computer-generated abstract effects that bombarded viewers in the mid-1980s has been used by some artists to critique the cultural impact of the information explosion directly (Meigh-Andrews 2006: 262). British artist Jeremy Walsh's (b. 1954) video *IOD* (1984) challenges the relationship between reality and mediation by providing collages of television station logos, indents, advertisements and captions to deliberately bombard and saturate the viewer (Meigh-Andrews 2006: 262).

The fundamental difference between video art and cinema has traditionally been the treatment of time (Popper 1993: 56). Video initially offered the instantaneous view, revealed on the tape in the moment, and made possible the ability to rewind and fast forward 'on the fly', whereas film required lengthier developing and editing times. This difference dissolved as the digital cameras and editing systems used in the cinema industry became readily available to consumers. Video art's relationship to television continues to evolve and, similarly, the boundaries between it and the other moving image forms have almost been eradicated. This coalescing of genres has been both aesthetic and technological, making 'video art' an art form that defined a period of social and aesthetic change. Importantly, video art accelerated an interest in installation art, where the focus moved from video content to one of situating video in a space. Bill Viola's work in Case Study 3.3 provides a good example of 'installed' video art.

The sculptural elements of video art and installation led to important developments in interactivity and virtual reality, and also helped redefine the possibilities of cinema. As Austrian artist, curator and theorist Peter Weibel states, 'the video and digital art of today have taken up the lance left behind by the cinematic avant-garde of the 1960s and developed one step further the universe of the cinematic code' (Weibel and Shaw 2003: 125).

Case Study 3.3
Bill Viola *The Quintet Series* (2000)

American artist Bill Viola (b. 1951) creates large-scale video installations that deal with the central themes of human consciousness and experience, and capture the essence of emotion through recording its extreme display as ultra-slow-motion, large video projections. His works invite the viewer to almost sink into and connect with the meanings within the image.

The Quintet Series is a set of four silent videos depicting the extremely slow unfolding expressions of five actors, where every minute detail of their changing expressions can be detected. The distortion of time and the detail it reveals in the large, high-resolution images is confronting for the viewer.

Excerpts of *The Quintet Series* can be found on YouTube.

ANIMATION

Animation is the process of putting images in motion, which can also involve the rendering of the images into three dimensions. The realization of animations has long been a time-consuming and difficult process. The effort required to create complex three-dimensional animations has even been dubbed the 'one frame movie' (Goodman 1987: 108–10). Like television, animation sits on the border of entertainment and art. Yet unlike video art, television's ongoing engagement with animation led to the popularity of Anime and cartoons, where the interaction between drawing and video was developed and refined.

Many animators have been software engineers, testing the boundaries of programming by giving life to still images and drawings. A significant development in animation was the ability to create three-dimensional moving images, often from two-dimensional drawings. American programmer-artist A. Michael Noll is one of the earliest pioneers to use a digital computer to create patterns and animations solely for their artistic and aesthetic value. His *Computer-Generated Ballet* (1965) is rendered for three-dimensional stereographic (using two screens) and two-dimensional (single screen) versions of white stick figures moving randomly on a stage. *Man and His World* (1965) was an early computer-generated animation created at Bell Labs by American artist Stan Vanderbeek (1927–84) with assistance from a resident programmer Ken Knowlton (Vanderbeek and Knowlton 1965). The contribution of institutions such as Bell Labs and the IBM workshops in the USA in the 1960s and 1970s cannot be understated, where the partnering of programmers with artists enabled approaches that masked the mathematical problems behind computer functions for many artists, allowing them to focus on the aesthetic if they wished.

Two early innovators in computer animation are the Americans Larry Cuba (b. 1950) and Karl Sims (b. 1962). Sims established computer programing as a new and valid animation technique – and as something different from traditional hand-animated, team-designed narrative. His work *Panspermia* (1990) creates and animates forests of three-dimensional plant structures using the evolutionary software systems that he pioneered (Wands 2006: 159). Cuba developed important techniques, such as the 'enveloped particle systems', that enabled computer programs to simulate natural phenomena including water, fire, smoke and rain (Wands 2006). A further example is that of Japanese artist Yoichiro Kawaguchi (b. 1952), one of the first artists to use algorithms to control computer graphics with the aim to make films for purely artistic purposes. He looked to create 'realistic depictions of fantasies' using his program, *Growth Model* (1982) (Goodman 1987: 165).

The work of Charles Csuri also exemplifies early computer art, which included experiments in animation. *Hummingbird* (1967) was made in collaboration with computer programmer James Shaffer, who enabled Csuri to digitize hand drawings, which were later animated in real time using a computer animation program. Another important artist in early animation was Lillian Schwartz, whose work *Pixillation* (1970) was a full-colour animation generated by a combination of hand and computer drawing. This also featured electronic sound described as 'drumbeats on the eyeballs' (Goodman 1987: 160). Some of her animation works required three-dimensional glasses to be viewed, such as *Flower 1* (2000). This trend can be aligned with the development of video goggles often used in virtual reality scenarios. An interest in colour and visual perception was common among artists working in early computer animations, and their investigations have led to common techniques such as cell-shaded animation, (using computer graphics to imitate hand-drawn animations), machinima (integrating graphics engines from video games and virtual worlds), motion capture and photo-realistic animation.

Case Study 3.4
Sin City (2005)

This film is a neo-noir thriller based on American artist Frank Miller's graphic novel series of the same name, and won the Technical Grand Prize at the Cannes Film Festival in 2005. *Sin City* is one of the first films to be shot primarily on a 'digital backlot', where actors perform in front of a green screen, and everything else is added in post-production. The combination of high-end digital cameras and the digital backlot made *Sin City* one of the few fully digital live action films of its time. The whole film was initially shot in full colour, and was converted to black and white with some colour added digitally later. True to the *film noir* tradition, the film was treated for heightened contrast. This combination of new and old techniques gave the film a hyperreal appearance, which emphasized the 'comic fantasy' element of the film. French postmodernist theorist Jean Baudrillard uses the term 'simulacrum' to signify a representation of the real, without the substance of the original. He argues that a simulacrum is not a copy of the real, but becomes truth in its own right, and coined the term 'the hyperreal' (see Chapter 9).

It is not surprising that animation has strong links with cinema. In addition to Case Study 3.4, *Waking Life* (2001) by American artist Richard Linklater (b. 1960), for example, uses a software version of 'rotoscoping', a cinematic tool that enables drawing onto film. In this work, real action was filmed on digital video, onto which a team of different artists then drew stylized lines and colours over each frame using off-the-shelf desktop computers. By way of another example, *Final Fantasy: The Spirits Within* (2001) by Japanese video game designer Hironobu Sakaguchi was an important computer-animated science fiction film created from the *Final Fantasy* series of role-playing video games. It was the first photo-realistic computer-animated feature film, and paved the way for developing photo-realistic animations in films.

CINEMA

> 3D animation, compositing, mapping, retouching: In commercial cinema, these radical new techniques are used mostly to solve technical problems while traditional cinematic language is preserved and unchanged. (Manovich 2001a: 209)

As video art was born of technological development, digitization also hastened the transformation of classical cinema. The innovative French illusionist and filmmaker Georges Méliès, working in analogue formats at the start of the twentieth century, could be seen as the father of special effects in cinema, just as the later work of Soviet documentary filmmaker Dziga Vertov challenged narrative and established the *cinéma verité* style of documentary movie-making (Manovich 2001a: 52). The broadening of the cinematic code presented in the expanded cinema movement of the 1960s, combined with the liberation signalled by the digitization of the industry in the 1990s, led to faster post-production processes informed by digital processing. Digital cameras with on-board hard drive storage streamlined the filming process, by making smaller, cheaper and high-quality tools widely available. Therefore, while complex equipment continues to evolve in large budget studios working with the latest special effect possibilities, independent experimental and personal cinema expands elsewhere. Despite the advances in computer art and animation enabling advanced post-production simulation tools, cinema has remained the art form most grounded in the recording and representation of reality – even though these digital effects and modelling only depict reality. Manovich argues that cinema in its analogue form already contained the multimedia and random access processes we associate with computers, and that the impact of the digital is ambiguous in cinema (other than its role in establishing programmable data as part of the process of film making) (Manovich 2001a: 52).

Applying early digital effects to moving images required cinema studios to engage large teams to program different elements of what the audience would see as a simple image sequence. For example, the holograph that appeared on screen for 37 seconds in the film *Return of the Jedi* (1983) by American film producer George Lucas took four months to create (Goodman 1987: 179). The early predictions that actors could be replaced by digital imitations has been getting closer to reality, as computer-generated imagery (CGI) is taken for granted in almost all cinema experiences. When actor Oliver Reed died of a heart attack during the filming of *Gladiator* (2000), directed by Ridley Scott, the post-production team produced his simulation to enable completion of the film. A live action body double was filmed in the shadows, which then had a three-dimensional computer-generated mask of Reed's face mapped to it, creating a digital body double that could be added to scenes (Landau 2000: 123). The same post-production crew used 2,000 live actors to create a computer-generated crowd of 35,000 virtual actors, which were required to look believable and react to fight scenes. This was accomplished by filming live actors at different angles, giving various performances, and then mapping these images onto cards using motion capture tools to track their movements, which were then used in three dimensional compositing (Landau 2000: 122).

Case Study 3.5
Jeffrey Shaw's *Legible City* (1988–91)

Australian new media artist Jeffrey Shaw (b. 1944) has pioneered interactive cinema, which combines the screen-based traditions of moving image with the potential of digital technologies to immerse the spectator in the experience. He integrated multiple media in work for rock bands Pink Floyd and Genesis through the 1980s, and actively sought alternatives to the flat screen – leading to his involvement in the iCinema Centre for Interactive Cinema Research in Australia, established in 2002 (Tofts 2005: 52).

Legible City is an interactive work where the viewer navigates a city on a fixed bicycle. The city is not tied to physical reality; it is made of three-dimensional letters that change as the cyclist changes speed or direction. Shaw examines the relationship of the virtual and the real, one of the central questions for the computer age (Manovich 1995: 260; also see Chapter 9).

Experiments in video art bled into cinema as multiple projections, multi-perspective narratives, the suspension of linear time in temporal and spatial asynchrony, and multiform plots, as shown in Figure 3.3 (Weibel and Shaw 2003: 120).

Non-visual aspects of digital art have fed into cinematic practice, particularly in regard to narrative, as above. While theorists such as Malcolm Le Grice discuss the influence of non-linear editing technologies on narrative, others suggest the influence of hypertext, which, as we discussed in Chapter 2, is a term coined by Theodor H. Nelson in the 1960s. Hypertext is the non-linear, non-chronological, non-hierarchical and multiple narrative structure featured predominantly on the internet, and has led to what has become known as 'hypernarrative'. Writing a narrative using hypertext technology allows the meaning of the story to be conveyed through a sense of spatiality and perspective drawn from digitally networked environments such as the internet, decentralizing a viewer's orientation, and giving different meaning to a script – while still allowing visual imagery to determine and pronounce place, time and characters (see Chapter 2). Again referring to the indexed database so fundamental in digital art, a hypernarrative may seek a range of trajectories through possible outcomes from within that database, not unlike the processes at work in video games. These traits have become common in interactive film works. Mark Amerika's *FILMTEXT 2.0* (2002), for example, is a digital narrative created for cross-media platforms. It has been exhibited as a museum installation, a website, a conceptual art e-book, an MP3 concept album, a series of live performances and a looping DVD (Amerika 2011). When visited as a website, *FILMTEXT 2.0* delivers text, sound and different trajectories in response to clicking the mouse on objects on the screen. A cinematic example of alternative narrative structures can be found in the film *Timecode* (2000) by English director Mike Figgis, which is constructed from four continuous 90-minute takes that were filmed simultaneously by four video cameras, shown at the same time on the cinema screen. The impact of these developments means that 'the narrative universe becomes reversible in the field of digitally expanded cinema and no longer reflects the psychology of cause and effect' (Weibel and Shaw 2003: 124). These experiments signalled the beginning of immersive, interactive and virtual worlds, and perhaps some of the biggest developments in cinema in these directions are yet to come. The facility of film distribution through the internet and portable storage media in itself offers new possibilities for filmmakers, including the impact and potential of internet film.

While digital arts expand the possibilities of cinematic forms, the very notion of cinema itself has also been examined and critiqued by digital film artists. Films by artists such as Mathew Barney and Jesper Just feature the grand production qualities of major commercial cinema releases, yet present very artist-driven content. Cinema, therefore, continues its journey in the digital realm, towards holographic cinema, haptic interfaces, internet film and more.

Figure 3.3 Jeffrey Shaw, *Legible City*, 1988–91. Performance still. Image courtesy of the artist.

INSTALLATION ART

Enhanced cinematic experiences and projection possibilities have demanded expanded options to present such work, and *Legible City* (Figure 3.3) provides an early example of what is possible. The capitalization of the image in physical space is an important element of installation art – an art form developed in analogue at the beginning of the twentieth century that has accelerated considerably in popularity as computers have developed. Installations are three-dimensional artworks where space is a key element. They are often site-specific, and involve the viewer's perception of a space as a fundamental point of engagement with the work. Growing out of the works of Surrealist and Dada artists in the early twentieth century – such as Marcel Duchamp's ready-mades or German painter Kurt Schwitters' (1887–1948) *merz art objects* – installation art was particularly favoured by the conceptual artists of the 1960s, where the intention of the artist overcomes the preoccupation with form (see Chapter 2). Installation art has an immersive quality, and can involve different kinds of still or moving images, interfaces, lighting, virtual reality environments, internet hook-ups and spatialized sound. Works by artists such as American multimedia artist

Tony Oursler (b. 1957), for example, integrate innovate projection ideas with sound that can only be shown in an installation environment. *Blue/White State* (1997) features a rag doll-like abstract figure of someone who has fallen out of a chair. The face is projected onto a fabric head, and appears to talk as viewers pass through the gallery.

Installation is the only environment for experiments in 'kinetic art', which includes optical art and other moving artworks that have been significantly facilitated by the involvement of computers. Installations will often absorb digital technologies not often associated with art, such as surveillance cameras and time-lapse technologies. While there is perhaps no such thing as a 'digital installation' (Wands 2006: 100), they are an important component in the digital art world for the way they blend different elements of digital art together. British artist Lei Cox (b. 1965) makes installations that feature both video paintings and interactive objects, where digital imaging creates hybrid creatures within fantastical landscapes. *Skies over FlowerField* (1995–8), part of the *Ultra Reality Series*, is inspired by computer games, poking fun at the environmental messages often contained in virtual reality environments. It uses clay animation (or claymation) on interconnected screens, as well as an interactive component where pressure pads hidden under astroturf trigger talking flowers.

Chapter Summary

This chapter discussed a range of theoretical concepts that have informed historical and technical trends in digital art imagery, and has examined photography, computer-generated drawings, sculpture, animations, video art, cinema and images within installation art.

■ Digital image-making has been shaped by techniques laid out by artists from the Surrealist, Dada and conceptual art movements.

■ Technologies for the creation, editing, storing and reproducing of images have developed very quickly and continue to do so.

■ Digital image creation and distribution has seen a democratization of the image and its making.

■ Digital art is often hybrid, and digital artists will often work across different media.

4 DANCING AT THE SPEED OF LIGHT: THE DIGITAL IN PERFORMANCE

Performance has become one the most significant art practices in the last hundred years, and its surge in popularity has been aided by its fast integration of new technologies that enable an ever-growing world of possibilities. As narrative and character were no longer the focus of performance work in the twentieth century, interactivity and multimedia presentation have played an important role in the development of new performance forms. The digital facilitates and mediates live performance, through a computer screen, enhanced by projections, in cybertheatre events over the internet or immersed in a virtual world. Digital technologies provide a toolbox of items that inevitably become characters on a stage; robots are choreographed, cyborgs react to messages from the internet and microscopic cells perform on glass slides. Digital aesthetics have influenced and shaped the content and performative qualities of various art forms, often from unexpected directions. The computer has acted as an agent of action and creation, blurring communication, scriptwriting, acting, visual art, science, design, theatre, choreography, video and performance art in its path. Performative forms highlight that digital aesthetics cannot be broken down into a simple opposition between technology and humanity – the performative arts make it apparent that humans are a kind of technology too, and our brains have come to be termed 'wetware'. This chapter discusses how digital technology has become an integral part of performance practice, exploring its adoption in 'live' art and its various permutations.

The term 'digital performance' includes all performance works in which computer technologies play a key rather than a subsidiary role in the generation of content, techniques, aesthetics or delivery forms. Howard Rheingold's claim that virtual reality is ultimately a theatrical medium, drawing on the use of sets, performances and scripts, merits inclusion here (Rheingold 1991). The performative presentation of robots and cyborgs has replaced puppetry and brought the body into close scrutiny. Digital technologies have enabled the experience of live performance on the smallest of scales, where artists can now choreograph cells under microscopes and grow additions for their bodies. A new form, performance art, grew from artists' desire for a more visceral, body-centric element not found in existing forms, running in direct contrast to the appeal of the virtual in other art forms. Engaging with the tangibility of the physical body and its relationship to technology, performance art provides a refreshing alternative to the discussions around disembodiment that are often at the core of debates related to the impact of digital arts (Dixon 2007: 24; also see Chapter 2).

There is an exciting tension between the liveness of performance and pre-set digital technologies. Virtual technologies, whose attributes can be present without sharing any of their real or imagined physical form, are a direct outcome of digital technology. This relationship between the actual and the virtual has a long history in performing arts and, since the eighteenth century, the virtual had moved from a role of fiction to assuming the negative qualities of the fake. Postmodernism, however, has brought the fake back into favour, and many digital performance works examine the tensions between the actual, the fake and the virtual, and the potential of the virtual to morph and extend the possibilities of the performing body.

CYBERPUNKS IN CYBERSPACE

Cyberspace is the electronic medium where online communication takes place on computer networks. The term was first used by cyberpunk science fiction writer William Gibson, who later went on to call it an 'evocative and meaningless' term (Thill 2009). Gibson's book *Neuromancer* (1984) describes a society made up of human/machine hybrids, and is one of the most influential pieces of cyberpunk writing. Many terms have been derived from cyberpunk literature. For example, Michael Swanwick's novel *Vacuum Flowers* (1987) was the first to use the term 'wetware' to describe human parts, a play on the words 'hardware' and 'software'. The genesis of 'cyber' is the term 'cybernetics', coined by Norman Wiener in 1948 (Kellner 1995), which has led to a plethora of other words such as cyberspace – the electronic medium of computer networks – and even cyborg. A 'cyborg' is a real or imagined being with both biological and artificial (i.e. electronic, mechanical or robotic) parts, often an organism that has technologically enhanced abilities. The term was coined in 1960 when Manfred Clynes and Nathan Kline (1960) used it in an article about the advantages of self-regulating human-machine systems in outer space.

THEORETICAL TERMS

REMEDIATION

This is an idea proposed by Jay Bolter and Richard Grusin, who argue that new visual media achieve their cultural significance precisely by paying homage to, rivalling and refashioning earlier media (Bolter and Grusin 1996). They call this process of refashioning 'remediation', and they note that earlier media have also refashioned one another: photography remediated painting; film remediated stage production and photography; and television remediated film, vaudeville and radio.

ABJECTION

This literally means 'the state of being cast off', a state that is rejected by and disturbs social reason, implying degradation and baseness as well as intentionally disturbing conventional identity and cultural concepts. The term was developed by philosopher Julia Kristeva as a communal consensus that underpins a social order, and can be seen as an important theoretical framework for performance art in particular.

Two other important French theorists are Jean Baudrillard and Paul Virilio. Baudrillard sees the digital as being able to turn dualities and polarities into norms and models, moving from a cultural structure of relationships to one of connections (Auslander 2008). Virilio, however, foresaw the speeding-up of society as facilitated by digital technology (Virilio 1977 [1986]).

THEORETICAL CONSIDERATIONS

Central to many discussions around performance and digital technologies is the idea of the Cartesian split. A philosophical concept that began with Socrates, and was later confirmed by René Descartes in his 1637 book *Discourse on Method and Mediations* on Philosophy (1960), the Cartesian split distinguishes, divides and separates the mind from the body (see Chapter 2). The body is abstracted and depersonalized, and the self remains firmly planted in the mind (Dixon 2007: 213). This way of thinking, that enables a separation of things that happen to our body from that of our mind, is firmly embedded in modern humanity. Disembodiment is a term used to describe this separation, a state of being often claimed to occur when inhabiting virtual environments where the mind can wander without the physical inhibitions of the body (Balsamo 2000), as when a person connected to the internet can be virtually represented and interact within cyberspace. The virtual body can be seen as a kind of theatrical entity – an unreal, constructed version of ourselves. Virtual reality has been embodied in theatre for hundreds of years, where performers use a type of 'virtual' to examine the interaction between virtual and physical. This emphasis on liveness and the body's new emphasized role in art was facilitated by digital technologies.

The ideas posited by French playwright Antonin Artaud (1896–1948) provide us with some useful touchstones when discussing the impact of digital technology on performance. Seen as a 'philosopher of the theatre' (Dixon 2007: 18), important theoretical notions were developed by Artaud in his collection of essays *The Theatre and its Double* (1958 [1938]). One of the essays in this collection, 'The Theatre of Cruelty', calls for a kind of total theatre that shatters false reality. He imagined a duplication of theatre, which he called theatre's 'double', that was its own, magical self. Artaud considered dreams and thoughts no less real than the outside world, foreseeing the possibilities of virtual reality, a term he coined by linking alchemy and theatre (Dixon 2007: 242). Virtuality is the fulcrum for his theatre of cruelty: it can be seen as a shadow figure, an uncanny component of every work. Artaud's idea of the double is actually enabled by digital technology in four possible ways:

1. Reflection (technology as a mirror – video and surveillance)
2. Alter ego (robots, cyborgs, body art, avatars)
3. Spirits (telematics and internet transmissions)
4. Manipulable mannequins (robots, cyborgs, virtual reality)
   (Dixon 2007: 242)

The lack of difference between reality and representation, as envisioned by Artaud, is being realized as a result of digital developments, leading to an imagined future where the real world and fiction might no longer need to be distinct categories.

Another influential theorist was French theorist Guy Debord (1931–94) and the Situationist International movement that was active in the early 1960s. This movement combined Marxism, psychoanalysis and existentialism as a theory for life and art that rejected art as something separate from politics. Debord's 1967 work *The Society of the Spectacle* (Debord 1995) urges popular control of urban spaces, and the use of theory as a locus for 'aesthetic actions' (Rush 1999: 64). Artists took this on by using public events and politics as topics for artworks, creating and developing a sociopolitical approach to art that was most effectively realized in performance. This led to the integration of media never intended for artistic consumption, such as news event footage and the re-enactment of events. Media watchdog group Ant Farm produced *The Eternal Frame* (1975), a performance that re-enacts and re-stages public events including John F. Kennedy's 1963 assassination.

Philip Auslander's important book *Liveness: Performance in a Mediatized Culture* (2008) claims that performance, as well as audiences' perception of it, is largely affected by the form of mediation supplied by the dominant media of the time. Auslander uses the term 'cultural economy' to describe the way different media enjoy various degrees of cultural presence, power and prestige at different points on the historic timeline.

His ideas depart from two major premises. The first is that human sense perception is not simply a biological given: it is culturally and historically influenced, including by the popularity of technology, as discussed in the works of Walter Benjamin. The second is that all media are not equal. At the time of writing *Liveness*, Auslander saw television (or the televisual) as the dominant media, but has since claimed that digital is the new important media, since the televisual is now experienced through digital remediations (cited in Breznican and Strauss 2005: 196). Auslander concludes that older performative forms, such as theatre, have a lesser cultural presence than cinema or the internet, yet survive due to the 'prestige factor', a perception of theatre as 'high art' that requires specific educational and cultural capital for its appreciation. Video screening on stage or in an installation becomes art, yet the same images on television remain entertainment (Breznican and Strauss 2005: 195).

HISTORY

Futurism was an important art and social movement in the early part of the twentieth century, originating in Italy. It emphasized and glorified themes associated with contemporary concepts of the future, including speed, technology, violence, objects such as the car, the airplane and the industrial city, and was practised across all genres of art. The work of the Futurists can be seen as the basis for movements such as cyberpunk, and a foundation for the development of new and existing technologies leading to cyborgs and robotics. The approach of the Futurists can be found in *The Futurist Manifesto* penned by the group's leader Filippo Marinetti (Joll 1960 [1909]). Other manifestos generated by the Futurists were influential in the areas of digital music, as discussed in Chapter 5.

The Dada movement, which began as a reaction to the horrors of World War I in Switzerland around 1916, rejected reason and logic, prizing nonsense, irrationality and intuition as an approach to art (Budd 2005; also see Chapter 2). A key figure of the movement, Marcel Duchamp, is largely considered to be the founder of conceptual art, where the emphasis is on the idea, rather than the subject or any object created. The artist selects material for aesthetic consideration, rather than forming something from traditional raw materials of art – and this thinking led Duchamp to create what he called 'ready-mades' and to see real life activities as art (see Chapter 2). Other artists followed this focus on process, perception and revelation of the body in the environment (Carlson 2004: 111). The Dadaists championed interactivity, and Duchamp's *Rotary Glass Plates* (1920), made with surrealist photographer Man Ray, is often cited as one of the first interactive works. As also described in Chapter 2, the work is activated by the movement of the viewer, who must stand a metre away to see it properly. Importantly, Dada is seen as the starting point of performance art.

In addition to the desire of the surrealists to create dreamlike imagery, as discussed in Chapter 3, the Fluxus artists, active in the 1960s and 1970s, sought audience involvement and artist autonomy in their works. These artists combined artistic experimentation and social and political activism. Where the Futurists practised within many different genres, the Fluxus artists combined genres in single works. The social and sexual revolution of the 1960s found expression in art away from the canvas and into actions where the viewer became involved. An important characteristic of Fluxus art is the use of instructions, which are given to participants who then make their own narrative or associations, a trend that was later facilitated by digital technologies. The act of inviting participation was itself a sociopolitical act and it freed artists from the influence of art history by eliminating aspects of craft, leaving only process (Rush 1999: 48). A characteristic form of the Fluxus movement was 'happenings' – events where different art forms came together in the moment, leading to the use of the term 'mixed media'. The dance and media experiments in New York City during the 1960s were a vital development of what then came to be known as 'multimedia' performance, where fertilizations between theatre, dance,

Figure 4.1 John Cage, *Variations V* (1965). John Cage, David Tudor, Gordon Mumma (foreground), Carolyn Brown, Merce Cunningham, Barbara Dilley Lloyd (background). Photograph by Hervé Gloaguen. Image courtesy of the John Cage Trust.

film/video, visual art and sound knitted in single events. During this time, the American painter Robert Rauschenberg was an early proponent of intermingling art and technology, and he collaborated with composer/musician John Cage and dancer/choreographer Merce Cunningham to create some of the first multimedia events. Together they developed what is thought to be the first multimedia work, *Variations V* (1965), with a large team of collaborators contributing film, choreography, dance, sound and builders of the technology to facilitate these interactions (see Chapter 1 for a discussion of the term 'media'). The technical equipment developed for this work, some of which may be seen in Figure 4.1, anticipated the computer-controlled interaction between live performance and sound effects seen in theatre and dance since the 1990s (Rush 1999: 37).

The Wiener Aktionisten (Viennese actionists) were a group of artists also repelled by war (by then, World War II), and who rejected museums as places to show art. Building on the reactionary nature of the Dadaists and the happenings of the Fluxus artists, they created works in the 1960s in which destruction was often the primary path (Rush 1999: 55). They staged what they named 'actions' – precisely scored works in controlled environments that emphasized the body through transgressive, violent and destructive performances. The American painter Jackson Pollock, Italian painter Lucio Fontana and Japanese painter Shozo Shimamoto made paintings about the creative act, not just the object or its subject (Rush 1999: 36). These artists painted in a way that was spectacular to witness – full of action, movement and drama, encapsulating Duchamp's focus on process as performance.

TECHNOLOGY

> A new medium is never an addition to an old one, nor does it leave the old
> one in peace. (McLuhan [1964] cited in Auslander 2008: 194)

The 1990s saw a blossoming of experimentation with performance and computers, and early performances were characterized by an audience enchanted by technological spectacle and novelty, a reaction that focused on the 'how'd-they-do-it' factor (Auslander 2008: 195). Computer-simulated environments offered performance a new space in which to occur, and new tools to construct and control different elements of a performance quickly and easily. The integration of film into theatre performance challenged the distinction between what is live and what is not by confusing live and pre-recorded action on stage and screen. Computers provided a new level of control in performance – sensors could relay tactile or visual information to trigger or manipulate data, controlling machines and the media stored, generated or relayed by them. These signals can be triggered by audience or performers alike, and can facilitate changes on performers, sets and sounds even to remote locations. These were very responsive technologies, and ongoing software innovations maintained a steady pace that would mediate performance and all its components.

The screen became an important part of performance, providing a portal to uniquely flexible spaces, challenging the fixed point of view that a traditional theatre provides to the members of the audience. As higher-resolution projectors became available to most consumers and were readily connected to any computer, projections gradually removed the need for screens at all. Video was adapted to create virtual sets in performance spaces that offered unique moving environments, and projectors were turned onto bodies instead of screens. Stereoscopic (double screen) projections and three-dimensional visualization paved the way for virtual reality environments in installation and internet spaces.

As with installations, collaborations between artists and scientists provided key developments in many areas of performance, and interactive software gradually became more user-friendly, with interfaces that enabled artists to do their own programming and operate technologies themselves, allowing artists themselves to be the creators of unique control environments that operate interactive combinations of technologies. Similarly, the ongoing fascination with living bodies was another avenue for teams of artists and scientists, using the latest digital technologies available to explore the possibilities of robotics, body modification and cellular manipulation.

The internet provided a significant contribution to performance. Early experiments where collaborations took place over phone lines and expensive satellite relays suddenly became available to anyone with an internet connection. The internet has enabled extended forms of interaction that cross continents and time zones, providing a 'soft space' for performances to take place. It has been used as a performance collaborator in its own right, and has provided an interactive database and distribution tool for performers since its adoption by the public. Performance works that use the internet as a key formal component in their conception are touched on here, but will be discussed in detail in Chapter 6 alongside trends such as telepresence, networked performance and the possibilities of transcription and replay.

CASE STUDIES

DANCE AND CHOREOGRAPHY

It is important to remember that interactivity and multimedia presentation have always been part of performance; actors respond to audiences in subtle ways, for example, and dancers have long interacted with paintings and music during their performances. Yet digital technologies have enabled a machine-facilitated interactivity and multimedia presentation in ways previously unimaginable. Dance in particular has had a sustained engagement with digital technology due to a pre-existing tradition of recorded and mechanized performances. Yet the clarity and speed of digital facilities that facilitated developments such as motion tracking, real time and remote audio-visual connections have propelled dance into new performance environments.

American dancer Loie Fuller (1862–1928) is often cited as the first modern dance choreographer to integrate new media within her performance work. As Fuller danced in works such as *Serpentine Dance* (1881), the robes she wore became a sort of 'screen' for multicoloured lights to project upon, beginning a long tradition of electronic technology adoption in dance works. Later, a digital aesthetic was evident in dance performances as a result of computer-generated choreography, which offered new and wide ranging indeterminate possibilities for movement. New kinds of fluid, indeterminate shapes became possible, as the dancing body is transformed into digital information through motion tracking, photography and video. In works such as Sophia Lycouris's *string* (2000) the performer dances around a projection that eventually integrates with her own body, creating an interesting kinetic liquidity (Dixon 2007: 406). Digital processing is also able to generate technical solutions and three-dimensional renderings of astonishingly complex and fragmentary designs for sets where dancers interact within. In the San Francisco Ballet's dance production *Pixellage* (1983), computer-generated imagery was incorporated with live performance for the first time in a major venue, with the projection being shown on a screen behind the performers (Goodman 1987: 182). The internet also provided new spaces for dance to occur, and for new types of collaborations to take place.

In the realm of new technologies, content, not just the mechanism for delivery, is key. Projected content was explored in a number of ways, and the possibilities of motion-capture technology were of particular interest to dancers and choreographers. Sensors or markers can be applied to the performer's body, whose movement is then tracked and captured, originally with magnets and later with cameras. A computer can then combine and interpret all the data coordinates and provide a three-dimensional rendering of the markers moving in space. The dots are joined up to create the kinetically accurate dance animations (Dixon 2007: 189). Australian dance company Company in Space created a dance theatre performance *Incarnate* (2001) in which a computer-generated female body shape is projected and filled with points of brightly coloured lights that appear to choreograph the virtual dancer for the audience, dragging it into different shapes and dimensions, while disintegrating and re-materializing the body itself (Dixon 2007: 255). It is a wonderful example of how the digital can remind us of our very materiality and mortality. Animations can be generated from motion tracked coordinates. In *BIPED* (1999), choreographer Merce Cunningham, one of the early explorers of motion tracking, worked with software company Riverbed to create natural-looking, fluid animations derived from dancer movement, with which actual dancers would interact during the performance. Dancer movement was captured using reflective markers on joints and the dancer's body as reflective nodes detected and traced by a ring of cameras. The projections were presented on a scrim in the performance spaces, creating a perception that the live dancers appear to interrelate with the virtual dancers. With music by Gavin Bryars, this performance put digital dance on the map.

Computers can be used to choreograph dancers by way of random pattern generation for choreographic scores or the manipulation of projections or motion tracking as well as through cameras, screens and video (Dodds 2004: 68). Cunningham used one of the first dance simulation and animation software packages in his work *Trackers* (1989). The software translated Cunningham's choreography into three-dimensional wireframe figures (Dixon 2007: 184), complementing and extending objectives and thematic principles for the choreographer. Having already made use of chance procedures in his earlier choreography since the 1950s, Cunningham used the computer's possibility to generate random data to choreograph works. However, these were not always physically possible for dancers to enact.

The motion tracking sensors can be used to control machines and the media contained within them, and placed on the floor to pick up steps or to affect sound, visuals, lighting and video. In this way the computer becomes a live, real-time collaborator for the range of elements involved in a dance production. Indeed, set design, choreography, costumes, sound and text and software that responds and interacts with dancers in real time became common by the 1990s. New York City-based performance collective Troika Ranch created systems designed to bring dead electronic media to life by imbuing them with the liveness we experience in corporeal performance (Dixon 2007: 196). Director Mark Coniglio developed media-activating computer systems, and likens these to a musical instrument. Troika Ranch also use non-wearable interactive tracking systems, such as laser beams and lights across the stage, that activate when dancers 'break' the beam. In their work *Bank/Perspective 1* (1998), dancers' steps activate stored video images on a database, and were able to alter the music key, tempo and volume, using piezo and flux sensors fitted on their bodies. Coniglio embraces the inherent risk in using new, often untried technologies, commenting that digital technologies are 'seductive in a way that is difficult to control'. The proprietary qualities and complexity of much early movement tracking software were hard for artists to adapt to their use, a problem that was rectified in the 1990s when programs that enabled easy adjustment and building came on the market. Dance simulation programs would often feature input from choreographers and dancers, and were used to push the capacity of computers to track and replicate movement digitally. The Germany company Palindrome designed its own camera tracking interfaces and software system. The interplay of proximity and touch was used to trigger audio, lighting and video effects in their groundbreaking work *Touching* (2003).

Interactivity has always been at the heart of dance and choreography, but the wealth of new techniques and systems has enabled the audience into the dancers' world like never before, where viewers enter the work. Diane Gromala and Yacov Sharir created *Dancing with the Virtual Dervish: Virtual Bodies* (1994–6), a work that explored the construction of the digital body through virtual reality. In this work, the audience enters the dancing world using the tools of virtual experience. Working with Sharir, who is a choreographer and computer scientist, Gromala constructs an environment from computer-based visualizations of her own body which she manipulated and animated to represent decay and reformation (Rush 1999: 235). Presented as an installation with three-dimensional sound in which the audience enters an animated world wearing a head-mounted video display, users feel immersed within the virtual body they enter, and interact with it by touching text, and flying into organs. There is a dancer in the space, and another in the 'virtual' space that interacts with the participant (Dixon 2007: 376). The integration of architectural elements into dance performance was explored by Deborah Hay in her work *Group One* (1967), an important work in the history of media and performance, in which people and film were used as architectural elements (Rush 1999: 31). In Stephan Silver's *Sinfonica* (2000) dance installation, visitors move through sensor-activated corridors that trigger images and sounds using pressure pads, light sensors and ultrasonic devices. Dancers in the space are lit only by the light of the projections of computer animations describing the geometric shapes of the choreography (Dixon 2007: 398). These are multi-sensory experiential environments designed to be inhabited rather than viewed as an artefact.

Mimi Garrard Dance Company's *Phosphones* (1969) is an early example of light and electronic music systems being synchronized using real-time music systems (Goodman 1987: 181). These early pre-digital iterations required intensive programming and building before show time, whereas more recent technology enables programming on the fly. A collaboration between Rebecca Allen, Twyla Tharp and musician David Byrne, entitled *The Catherine Wheel* (1983), featured an intricate example of computer-animated human motion possible at the time, where videotape showed computer-generated images integrated with choreographed live dancing, using a computer to represent the non-corporeal nature of the subject of the performance, a fourth-century saint (Goodman 1987: 182).

Telematic performances make use of remote hook-ups, initially on phone lines, then on the internet, making a significant impact on the possibilities of collaborative dance and choreography. In an early work using phone line hook-up made by Kit Galloway and Sherrie Rabinowitz, *Virtual Space/Composition Image – Space Dance from Satellite Art Project* (1977), the image of one performer in Maryland was mixed with the image of dance partners in California, the final product being a screen image of the dancers in the same image space (Popper 1993: 137).

<hr>

Reflection

> Interactivity deeply entwines the functions of viewer and artist. In the process, the artist's role changes. This convergence transforms what had been two very different identities of artist and viewer. What interactive art now solicits from the viewer is not simply reception but an independent construction of meaning. In interactively participating, the viewer derives power somewhat parallel with that of the artist: to choose one's own path and discover one's own insights through the interactive work. (Lovejoy 2004: 167)

Margot Lovejoy views interactivity as a fundamental alteration of artistic process, since creates potential for the arts to expand into new territories that have not been possible until the integration of computing. Audiences are essential to the completion of an interactive artwork, as they have the power to be an active participant in the unfolding of a work's flow of events, influencing or modifying its form. She argues that interactivity provides a system-based approach to creating work in which participation is the primary focus, fundamentally changing the artist's role. They must create specific content but also build in a democratic and collaborative dialogue as well as new processes for generating new elements. The work then becomes a frame or context providing an environment for new experiences of exchange and learning (Lovejoy 2004: 168). The real-time realization of interaction facilitated by the digital has essentially changed the artist's role in the creation of a work.

<hr>

THEATRE AND PERFORMANCE ART

As in dance productions, projections, sensors, internet hook-ups and virtual reality became important parts of theatre once they become affordable for small production companies and individual practitioners. In fact, the use of media technology including the likes of film, video and sound equipment became some of the identifying characteristics of experimental theatre. Early experiments in staging were conducted by the likes of Oskar Schlemmer, head of the theatre workshop at the Bauhaus, who acknowledged the stage as a three-dimensional space (Wands 2006: 122). In 1968, conductor Andre Kostelanetz coined the term 'theatre of mixed means', in which he referred to theatre that rejected the verbal and narrative emphasis in favour of presentational means such as sound, light, movement, film and television (Carlson 2004: 115).

The introduction of media screens on the set provided a new, flexible space, challenging the fixed point of view a traditional theatre provided to the members of the audience. Multimedia performances become central to the ongoing development of theatre, and digital technologies played a large part in this development. In a music theatre work by Beryl Korot and Steve Reich, *Three Tales* (2002), events

Figure 4.2 Michel van der Aa, *After Life* (2005–6). Performance still. Image courtesy of the artist.

from the last century are used to explore the implications of developing technology. Korot brings her experience as a multi-channel video artist to bring video into the theatre and its design, and Reich uses his minimal, repetitive compositional style to allude to mechanization (Wands 2006: 127). Film and video create architectural elements in the stage environment, which permit new interactions on stage and opportunities to negotiate scenes over different time periods (Rush 1999: 42). But, most importantly, the use of digital projection offers the possibility to alter viewers' versions of reality, as well as enlarge and confuse their perception of space. Video is not used as a prop in these theatre works, it *is* the set: an integral part of the work where the performers interact. These are sometimes called 'soft sets', although the term is more suited to productions that take place in cyberspace, such as on the internet. Dutch composer Michel van der Aa's opera *After Life* (2005–6) uses video projections on various layers through the set space, where the performers move easily between, in front of and behind the virtual characters and reflections of themselves, as seen in Figure 4.2.

Case Study 4.1
Monsters of Grace (1998) by Robert Wilson and Philip Glass

The works of American director Robert Wilson embraced new digital staging concepts in ambitious, large-scale productions for the first time. Wilson began as a performance artist, dancer and designer in the 1960s, and was very influenced by the happenings of that period. Together with composer Philip Glass, Wilson made *Monsters of Grace*, a digital opera featuring three-dimensional animation on film (by Jeffrey Kleiser and Diana Walczak), controlled using a computerized masterboard (Rush 1999: 61). This production was branded as a cutting-edge digital theatre work at its premiere and is an example of the issues around early digitally enhanced performance works and the debates they generated. Over 13 films were created for the production, some requiring the audience to wear three-dimensional glasses to view animated three-dimensional films. The production attracted considerable negative review — perhaps due to the high expectations for what new media would bring to the ancient form of opera, and to some lack of integration, theatricality or liveness, at the expense of its technological integration. It brought rise to the concerns of content versus technological wizardry. In fact Glass eschews the term 'opera' and stresses that opera houses just have the right kind of machinery to produce the theatrical demands of the works.

Not all large-scale works have large-scale budgets, as the prevalence of consumer-grade technologies and the use of social media have meant that many people can be contacted cheaply to attend large-scale events with modest production values. An early example – a remarkable achievement given that it predates most social media – was Desperate Optimists' work *Urban Shots* (1999). This was set with very modest production values in a large outdoor car park in Jena, Germany, yet it was seen by more than 10,000 people. Large-scale, free public events such as these bring digital art into public spaces, creating site-specific works. *Urban Shots* featured a live video feed, 16-millimetre films, contributions by students, live bands and performing police dogs (Dixon 2007: 414).

Video has also been employed to place the audience inside theatre works. Surveillance theatre refers to performance works in which surveillance technologies are used in the creation of the work (Dixon 2007: 440). An early work in this form was Les Levine's *Slipcover* (1966) in which visitors enter a space, where they find themselves looking at images of themselves on a screen. The paradigm turns the viewer into the performer, but not in a voluntarily interactive way, making it different from other interactive work. Joel Slayton's work *Telepresent Surveillance* (1997) features robots fitted out with filming cameras, which follow and move among the audience, projecting the images they capture in the space. Natalie Jeremijenko's *Suicide Box* (1996) involved a camera being left on the Golden Gate Bridge in San Francisco for 100 days, in which time she caught 17 suicides on film and compressed them into a projected artwork (Dixon 2007: 441). The concept was also employed in larger-scale theatre works. David Saltz's production of Peter Handke's *Kaspar* (1999) employs a giant eyeball projection – linked to a camera – that moves to follow every move of the character Kaspar. Sensors embedded in the furniture interact with the camera to indicate where it should point to capture and observe Kaspar's location. Digital technologies have made these works easier to create, public footage easier to access, surveillance cameras smaller and clearer to see.

The Builders Association claims to 'reanimate classic theatrical texts by infusing them with new media, and then reworking them within the chaotic context of contemporary global culture' (Rush 1999: 70). Priding itself on using the most sophisticated on-stage digital technology available at the time, the Builders Association creates virtual soft sets through projection, producing a curiously flat effect in which live actors seem collapsed into a virtual screen. Director Marianne Weems highlights aspects of digital culture in her work *Super Vision* (2006), which deals with a number of characters whose interactions with others occur via digital mediation, echoing the form of the piece. Weems' work principally employs digital technology and projection toward two ends: to create 'soft space' or virtual sets, which exist as light or upon the screen, thus complicating and expanding spatial relations on stage; and to mediate and de-materialize actors within the performance using virtual performance and avatars. It is no coincidence here that the dramaturgical themes of many of these pieces touch upon geography and identity.

New York's The Wooster Group creates energetic theatre works presented as multi-media theatre. The group turns classic plays into media works by employing multiple video monitors, high levels of amplification, video, live feeds of sound and image and various low-technology aspects. In works like *The Hairy Ape* (1994–2001) microphones were taped into the hands of the actors and around the set, expanding and exploding the production beyond physical space and presence. Moving away from classic texts and more open, fluid scripts, the integration of the everyday into theatre begun by Fluxus artists has been facilitated by the ever-increasing level of digital interactions in society. Figure 4.3 shows a still from Blast Theory's *10 Backwards* (1999), in which Artaud's double is represented as a technological reflection. During the performance, everyday actions are video-recorded, then repeated, re-enacted, enlarged, frozen and analysed. The central character Niki uses the video for her own self-analysis, but the duplicate eventually becomes the reality she must copy. Here, it is a consumer's digital aesthetic that is central to the content of the work. The computer avatar is another subject of many theatre works. *Avatar Farm* (2000) uses the University of Nottingham Computer Research Group's virtual environment to bring together avatars of local and remote actors with members of the public, demonstrating Artaud's fourth quality, that of malleable mannequins (Dixon 2007: 261).

Figure 4.3 Blast Theory, *10 Backwards* (1999). Performance still. Image courtesy of the artist.

Case Study 4.2
Dumb Type and the Here-Now Technology Culture in Japan

Dumb Type is an important Japanese performance group for whom digital technologies and aesthetics are central. The members totally integrate digital technologies into their multimedia live performances — aesthetically, technically and structurally. At the time Dumb Type arose and had achieved international exposure in the 1990s, Japan was often viewed as an already realized example of our digital future. In the midst of Japan's so-called 'Bubble Economy', fuelled by the trade in digital goods, the urban landscape had become so thoroughly infused with digital screens, images, projections and designs that sections of the futuristic film *Blade Runner* were shot there. Dumb Type developed sophisticated sets where mechanical stands, projections, lighting and objects shift and move across and within the stage during the performance. The group has collaborated with numerous digital musicians and artists, including Ryoji Ikeda (discussed in the following chapter), and the content of their works, notably *Memorandum* (1998), explicitly addresses issues raised by digital media, notably memory, transience and transcription. *Memorandum* begins with a performer on stage writing, and the words he transcribes are projected behind him, the sound of his pen amplified and expanded. Dumb Type exposes the juxtaposition of the possible ecstasy that digital media might engender, with the unwanted noise and moments of apparent breakdown in which identity is erased and crushed by the omnipresence of technology. Nevertheless, as works such as *Memorandum* demonstrate, digital aesthetics cannot be broken down to a simply binary — positive or negative — between technology and humanity. Where digital forms so closely echo our own perceptual structures and mechanisms, it becomes apparent that humans too are technology.

Figure 4.4 Dumb Type, *Memorandum* (1998), by Emmanuelle Valette. Performance photograph by Florence Berthaud. Image courtesy of the artist.

The creation of scripts has been likewise influenced by digital forms. The exploration of the nature of hypertext, used to write web pages, has created a rhizomatic structure for writers. This is known as 'hypertext narrative' and was first explored by Michael Joyce's *Afternoon* (1987), in which the user may choose segments of text in 539 narrative branches of a story called 'lexias'. While *Afternoon* exists in a computer, these texts can also be performed as theatre works, creating 'hypertextual performances' where the text is central to the work (Dixon 2007: 483). Simulated voices generated by computers have featured in numerous artworks across many genres, often performing in real time in response to human questions. Chatterbots, software robots living in cyberspace, are constantly reprogrammed to seem more and more like a 'real person' (see Chapter 9 on hyperreality). These feature in many live coding music performances, discussed in the following chapter.

Performance art has been defined as a visual and performative hybrid that incorporates recent installation, site-specific and body art practices (Carlson 1994). Emerging in the 1970s in America, Europe and Japan, its strong link to hybridity and conceptual art has meant that it has often incorporated a high degree of multimedia, facilitating its emphasis on bodily presence and movement. Often confronting, sometimes closer to circus, performance art blurs boundaries between art, technology and popular media (Carlson 2004: 134). It can be scripted or unscripted, random or carefully orchestrated, spontaneous or otherwise carefully planned, with or without audience participation. The performance can be live or via media; the performer can be present or absent. It can be any situation that involves four basic elements: time, space, the performer's body (or presence in a medium) and a relationship between performer and audience. Performance art can happen anywhere, in any venue or setting and for any length of time and has been a vehicle for many developments in digital art and performance. Performance art developed from early twentieth-century movements in art, in particular Futurism, Fluxus and Dada, and became a genre distinct from theatre in the 1970s. Performance art has relied on some theatrical tools, while generally appearing more experimental than theatre (Carlson 2004: 114).

In particular, performance artists pioneered the way video was used in performance. The early experiments with video by artists such as Vito Acconci (b. 1940) and Bruce Nauman (b. 1941) often employed video as a frame to separate themselves from the outside world, in opposition to how theatre was using projections to create interior worlds where actors would interact. Early works by Carolee Schneemann created a forum for the artist's body to be the material of a performance in conjunction with photography and video. In *Snows* (1967), 16 mm and 8 mm film slides, revolving light sculptures and strobe lighting are featured in a production involving eight different performers. Motion in the audience is picked up by microphones under the seats, which would then set off active media elements (Rush 1999: 41). These techniques have been duplicated digitally ever since, enhanced by faster communication speeds and wireless technologies. Another early influence on later digital works was video-maker Nam June Paik and cellist Charlotte Moorman's collaboration, *TV Bra* (1968). Moorman is taped playing the cello topless, wearing two mirrors on her breasts that reflect cameras focused on her face that play back onto television monitors fashioned as a bra. In *Concerto for TV Cello and Videotapes* (1971) she ran the cello bow across stacks of television sets with pre-recorded and simultaneous images of her doing it (Rush 2003: 49). While Paik abandoned live performance in the 1980s, his influence was immense and inspired many other performance artists (see Chapter 2).

What the digital realm has contributed to these next phases of developments in performance art has been a different quality of image, sound, transmission and location. The analogue distortion favoured by Paik has been replaced with a pixelated distortion unique to digital equipment. Projectors and monitors are smaller and more portable, more easily hidden and transported. American performance artist Laurie Anderson has revelled in the ongoing possibilities of digital technologies, and each of her works builds upon new developments. Her autobiographical work *United States* (1980) is widely considered to be the work that brought performance art into the 'mainstream cultural consciousness' (Carlson 2004: 115). The work epitomized

Figure 4.5 Laurie Anderson performing live in Milan, 2007. Photograph by Lanz Vanzella. Licensed under the Creative Commons Attribution-Share Alike 2.0 Generic License.

many facets of performance art – it is that of a single artist, it uses material from everyday life and exhibits a preference for movement of the body in space and time over any conventional 'character'. It swings from virtuosic and physically demanding skills to everyday chat, yet always mediated by digital technology in some way. Other performance artists, such as Mona Hatoum and Marina Abramović, have produced works that engage digital technologies from a variety of forums – photography, internet, video and sound, often used to investigate ideas around the object.

CYBORGS, ROBOTS AND BIOARTISTS

Much performance art poses questions about the human relationship to the technologies we use in our lives. Artists share a fear and fascination with the concurrent humanization of machines and the dehumanization of humans by using their artworks to comment on anything from artificial intelligence to the loss of intimacy. Often, this topic is handled in a very personal way, by using the artist's own body as a site for investigation. The cyborg is one model for this kind of investigation. Donna Haraway's essay 'A Cyborg Manifesto' (1985) investigates this idea from a socialist feminist perspective, asking to what extent are we already experiencing a human – machine symbiosis. Virtual and physical existence is not a simple dichotomy, but a complex interplay (Paul 2008: 166). That the cyborg can be seen as an extended body, a kind of post-human, often comes up in digital art projects, as digital technologies enable an almost seamless fusion of body and machine. This is exemplified in the practice of Australian artist Stelarc, in Case Study 4.3.

Case Study 4.3
Stelarc and His Evolving Body Dialogue

As we saw in Chapter 2, one of the most written-about performance artists working in this area would have to be Stelarc, who actively engages his body with various forms of technology, most recently robotics and virtual perception. Rather than submit his body passively to the role of technology, he creates an 'active dialogue between corporality and cybernetics' (Carlson 2004: 133). Dubbed the 'cyborgic performance artist par excellence' (Dixon 2007: 312), Stelarc is perhaps one of the most documented performance artists of our time. In his work *Ping Body* (1996) his body jerks spasmodically and involuntarily as his muscles are stimulated by electronic signals sent to his arm remotely over the internet, connected via a mass of cables. Remote audience on the internet can also activate the artist's body this way. Stelarc often collaborates with other artists (and Cat Hope has been a musician in one of his *Ping Body* performances) to enrich the spectacle, and commissions technicians to build specialist equipment for him. A custom-built third arm was designed for him in Japan from metal and Perspex, which he attaches to one of his own arms and uses in numerous performances which showcase the movements of this human-metal cyborg. As Chapter 2 explained, Stelarc considers the body to be somewhat obsolete or absent, unable to compete with machines and technology (Dixon 2007: 316). Rather than using technology to seek ways the body can transcend corporeality, he is interested in how it can be extended and modified. Perhaps the most dramatic of these is his *Exoskeleton* (1998), a large six-legged pneumatically powered robot that he stands in – positioned on a rotating turntable – and activates to move with spider-like movements in association with a dramatic soundscape.

A different approach to the body's interactions with technology can be found in the work of French performance artist Orlan, who employs the digital technology used in surgical procedures to alter her own body, rather than add machinery to it. In a series of performances entitled *The Reincarnation of St Orlan* (from 1990) she transmits a plastic surgery operation being performed on her face over satellite video connections, while she concurrently reads text and talks to her remote audience while under local anaesthetic. The composite alterations to her face are drawn from classic artworks in history. For example, her forehead has been remodelled to resemble da Vinci's *Mona Lisa* (Giannaci 2004: 49). Her corporeal body becomes a kind of virtual body itself, with the same malleability and potential for change as a digital image (Dixon 2007: 231).

Microscopic and macroscopic performances can be developed in science laboratories for exhibition online or in galleries. The activity of human and animal cells and other microorganisms can be visible using very powerful digital imaging devices connected to optical microscopes that enable artists to activate and control biological procedures. The SymbioticA Biological Arts Laboratory at the University of Western Australia has facilitated some important work in this area, directly exploring the use of contemporary biotechnological tools such as tissue engineering. The Tissue Culture and Art Project, based at SymbioticA, created *Semi Living Worry Dolls* (2000), the first living tissue engineered sculptures to be presented in a gallery context (Catts and Zurr, personal communication), shown in Figure 4.6. Moreover, Eduardo Kac is an artist who investigates the idea of disembodiment by looking at the materiality of interfaces and the effect they have on our bodies (Paul 2003: 170). *Time Capsule* (1997) was a performance in Brazil where Kac was televised live using a special needle to insert a microchip with a programmed identity number into his left leg. He then registered himself on a web database for lost animals, and

Figure 4.6 Tissue Culture and Art Project, *Semi Living Worry Dolls* (2000). Image courtesy of the artists.

interactive tele-robotic webscanning was used to read his implant as he lived his life. An important examination of surveillance and liberation, the work takes digital technology and literally places it at the centre of its inventor (Paul 2003: 171, 173; Rush 1999: 230; see also Chapter 9).

Digital technology has enabled new ways of looking at the body and its relationship with machines. Yet machines can also look at us – the eerie and precise digital dissections in the *Visible Human Project* (1994) consist of a collection of images stored at the US National Library of Medicine. This is an archive of detailed digital dissections of two human bodies which were MRI scanned, frozen in gelatine, quartered, re-scanned, then sliced into thousands of layers 0.3 to 1 mm thick and photographed repeatedly, as the fine layers turned to dust (Bell 2000: 156). The corpses were of an anonymous 59-year-old housewife who died of a heart attack and executed prisoner Joseph Paul Jernigan. The archive has provided a stimulus for a number of performance works, such as Paul Vanouse's *Items 1–2000* (1996). The work reflects on this cyber incarceration by placing the archive images alongside Vanouse's own sketches and memories as a student in an anatomy morgue. These images are triggered by visitors who use a pen in a scalpel-like way to read a bar code hanging over a body partially submerged in wax, to liberate an image from that part of the body (Dixon 2007: 222).

Robotics is a fascinating field that has informed artworks since its inception, and many technological developments in robotics have been driven by artists. The first computer-controlled robot artwork was based on the imitation of an animal. Edward Ihnatowicz's *The Senster* (1971) was a 3-metre-long metal construction resembling a lobster claw that moved towards quiet observers and shied from loud or animated ones. Motion detectors and a microphone captured observers' movements and sound. This was fed into a digital computer that processed the data and activated kinetic responses in the robot. Survival Research Laboratories, founded by Mark Pauline in 1994, blends influences from theatre, sport, art, military science and engineering using remote-controlled robots and reanimated roadkill to stage spectacular and messy battles. Here, the destructive, dirty power of machines is examined and at times glorified and mocked in performances such as *Illusion of Shameless Abundance: Degenerating into an Uninterrupted Sequence of Hostile Encounters* (1989), in which brutal battles emphasize entertainment in ways not dissimilar to some television programmes, yet always with a political message.

VIRTUAL REALITY

In Chapter 2 we saw how Dada broke down the boundaries that separated different art forms from each other and from everyday life. Virtual reality continues this evolution, shaping elements of architecture, video, sculpture, audience interaction and performance. Virtual reality is an industrial computer graphics format that simulates navigable three-dimensional environments. Howard Rheingold defines virtual reality in terms of three aspects:

1. Immersion (being enveloped in it)
2. The ability to move around in the world it creates, and choose your point of view
3. Manipulation – of the environment and your place in it
   (Rheingold 1991: 34)

The passive watching associated with most art forms is replaced by a total immersion beyond interactivity where the difference between modelling and copying, real and fake, is blurred (see Chapter 9). It is useful to remember that the perfection of mathematical modelling and fast computing is what created virtual reality in the first place (Lovejoy 2004: 160).

Like early digital printmaking, early virtual reality works needed to be programmed and electronic circuits tailor-built, and many early works in the 1980s were limited to specially constructed virtual reality rooms or centres in universities. American technician Jaron Lanier coined the term 'virtual reality' to distinguish between immersive digital worlds and traditional computer simulations. By the late 1990s, more artists were able to experiment with virtual reality as user-programmable interfaces enabling sophisticated computer control became increasingly available. Pieces of hardware, such as head-mounted cameras, video goggles, datagloves (that show your hand in the space, letting you touch and point), wands and suits have been integral to the development of the virtual reality experience. While initially clumsy, these tools continue to develop and continue to integrate human elements such as the sense of touch.

Char Davies' *Osmose* (1994–5) was designed to make an immersive virtual space where mental constructs of the world can be given a three-dimensional form that is then kinaesthetically explored (Davies 1998: 65). This work was revolutionary in its time for the way it used full-bodied immersion facilitated by a datasuit, unlike the head-mounted devices used up to that point, which emphasize the mind–body split. *Osmose* read the participant's action from the waist up, and monitored breathing. The participants (or 'immersants', as Davies called them) can see themselves in the nature imagery which they travel through. The participant's actions are witnessed from outside the virtual reality booth as a silhouette, and the spatialized soundscape responds to the user's location, direction and speed of movement.

The impact of virtual reality technologies is realized in many aspects of theatre. While the use of video to create virtual or soft sets has been discussed, this technology has also been used for historical purposes. English academic Richard

Beacham's models reconstruct old theatres using virtual reality tools to reassemble, enter and navigate ancient theatres, such as Rome's first, *Pompeii* (1997). Virtual reality technologies are also used to pre-model scenography in theatres. Yet despite many of these developments, theatre remains somewhat limited by the traditional presentation of sets and stage, the navigation of its world kept solely for the actors on the stage, leaving the audience some distance from the action. Only when theatre breaks out of the blackened room, into the open, disposing of the stage – virtual or otherwise – does it share the openness we may find in other performance forms such as performance art.

Chapter Summary

This chapter has discussed a range of theoretical concepts that have informed historical and technological trends in dance, theatre, performance art and science-driven art such as robotics, bio-art and virtual reality.

■ Performance has been informed by the ideas of Antonin Artaud, Jean Baudrillard, Philip Auslander and Paul Virilio and developments in the Fluxus, Dada and Situationist movements.
■ Digital technologies have changed the way performance is presented, conceived and experienced through interactivity, virtual reality, the internet, video projection, robotics and motion-tracking software.
■ New forms of performance have been facilitated by the digital, such as the case with performance art.
■ Digital performance is often characterized by hybridity and the desire to examine the impact of digital culture on our lives.

5 FROM SCRATCHY TO GLITCHY: THE CREATION, PERFORMANCE AND INSTALLATION OF DIGITAL MUSIC

The role of the digital in the performance, recording and reproduction of sound has exercised a considerable impact on music, as touched on in Chapter 2. Music changed rapidly with the introduction of digital technologies, which ushered in the development of new sounds, new instruments and the potential of digital recording. The manipulation of sound itself became central to new music, a significant artistic practice that crosses into almost every other digital art form and has revolutionized as well as fragmented music practice. This chapter focuses on the impact digital technologies have had on the creation and performance of new music and its fragmentation into multiple sub-genres. The rapid development and popularity of computers saw a democratization of music-making similar to the changes impacting digital photography, taking sound recording and processing out of expensive studios and onto people's home computers. The synthesis of sound and high-quality recording has offered up a new and extensive range of materials for composers. Digital audio is an immaterial stream of numerical data, an essence felt in different degrees within all music mediated by the digital, which has offered a platform for the reinterpretation of existing materials through basic editing, sampling, mixing and remixing. A range of new music genres has been created in addition to the enhancement of existing works through recording, adaptation and distribution. Digital audio continues to evolve, offering up new performative approaches that use the potential of the computer as an instrument and the internet as a conduit. Digital technologies have moved music into new realms of sonic complexity while simplifying their manipulation.

A DRASTIC CHANGE FOR THE DIRECTION OF MUSIC

The twentieth century saw the development of electronic music, cited as the third most important development in the history of music after vocal and instrumental music (Stuckenschmidt 1995: 11). Electronic music introduced new ways to make and organize sounds using a range of machines and our interaction with them. The invention of sound recording in the late nineteenth century revolutionized the way music would be experienced by audiences. The record presented a potent new *aura* created by the magic of technology – one of displacement, the magic of hearing music emanating from a different place and time by people not physically present (Cascone 2000). Recording soon moved from a technology of duplicating existing music to one of invention, offering a range of new materials for artists to use and manipulate in the creation of new work. These developments saw a fundamental change in the way music could be created and enjoyed.

As well as these technology-driven developments, the twentieth century saw music moving away from some of the basic structures that had formed its core for hundreds of years: melody and harmony. Many composers of instrumental music were changing their focus from tunes to textures, from structure to open forms, employing extended and improvisatory techniques for performers. Ferruccio Busoni (2010) wrote an influential essay in 1906 entitled 'A Sketch for a New Aesthetic of Music', which looked for a break from established musical conventions into new sound worlds. A new musical convention, known as serialism, to replace tonal systems was developed by Viennese composer Arnold Schoenberg (1874–1951). This was a system that posited a 'row', or a fixed set of notes, chosen by the composer, rather than as part of a musical scale. This created what could be thought of as a more mathematical approach to music composition, as Schoenberg also proposed predetermined ways to manipulate the row, by arranging it forwards, backwards and even upside down, in what could be thought of as a kind of paper-based algorithm. Serialism provided a methodology similar to the computer's ability to perform functions on set blocks of pre-recorded sound that was yet to come.

As with other art forms, the Italian Futurists made important and specific contributions to the future of music. Luigi Russolo's Futurist manifesto published in 1913, 'The Art of Noises' (Russolo 1987), acknowledged that life was being reshaped by technology, and demanded that the sounds of the new industrial world become part of the musical toolbox. The flourishing of electronic music involved the realization of these ideals, and digital technologies accelerated these developments at an unprecedented pace and scale.

Perhaps one of the most influential thinkers of twentieth-century music was John Cage. His writing and conceptual approach to music are key in the shift of music into the world of 'sound' – where all sounds could be thought of as music, not just those of traditional musical instruments. His work examined the implications of silence in the key piece *4'33"* (1952). In this three-movement work, there is no music written on the page of the score; the performer sits at his or her instrument for 4 minutes and 33 seconds, leaving the audience to examine the meaning of the absence of music, or, rather, how everyday sounds could also be musical (also see Chapter 9). His 1937 essay 'The Future of Music: Credo' (2006) discusses an open music that incorporates noise and all the new tools possible to make it. For the first time in history sound artists could shift their focus from the foreground of musical notes to the background of incidental sound (Cascone 2000).

The use of recorded media to create new music was pioneered by the French composers Pierre Schaeffer (1910–95) and Pierre Henry (b. 1927), who worked with tape in *musique concrète*, an approach that took recorded sound as the start, rather than the end, of the compositional process. Schaeffer introduced a philosophy of how to listen to such music, where no performers are present, called *acousmatics*. He conceived of sound as an object that could be subjected to compositional processes, dissociated from instruments or performers, and experienced through loudspeakers. Acousmatics had a profound effect on how people could create and engage with music, and digital technologies pushed music even beyond speakers and into inter-active live environments where playback and live performance could be combined, shared and dissected, beyond concerts halls and into people's homes and headphones.

Reflection

French composer Edgard Varèse (1883–1965) was an early explorer of electronic music, who famously redefined music as 'organized sound' (Varèse 1975). Can you think of a piece of music constructed of 'sounds' rather than musical instruments?

Given that the roots of digital music lie in electronic music, an examination of the fundamental and crucial differences between electronic and acoustic music is worth-while. Thom Holmes outlines seven traits of electronic music in his book *Electronic and Experimental Music: Technology, Music and Culture*.

1. *The sound recourses available to electronic music are unlimited.* Rather than different arrangements of existing acoustic instruments, electronic music provides new sounds altogether.
2. *Electronic music can expand the perception of tonality.* Electronic sounds do not have to be 'designed' to any scale or music system, and new systems can be developed.

3. *Electronic music exists in a state of actualization.* A work of electronic music is not realized until it is performed or played back in real time. This is different from acoustic instruments, for which music is written on manuscripts and passed down the centuries.

4. *Electronic music has a special relationship with the temporal nature of music.* Music, like dance and video, takes place during the passing of time (i.e. it has a start, an end and a duration). Electronic music explores this in new ways.

5. *Sound itself becomes the material of composition.* Making new sounds from first principles (basic electronic signals) and arranging recorded sounds is a more hands-on way of composing music.

6. *Electronic music is not affected by the limitations of human performance.* Machines can do things humans cannot! Sound is not interrupted by the need to take a breath or the speed at which a finger can move.

7. *Electronic music often lacks a point of comparison with the natural world of sounds, providing a largely mental and imaginative experience.* A new range of sounds have been made available by electronics, different from those experienced in the natural world, and these create different responses.
(Holmes 2008: 121–2).

Digital technologies extend these characteristics, and have moved electronic music from a marginal form of music production to a more dominant one through the marketing of cheaper, smaller devices and systems. In addition to new electronic sounds, acoustic instruments are mediated through digital equipment when they are recorded, amplified and distributed.

WHAT IS A DIGITAL SOUND?

The digital soundscape is a blend of real and illusory, recognizable and strange, old and new (Sexton 2008: 94). It can be argued that the digital has somehow reached everyone (Cascone 2000). But how is a digital sound different from the sounds that came before it?

The material of the digital sound world is comprised of numerical data patterns, which differs from earlier electronic sounds, known as 'analogue' sounds. An analogue sound is a continuous signal that unfolds in real time and is stored in linear media such as tape. Analogue synthesis created some of the first electronic instruments. A digital sound is stored in data fragments, known as 'bytes', on a computer. Each byte is a binary number, a number for which a digit may have two values – 1 or 0, or on and off (Holmes 2008: 296; also see Chapter 1). To hear a sound from these bytes, a digital to analogue converter is required to turn the electrical signals into sound that can be listened to in speakers or headphones. Arguably, Ryoji Ikeda's music and installation work provide examples of what could be the quintessential digital art, as discussed in Case Study 5.1.

Case Study 5.1
Ryoji Ikeda and the Digital Sublime

Ryoji Ikeda (b. 1966) is a sound artist from Japan who exemplifies many traits associated with digital music, creating sounds and visual images that appear as pure digitization of data, sound and light, resulting in a modernist, digital sublime. His first recorded release, *+/-* (1996, Touch), introduced very high frequencies and short blips of sound that waver between almost imperceptible high-pitched tones to ear-splitting noise. Ikeda's works often take different forms with the same title – appearing as composition, installation and recording. His work *test pattern* (2008, ongoing) features a system that converts any type of data (text, sounds, photos and movies) into barcode patterns and binary patterns of 0s and 1s. A still of this work is featured in Figure 5.1. Using a real-time computer program designed by Tomonaga Tokuyama, the installations and live performances feature intense flickering black and white 'barcode' imagery that results from Ikeda's audio, a tightly synchronized and powerful soundtrack that explores both cold, machine-like beeps and blips as well as dense noise. The installations present on a very large scale with multiple projectors and speakers, and the public can walk onto the projection surface, which is often mostly on the floor, where they find themselves covered in the barcode-like black and white shapes, with their silhouettes now inside the installation. The work explores the possibility of perceiving a multitude of 'invisible' data moving in our world, allowing the participants to reflect upon human perception as well as the limits of mechanical possibilities.

Figure 5.1 Ryoji Ikeda, *test pattern [no. 5]* (2013). Audiovisual installation at Carriageworks, Sydney, Australia. Commissioned and presented by Carriageworks and ISEA2013 in collaboration with Vivid Sydney. Image by Zan Wimberly.

There are two key processes at the foundation of digital sound. 'Synthesis' is the creation of new sounds using electronic signals. 'Sampling' is the electronic copying, and subsequent repetition of the copied sounds (Holmes 2008: 131). When recording acoustic sounds to be manipulated on a computer, an analogue-to-digital converter is required to convert the material to bytes, in order to subject it to digital processes, such as detailed analysis and manipulation.

Digital synthesis has meant that there is no limit to the range of sounds that can be made from electrical signals, and it can be categorized into four different methods:

1. *Direct digital synthesis*, where numeric values are converted into an analogue electrical signal that drives a speaker.
2. *Complete sampling*, where a sound from the real world is digitized.
3. *Note sampling*, where the sonic parameters of a tone on an instrument are captured and analysed, then played on a keyboard or other trigger device.
4. *Wavetable synthesis*, which is a complex process of adding, subtracting, breaking down (known as granulating) and modulating digital information to create and modify sounds.
(Holmes 2008: 297)

Case Study 5.2
John Chownings' *Turenas*

A pioneer of wavetable synthesis, John Chowning demonstrates these techniques in his work *Turenas* (1972), whose title is an anagram of the word 'natures'. A wide range of natural-sounding electronic percussive sounds is created and reproduced over four loudspeakers, creating a very musical work for such an early period in the development of digital synthesis, going a long way to bridging the gap between the computer laboratory — where such processes were taking place in the early days of computing — and the concert hall, where music listening has traditionally taken place (Holmes 2008: 258). Electronic percussion sounds were used in programmable drum machines, which became a cornerstone of 1980s pop, epitomized by musicians such as Gary Numan and Devo, and later dance, electro, house, techno, R&B and hip-hop music.

Curtis Roads calls the various processes of dissecting and reassembling sound that have come to characterize many digital sound works 'microsound' (Roads 2004).

The creation and manipulation of sound synthesis soon moved from the computer to a keyboard instrument where different sounds could be controlled more intuitively, and so the synthesizer was born. Commercial digital synthesizers intended for performance were developed in 1976 in the USA, the first portable version being the Synclavier (Manning 2004: 222). These originally had floppy disk drives to store samples that were made and push-button controls that meant no understanding of the complex procedures involved in synthesis was needed. One of the inventors of the Synclavier was Jon Appleton, and his work for the Synclavier entitled *Prelude* (1978) explores the possibilities for keyboard-controlled performance programs. Another synthesizer was the Fairlight CMI, developed in Australia in 1975 by Peter Vogel and Kim Ryrie. As well as being a synthesizer, it was the first commercially available digital sampler (Holmes 2008: 265). It had a light pen that could draw functions onto a cathode ray tube screen to facilitate synthesis. The notion of a 'computerized orchestra' was born, and a number of leading pop and rock musicians, such as John Paul Jones, Kate Bush, Peter Gabriel, the Pet Shop Boys and Stevie Wonder, used Fairlight sounds extensively in their works (Manning 2004: 225). Jean Michel Jarre composed a work entirely on the Fairlight, entitled *Zoolook* (1984). These instruments set the scene for separating composers and performers from the computer programming involved in synthesis, and when the first digital sampling keyboard, the EMUlator, was released in 1981 (Holmes 2008: 266), the computer was inside the instrument, and the fascination with samplers had begun. In France, Jean-Claude Risset (b. 1938) was combining software synthesis with acoustic instruments, analysing real sounds from a trumpet so they may be resynthesized to be played on a MIDI keyboard in a process known as Digital Signal Processing (Manning 2004: 199). His work *Dialogues* (1975) for flute, clarinet, piano, percussion and computer-generated sounds explores the dialogue between acoustic instruments and computer-generated sounds, leading the way in the digital processing of acoustic sounds (Manning 2004: 198). Risset worked in the centre of computer music development in France, IRCAM, which remains an important hub for electro-acoustic explorations today.

Digital sound quality, or fidelity, was an important attraction in the adoption of digital audio. Tape hiss and record crackle disappeared and digital recording offered better audio quality than cassette tape, and claimed to have more durability than vinyl. Debate continues today about the cold brittle sound of digital compared to the warm depth of analogue LPs, and improvements in the quality of digital-to-analogue converters addresses this issue to some degree. Digital sound quality relies on a high-quality sampling rate, which is how many times per second an analogue sound source will be sampled when reproducing a live sound. An early sampler would sample at eight bits per second (a bit being eight bytes), with current levels sitting around 49 bits, requiring more storage space. In the 1980s, a hard drive would typically have around 40 megabytes of storage, and less than 20 years later, 20 gigabytes was not uncommon (Manning 2004: 258). The compact disc (CD) was first introduced in 1982, one of the earliest high-capacity portable data storage devices. However, by the start of the twenty-first century, fixed media such as CDs and DVDs were increasingly replaced by internal hard drives and flash media.

THE TOOLS OF DIGITAL MUSIC

The key tool for the ease and intensity of manipulability in digital music has been the computer. While a detailed examination of the history of the development of the computer is beyond the scope of this book, an overview of relevant developments will be given here (also see Chapters 2 and 6).

The work being undertaken at Bell Labs in the mid-twentieth century, so key in the development of other areas in digital art, was fundamental in establishing the first steps toward computer music. Bell Labs' desire to transmit large amounts of voice data in a digital form over existing telephone wires drove them to experiment with a range of digital audio possibilities (Hass 2010). Max Mathews' (1927–2011) *Bicycle Built for 2* (1962) is an early example of speech synthesis made at Bell, where he was employed as an engineer, that gained a place in the popular culture when it appeared in the Stanley Kubrick film *2001: A Space Odyssey* (1968). Mathews, seen by many as the forefather of computer music, developed a program known as *Music 1* (1957), which created the first few notes of synthesized music from a computer. Mathews also developed *Graphic 1* (1968) with L. Rosler, an interactive computer system that could translate images drawn with a light pen onto a terminal into sound, a development that pre-empted the first touch screen technology in 1983 and introduced the concept of interactive, real-time composition on a computer, many years before desktop computers were commonplace (Holmes 2008: 254).

As discussed in Chapter 2, early computers were large mainframe machines designed to handle commercial data processing. Before the end of the 1960s, data preparation tasks were done outside the computer and no interaction between the computer and the programmer would occur while the program was executing these tasks. Processing power was limited, memory was expensive, and computer music makers had to be programmers or depend on engineers with those skills. Storage was originally on magnetic tape, which, while generous in its capacity, could only be read sequentially. The development of random access memory (RAM) enabled computers to perform multiple tasks simultaneously (Manning 2004: 184). By the 1970s, computers were smaller, less expensive and more accessible to the general public, and computer music had become a self-sufficient area of computing (Manning 2004: 182). In the 1980s, personal computers (PCs) appeared in people's homes, music software packages were on the market and the large mainframe computer in a university research centre was no longer the prevailing model. Programs were more user-friendly and were being designed for composers, rather than scientists, to use. This trend has continued to the point where most music software is designed to be used by anyone, not just trained musicians and composers, to create music.

The key development that enabled this change was the introduction of the micro-processor in 1971 (Manning 2004: 219). Bell Labs introduced the first integrated single-chip sound processor in a touch-tone telephone and they soon appeared in synthesizers, cell phones and other digital systems that produce or manipulate sound (Holmes 2008: 264). An early example of music using a microprocessor was made by American composer David Behrman (b. 1937), a member of the pioneering performance group Sonic Arts Union, in which the microprocessor controls time intervals between chord changes in the piece *Figure in a Clearing* (1977). In the early 1980s, the microprocessor had enabled a new market of consumer electronics instruments, with a programmable monophonic digital music synthesizer released by Casio in 1980 for around 100 dollars, making it the cheapest and smallest synthesizer that had ever been available (Holmes 2008: 266). It featured preset rhythms and instrument sounds and came with a memory that could hold a 100-note sequence. During the late 1990s, the development of the external sound card, expanded a personal computer's music-making capabilities by producing quality analogue output (Holmes 2008: 292).

The 1990s saw a focus on software, away from hardware, for music performance, synthesis and editing. By the mid-1990s, personal computers were running software that could outdo hardware peripherals in almost all tasks (Manning 2004: 327). Audio plug-ins, which were once literally equipment that plugged into computers to add expanded levels of functionality, were now realized in software. Computers dedicated to music began to appear in music stores. The first direct-to-disk digital multitrack recording system was developed in the late 1980s, and marked the end of the need for recording media such as tape and CDs. This was closely followed by the development of audio editing software for personal computers, enabling the digital audio workstation (DAW) where sounds can be recorded, edited, notated and published in one place.

Amacher's *Sound Characters* (Case Study 5.3) is an example of a music that could only be realized with the precision tools available to a musician through computing.

Case Study 5.3
Maryanne Amacher's *Sound Characters (Making the Third Ear)*

Amacher (1938–2009) was an American sound artist who studied composition in addition to acoustics and computer science, and collaborated with John Cage on projects such as *Lecture on the Weather* (1975) and *Empty Words* (1978). Her major works were mostly sound installations that often featured sound transmitted through architectural structures, as in *MUSIC FOR SOUND JOINED ROOMS* (1980–2009). An extension of this interest in structurally born sound can be seen in her works investigating the physiological phenomenon known as 'otoacoustic emission'. This is a phenomenon where the ears themselves make sound in response to what they hear. Amacher composed several 'ear dances' designed to stimulate clear 'third' tones that she claimed were coming from the listener's ears themselves in response to the music she had created using digitally manipulated electronic tones, as featured in her album *Sound Characters (Making the Third Ear)* (1999, Tzadik), filled with heavily processed sounds full of digital artefacts, extreme pitch interpolation and other software-driven manipulations. Her performances were often high-volume, sensory assaults with visceral results. She holds a unique place in digital practice, in the way she worked with sound as an ephemeral, living thing.

In 1999, the Prix Ars Electronica in Austria, the leading organization for presenting and rewarding digital art, changed the name of its music section from 'Computer Music' to 'Digital Music'. This signified the end of an era, reflecting an acknowledgement that digital music had moved on from the days of academic computer investigations and was now a much broader, more diverse field (Stuart 2002: 2).

COMPOSING AND PERFORMING WITH DIGITAL SOUNDS

In early sound synthesis, a sound would often take days to create and process, as early computers could not perform different tasks simultaneously. But as new sounds were being created, the control of them was also developing. The Musical Instrument Digital Interface (MIDI) protocol was developed in 1983 and standardized a language of communication between computers and music peripheries that is still used today (Manning 2004: 240). While keyboards were the main MIDI controllers for some ten years, other controllers, such as drum machines and wind controllers, opened the way to software versions, as well as synthesizers, controllers and a variety of instruments (Holmes 2008: 235). MIDI has enabled the hybridization so characteristic of digital arts, exemplified in American composer David Rokeby's *Very Nervous System* (1991), which turned video camera images of people moving into MIDI signals that could be played as audio. Rokeby wrote the software and configured specialized hardware for the piece, which involved an interactive interface linking video, motion tracking software, music and movement (Wands 2006: 125; also see Chapter 2).

Computers were being used to 'compose' music in the early days of computer music, as mentioned in Chapter 2, but also to facilitate simple notation. In 1970 American academic Leland Smith developed a program entitled *SCORE* that could specify pitch, rhythm and any changes of key (Chadabe 1997: 116). This simple composing facility can be seen as a forerunner to modern notation programs (Manning 2004: 197), which create music notation on a computer by being either played on a MIDI keyboard, or using the drop-and-drag facility of a mouse. As word processors changed the way writing occurs, so did these change the way music was composed. These programs facilitate music manuscript creation, and enable composers to hear pieces as they go, using synthesized musical sounds as a guide.

Key Digital Sound Editing Tools

Many aesthetic and artistic concepts relating to digital processes echo those of analogue electronic music, in particular the editing techniques that were used to manipulate tape. Below are some of the most common techniques applied when editing a digital audio file.

Looping	the process of repeating a sample, used in synthesis but also a composition tool. This term came from tape, where a tape would be joined to itself so that it would repeat.
Fade	gradually increase the volume at the beginning or end of an audio track.
Crossfade	fade from one audio track to another.
Cut and Paste	cut a section of audio out and put it somewhere else in the piece.
Magnify/Zoom	this is a way to look closely at the detail of a sound wave on a software audio editor. While not an editing technique specifically, this tool enables fine sampling and editing of digital audio.

Many composers made personal composition programs in collaboration with software engineers that were only ever developed for their own use. Iannis Xenakis (1922–2001) used the mathematical nature of computer operations as a foundation for composition systems, and used computer-generated statistical processes as compositional materials for works such as *Atrées* (1962) for ten solo performers. Later, Xenakis used computers to facilitate multimedia works. In collaboration with programmer Cornelia Colyer, he developed *Polytope de Cluny* (1972–4), a work that was both composed and controlled by a computer during the performance. It was an automated light and sound composition employing 600 electronic flashes, three lasers and a seven-track electronic tape (Manning 2004: 203). Important developments in computer composition were enabled by the American composer Laurie Spiegel. *A Harmonic Algorithm* (1981) was composed in a program that goes on composing music as long as the computer is allowed to run (Spiegel 1980: liner notes). Spiegel also created *Music Mouse* in 1995, one of the early intelligent musical instruments realized as software, in which performing and composing happen at the same time on the computer screen.

Automation and manipulation are key elements of digital media, offering different ways to change and perceive materials. This increasing manipulability entails a distancing from what was traditionally a staple of the musical experience: humans performing sound on instruments in real time, an issue examined by Schaeffer's acousmatic music idea discussed earlier. Digital music was becoming increasingly complex and many digitally created or manipulated tracks were becoming humanly impossible to perform. The broken and quashed drum beats in jungle or breakbeat tracks are excellent examples, and can be found on the album *Terminator* by Metalheads (1992, Synthetic). The album is full of rapid breakbeats and features a sample from the character Sarah Connor in the film *The Terminator* (1984) – 'you're talking about things I haven't done yet' – that reflects the process of time stretching and compression typically employed in the tracks. Software has also been used to mask mistakes or imperfections of an artist during live performance. The Auto-Tune facility that adjusts 'out of key' vocals in real time has been used by many musicians to correct the pitch of vocals in the production and performance of popular music in which a copy of the recorded performance is deemed essential.

DIGITAL AS A MEANS: COLLECTING AND PRODUCING

While new ways of composing and generating sound were being developed, digital technologies were also accelerating change in the production, distribution and consumption of sounds. Recording, storage and retrieval systems have enabled a culture of collecting and archiving, where music is so easily accessible, and hard drive capacity expands in more portable formats (see Chapter 7). Recording technology began to involve a dissemination of music to a broader listening base, largely responsible for the popularity of pop and rock music from the middle of the twentieth century. Through these recording processes, there is more music available to us than ever before, from all periods of history, enabling pre-existing music to be re-examined, re-contextualized, and re-valued, offering diverse opportunities to engage with the past, through remixing, the re-release of early recordings, and exposure to a range of musical influences. Creativity was now evident in the ability to find and rearrange musical materials as much as to create (synthesize) or organize (compose) them. While a digital file can be reproduced many times without losing quality (as with digital photographs, discussed in Chapter 3), digital tools and formats actually provide a catalyst for developing new and different versions of artworks (Manovich 2003: 36). Digital technology makes it easier to mix existing sounds into a new work, meaning that the range of creators involved in music making has diversified considerably.

This valuing of archives is reflected in the emergence of the DJ as a more creative, composer-like role. The studio, once the realm of specialist engineers with little specialist music knowledge, has become a creative hub and remixing sounds has become a central component of musical culture (Sexton 2008: 93). The roles of musician and producer, instrument and studio, have become blurred by access to cheap, free or pirated software for recording, mixing and making any sound you could imagine. The bedroom producer was born, conflating the creator and consumer (see Chapter 7 and the notion of 'prosumer'). While this has enabled a larger range of people to participate in the production of electronic music, it also isolates them, fragmenting their involvement, as more and more individual electronic music makers contribute from their homes rather than studios (Sexton 2008: 93). Despite these many new developments, there remains an ongoing engagement with analogue sounds and older technologies, such as vinyl and tape, for many producers and musicians. Irish-born artist Aphex Twin is best known for his experimentation with computer-dissected beats in works such as *Come to Daddy [Pappy Mix]* (1997, Warp), and for his subjection of analogue synthesizers and drum machines to digital processes in the *Analord* (2004, Warp) series of EPs.

CONSUMING DIGITAL MUSIC

The introduction of commercial music releases on CD in 1982 saw the confirmed arrival of digital music consumption (Sexton 2008: 95). Originally marketed as everlasting, with Philips Records using the motto 'perfect sound forever' (Sexton 2008: 96), it was soon realized that they were not, some estimating the average music CD would only last between seven and ten years (Freidberg 2002: 23). In fact, they were also susceptible to damage, a quality explored by artists such as Yasunao Tone (b. 1935). A Japanese artist who was active during the Fluxus movement in the 1960s, Tone was an early computer music composer in Japan, and member of the influential Japanese improvisation ensemble, Group Ongaku. Tone's album *Solo for Wounded CD* (1985, Tzadik) features recordings of what Tone calls 'wounded CDs' (Stuart 2002: 3). CDs are uniquely damaged and altered by Tone so that they will radically skip, jump and stutter in playback (Stuart 2002: 7). An important part of the work is that the CD player that playbacks the disks has a 'de-controlled' system, so it randomly selects fragments of sound from the CD, with Tone sometimes hitting the CD player during a live performance to make it jump (Stuart 2002: 7). Tone has stated that the error-correction functionality of modern CD players has made it hard to continue to use this technique and, for this reason, he continues to use older equipment (Cox and Warner 2006: 345). The clean silence characteristic of the digital is therefore corrupted in Tone's 'wounded CD' works.

Other digital recording media were launched, such as digital audio tape (DAT) and midi disc (MD), but without the same success enjoyed by the CD. The intro-duction of the MP3 compression format in 1987, and its consequent distribution on the internet in the mid-1990s, that took the record industry by surprise, despite the origins of the format in corporate strategies to standardize digital data (Sterne 2006: 829; also see Chapter 7). The MP3 format was developed to overcome the slow connection speeds characteristic of the early internet, and, as these sped up, new, higher-fidelity file formats have been developed, such as FLAC and Ogg

Vorbis, and will no doubt continue to be (see breakout box). The MP3 employs a compression system to reduce the amount of data required to playback audio files. This entails some reduction in quality. However this is often thought to be a worthwhile compromise given that the reduction in data size has led to an ease of portability that has changed the way we listen to music (Holmes 2008: 314). The MP3 enables many tracks to be stored on a small device, leading to the development and popularity of the portable audio player that, by the early 2000s, could store more songs than would be possible to listen to in a single lifetime.

Compression: Efficient Ways to Share and Store Audio

As we will explore in detail in Chapter 7, audio files are compressed using psychoacoustic principles to analyse and arrange the original audio into compact code which decompresses on playback. 'Lossless' compression is where the reduced data flow contains all the components necessary to restore the original signal and provides a 35 per cent reduction in data size. 'Lossy' compression is where elements of the signal are permanently lost (Manning 2004: 259). An early example of lossy compression was used on the Mini Disc, a format used for portable digital recorders. MP3 (MPEG-1 Audio Layer-3) files are a derivative of the widely used MPEG (Motion Pictures Experts Group) digital signal compression protocol, developed in 1987 and used for video. MP3 was the first compression standard accepted by the Industry Standards Organisation (ISO) (Holmes 2008: 202). MP3s reduce the file size by 90 per cent, and permanently remove imperceptible audio signals, compromising the audio fidelity in the process (Holmes 2008: 134). Uncompressed audio formats in common use are the AIFF and WAV formats.

The MP3 served its purpose well, with the emergence of file sharing services, as discussed in Chapter 7. This kind of music distribution saw a shift from the marketing of an 'album' format to the single track. An album was now a platform for creating future revenue from singular elements, such as songs and music videos (Sexton 2008: 97). Digital distribution has led to an increased focus on peripheral materials that could be easily linked using the internet, with the visual aspect of music marketing moving away from cover art and lyrics reproduction to music videos and websites (Sexton 2008: 99). Online music magazines and blogs have flourished on the internet, and they can easily link images, video and live information feeds to each other in order to promote music. British dance music duo Coldcut creates music featuring cut-up samples of hip-hop, breaks, jazz, spoken word and various other types of music. Their performances feature live video mixes, which also feed audio back into their music. The songs from their album *Let Us Play* (1997, Ninja Tunes) had videos made by the artist Hexstatic, who mirrored their musical approach through the use of stock footage mixed together. The multimedia potential of CDs was explored by the duo on their remix album *Let Us Replay!* (1999, Ninja Tunes), which came with real-time video manipulation software developed by the group included on a CD-ROM. In a different musical sphere, a key American early computer music pioneer Morton Subotnick's (b. 1933) *All My Hummingbirds Have Alibis* (1993) was the first musical work released on a CD-ROM (Chadabe 1997: 332). Once loaded onto a computer, the user chooses the order of sections of music, as well as a range of images to accompany the music as it plays.

THE FUTURE UNFOLDING: INTERACTIVITY AND LIVENESS

While digital technology did enable more music that could only be experienced on speakers, it did not kill live performance, even though the introduction of the sampler triggered concern about musicians being replaced by computers, leading to union disputes (Manning 2004: 225). Enhanced possibilities for interactivity is a key reward of digital audio technologies, as it requires fast, random access to data, provided by large-capacity hard drives and fast processors. The tradition of improvisation in electronic music goes back to the 1950s, and was benefitted by increasingly compact technologies bought on by digitization. New performance tools, such as the laptop, brought about different kinds of improvisation. The laptop, for example, could be operated by anyone, from any musical (or non-musical) background, offering a new scope in the performance of digital music (Stuart 2003: 61). John Cage had pioneered the performance of live electronic music, with some his works featuring turntables, computers, radios and often having electronic devices built especially for them by the likes of Max Mathews and others for works such as *Variations V* (1965). Artists have recently automated and digitized some of Cage's chance procedures in an attempt to realize his works more accurately. A music ensemble in Australia, Decibel, has digitized and automated all the scores of Cage's eight *Variations*, enabling the realization of chance processes in real time on what they call 'digital screen scores'. The scores are also released as a tablet computer application in conjunction with Cage's publisher, Peters Edition (Vickery et al. 2012).

Reflection

'Spectacle is the guarantor of presence and authenticity, whereas laptop performance represents artifice and absence, the alienation and deferment of presence. After approximately 40 years of electronic music, the issues surrounding how audiences receive the performance of electronic music have yet to be resolved' (Cascone 2000: 101). Do you think that an electronic music performance can be enjoyed in the same way as music made using traditional instruments in a live performance? Or is it a different, but still potentially enjoyable, experience?

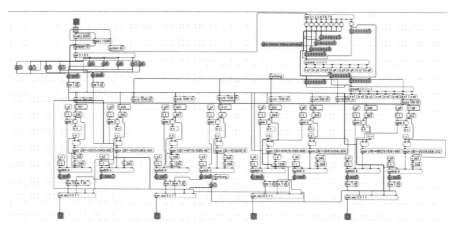

Figure 5.2 A Max patch created by Australian composer Lindsay Vickery for his and Cat Hope's composition *The Talking Board*, 2011. Image used with permission of the artist.

Initially, electronic music was featured alongside music performed on acoustic instruments, or used to affect it. But, in the 1990s, real-time audio processing facilitated improvising and interaction with electronics and led to the growth of new subcultures of music based on solely live electronic music performance, of genres such as such as hip-hop, techno and electronica, sustained by performance events at clubs and raves (Holmes 2008: 381). Software programs such as Max (named after Max Mathews, and developed at IRCAM in 1998), Pure Data and Super Collider provide modular GUIs that enable users to construct arrangements of instruments, from inside the computer and out, and manage the organization, playback and spatial deployment of sounds in real time. These programs went on to be used by artists such as Aphex Twin, Ikue Mori, Merzbow, Autechre and many others (Holmes 2008: 286). An example of how a Max patch looks on the screen is shown in Figure 5.2. Interactivity was also enhanced by the ongoing development of hardware controllers in lifelike computer accessories that use human gesture, including the real guitar controllers for programs such as Rocksmith and BandFuse (Heneghan 2013).

THE FRAGMENTATION OF MUSIC

Folk music and classical music existed side by side for hundreds of years. Then popular music attracted a new level of mass popularity, aided by the recording industry. However, the digital age has seen a fragmentation of musical style as at no time before. It would be impossible to name the hundreds of music genres today, especially as they are being invented all the time, but a range of works that epitomize digital approaches, from early to recent examples, will conclude the chapter.

A key work that bought together many new technological developments was the collaboration between Lejaren Hiller and John Cage that led to *HPSCHD* (1969), a work that launched the idea of computer-assisted composition (Manning 2004: 201). The computer proved to be the ideal means to generate the random processes that Cage had derived from the Chinese text, the *I Ching*. *HPSCHD* is for seven harpsichords, and between one and fifty-one tapes of computer-generated sound. It premiered in a sports arena where fifty-one loudspeakers were mounted on the ceiling, plus another seven for the harpsichords. Fifty-two slide projectors were also installed, and the performance lasted five hours (Holmes 2008: 380). The synthesized material for the tapes was created using routines specially adapted from Max Mathew's Music IV program, a newer version of *Music 1* discussed earlier. The computer provided the sound as well as its organization and control, realizing the full integration of both computer synthesis and computer composition (Manning 2004: 202).

British composer Jonathan Harvey's (1939–2012) *Mortuos Plango, Vivos Voco* (1980) exemplifies experiments with early Digital Signal Processing. The piece was developed at IRCAM, and is based on the recordings of a large church bell at Winchester Cathedral in England, and the voice of Harvey's own son Dominic. Its title is taken from the inscription around the bell, the full text providing the source material for the voice. The pitch and time structure of the work is based entirely on the rich irregular harmonic spectrum of the bell, using the breakdown of the bell sound as a foundation for chords, structure and modulations. The eight sections are each based on one of the principal eight lowest partials. Constant transformations between the sounds of the boy's voice and that of the bell unify the contrasting sources of material (Manning 2004: 201).

The work of Wendy Carlos (b. 1939) pioneered the synthesizing of orchestral sounds, but also popularized them in albums such as *Switched on Bach* (1968, Columbia), where popular classical music pieces are played on synthesizers. *Switched on Bach* was the first classical album to sell over half-a-million copies, and went on to sell over a million as well as winning three Grammy awards (2009, Classitronic). Her *Digital Moonscapes* (1984) uses a full digital orchestra, whereas other works, such as *Luna* (1984), modelled a single digital instrument that was then manipulated in real time between different sound qualities. Another application of electronic processes to existing music can be found in the digital process of time stretching, which has been used to take recordings of existing music to make new, drone-like works. *9 Beet Stretch* (2004) by Leif Inge is a 24-hour version of Ludwig van Beethoven's (1770–1827) *Ninth Symphony* (1824), produced using granular time stretching. The Canadian musician Barry Truax (b. 1947) uses the smallest particles of sound – known as grain – in his early computer works. *Nautilus* (1976) features subtle shadings of texture and a strong sense of organic development within the sounds. The work also investigates spatial qualities, where sound is distributed across different speakers, facilitated by software editing programs. In this work, musical material rotates in different directions, and the addition of reverberation leads to an illusion of closeness when the sound is moving rapidly, and an illusion of distance when the sound seems fixed (Manning 2004: 205). Digital technologies have offered more control for the spatialization of sound in multiple speakers, such as imaging or mapping movement in software sound editing programs. This has led to the employment of spatialization in cinema and computer games, working in tandem with imagery to enhance realism. Canadian sound artist Janet Cardiff's (b. 1957) audio walks employ spatial manipulation to recreate scenarios specific to particular locations, as listeners embark on walking tours wearing headphones, in works such as *The Munster Walk* (1997).

Laptop performers will often combine the laptop with other instruments, using the computer as a means to change their sounds in different ways. This integration of the laptop into performance combinations and ensembles (for example, the London Improvisers Orchestra often features laptop improvisers in its lineup) signifies an acceptability of the laptop as an instrument. Vienna-based artist Christian Fennesz (b. 1962) combines laptop and guitar in many of his performances. His album *Endless Summer* (2001, Mego) defied digital purism in favour of music that seemed retro and futuristic at the same time: the guitar sometimes plucked for rustic-folk flavour, and at others processed into a hazy background soundscape (Weidenbaum 2006). Another important performer, Ikue Mori (b. 1953), incorporates drum machines in combination with her laptop. Beginning her musical career as a drummer, Mori developed an interest in improvising, and continues to engage in a range of collaborations in New York City with artists such as Marian Zazeela, among others.

Case Study 5.4
Kim Cascone's 'The Aesthetics of Failure: "Post Digital" Tendencies in Contemporary Computer Music' (2000)

Cascone's essay explores the concept of the 'postdigital' as artists experimenting with a media in a way it was never designed to be used. Using the genre of glitch music as an example, Cascone presents the notion that good ideas can be generated from malfunction. Cascone claims that a postdigital movement occuring after the revolutionary period of the information age had passed and new work emerged from the failure of digital technologies, showing that the complete control of technology is an illusion (Cascone 2000). The digital malfunction in music can be generated by glitches, bugs, applications, system crashes, distortion and even the noise generated by the machinery itself, all able to be employed as creative material. We will further explore the notion of the postdigital in more detail in Chapter 9.

Digital music is perhaps best epitomized in the genre of glitch, as it accommodates both Cascone's postdigital approaches, discussed in Case Study 5.4, in conjunction with the microsound processes described by Curtis Roads. It arrived largely on the back of electronica, a genre of electronic music that is largely dance-based, and includes house, techno, drum 'n' bass, and ambient genres (Cascone 2000). Finnish group Pansonic create highly synthetic, hard-edged industrial sounds and fluorescent landscapes in their music, one of the earliest examples of glitch, on their album *Vakio* (1995, Blast First). Interestingly, Pansonic proudly confirm that all analogue equipment was used to record the album. Other artists find a more subtle approach and German artist Alva Noto bridges the gap between the harshness of Ikeda's biting digital sounds with a definite delicacy in works such as *Kerne* (1989, Plate Lunch). Glitch also offers a new musical take on noise music, in which the detritus of digital processes is used as the primary creative material, from dense, powerful and visceral works to more gentle explorations. The most delicate of explorations can be found in the work of the Japanese Onkyo movement, featuring composers such as Tetsu Inoue, Sachiko Matsubara and Nobukazu Takemura. Their work, while using small and delicate slices as well as digital noise, is very low in volume, demanding an intense and rewarding listening experience. *World Receiver* (1996) by Tetsu Inoue applies digital synthesis to world music, creating some wonderful house music as a result.

Figure 5.3 Live coding duo Slub performing at the Changing Grammars Symposium in Hamburg, 2004. Photograph by Renate Wieser. Image used with permission of the artists.

Other laptop performance techniques include networked performance and live coding. Carla Scaletti's *Public Organ: An Interactive, Networked Sound Installation* (1995) was premiered in ICMC in Banff, Canada and simultaneously on the web. Using a television, radio, telephone, camera, spray can and book, the artist provided an installation at a physical site while also inviting contributions via the internet. The work aims to reinforce the concept that while we act as individuals, we participate in a total world (Chadabe 1997: 337). Other artists have engaged with telecommunications in sound installations that use GPS systems, social media and mobile phones (Hope 2006). Australian artists Amanda Cole and Warren Armstrong created *Twitter Hymn Book* (2012), an installation that turns tweets into bite-size generative music compositions (also see Chapter 9 on social media art). The work searches for tweets with particular hash tags, turns letters and words into notes and chords, and translates them into MIDI and then into sound – fundamentally converting tweets about spirituality into a hymn. Live coding is a performance practice in which digital sounds are synthesized and improvised in real time, and the programming code used to do this is usually projected for all to see. Figure 5.3 shows a photograph from a performance by British duo Slub, formed in 2000. The performers have dedicated themselves to live coding since 2005, having developed their own generative software as well as employing game engines and other programming languages.

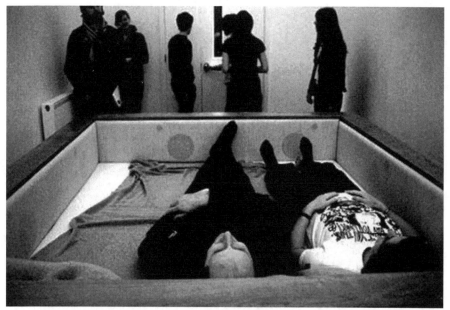

Figure 5.4 Kaffe Matthews, *Sonic Bed – London*, 2002, from the *Sonic Bed* series. Image used with permission of the artist.

An important element of digital sound practice comes in the form of installations. While many use complex pre-programmed coding processes to enact sophisticated routines in works involving movement and sound, others use programs that allow others to contribute, as seen in works that use internet and social networking platforms. The English sound artist Kaffe Matthews' career has spanned electronic laptop performance, spatialized works and installations. Her *Sonic Bed* (2002–5) is a purpose-built portable venue and instrument that combines digital software, audio reproduction and CAD design (see Chapter 3). Individuals or couples can lie in bed to listen to works played over a hidden 12-speaker system. *Sonic Bed* (as shown in Figure 5.4) is created in such a way that works can be commissioned for it, using the specially developed software interface developed by David Muth.

Digital recording technologies have also enabled the documentation of sounds previously inaudible. Japanese sound artist Toshiya Tsunoda (b. 1964) creates field recordings of vibrations which he then transposes into a higher-pitched audio range before mastering them to a CD. His album track *Gas Cylinder: Misaki-cho, Miura* (Infrigitive 2001, track 7) records shipping activity at sea as experienced through the reflective interior of a gas cylinder onshore. Tsunoda believes that identifying the original source of sounds in the recording is not as important as exploring how those sounds interact with each other and the space in which they exist – even when that 'space' is a CD recording (Tsunoda 2007). He manipulates the characteristics of very low-frequency sound (in particular, its ability to travel long distances) through CD reproduction by extending the CD frequency range that is usually limited to 20–20,000 Hertz down to around 10 Hertz (achieved by negotiating with CD manufacturers). A different approach can be seen in the work of German sound artist Christina Kubisch. Her *Fünf elektromagnetische Raster* (2012), presented at the Basel House of Electronic Arts, features recordings of electromagnetic fields. Kubisch translates the inaudible sounds of structures using a recording device she developed herself, listening into banks, security gates, servers, power stations, transmitters, subways and trains. The sounds are original recordings that have not been modified electronically, as they offer an interesting aural window into hidden sounds, without the need for any 'enhancement'.

Chapter Summary

This chapter has discussed a range of historical, theoretical and technical trends that have led to the development of digital music, and enable its ongoing development. Through an examination of the history of computer music, cultural change and the new editing, performance and distribution modes available to music through digital technologies, a range of digital music works have been examined.

- The influence of Futurism, serialism, musique concrète and the writing of John Cage provided key foundations for the development of digital electronic music.
- The twentieth century saw a radical change in the approach to music composition through the introduction of recording and electronic music processes.
- The development of the computer facilitated a move from analogue to digital tools. Digital synthesis and sampling are the key components in the construction of digital sound as facilitated by computing.
- Digital technologies have enabled new levels of interactivity in music through interactive software programs and internet connectivity. They have also enabled greater accessibility, portability and the miniaturization of music equipment.
- Music has fragmented into many smaller sub-genres, with the multi-format presentation of music a characteristic of digital practice.

6 THE POSSIBILITIES OF A WEB: INTERNET ART

Like digital music, internet art is an emerging area of the digital arts that helps to redefine arts practices in contemporary society. The development of internet-based art further demonstrates the hybridization of the arts made possible by digital technologies, discussed in Chapters 1 and 2. Responding to the increasing facility, availability and user-friendly nature of computer hardware and software, internet art has become an ever-growing area of the digital arts that incorporates all the art forms discussed in previous chapters. As this chapter highlights, the rise of internet art parallels the growth of internet technologies since the 1990s. Indeed, artists manipulate new technologies while also contributing to their evolution. Although different factors contributed to its initial development, internet art has been enabled primarily through advances in digital interface technologies related to the invention of HTML and popularized by graphical web browsing after the appearance of the browser Mosaic – both in 1993 (Greene 2004). While developments in web-based browsing technologies and coding supplied artists with new graphical methods, internet artists had already been devising interactive, text-based digital works even before then. As we will discuss, the forerunners of internet art are found in mid-twentieth-century participatory and conceptual artworks, notably Korean-American video artist Nam June Paik's *Participation TV* (1963) – a user-driven interactive experience that 'prefigured browser art' (Greene 2004: 9) and allowed 'the visitor to produce voice-generated television images' (Carpentier 2011: 58).

Chapter 6 will explore internet art from theoretical, historical and technological perspectives. It begins with the frameworks applicable to the interpretation of internet art, specifically the theories of Canadian media theorist Marshall McLuhan, Jean Baudrillard, Nicolas Bourriaud, Gilles Deleuze and Félix Guattari. Through the 'global village' of McLuhan, the 'simulacra' of Baudrillard, the 'relational aesthetics' of Bourriaud and the 'rhizome' of Deleuze and Guattari, we examine the democratization of art set in motion by the web and interrelated digital media. We also consider formative art-historical moments, including the influence of Dadaism, the

Fluxus movement, conceptual art, participatory art and pre-internet media-based works, such as *Participation TV*, some of which have already been explored for their impact on the digital arts (see Chapters 2, 3 and 5 in particular). The emergence of digital technologies has propelled internet art forward as an ever-increasing area within the digital arts (also see Chapters 2 and 9). While exploring the effects of emerging technologies on internet art, we also reflect on the technological innovations that have been catalyzed by artists innovating across a number of digital media.

Furthermore, we will discuss the impact of social networking, open-source software, new operating systems and programming environments (including recent developments in Java applets, Flash and Shockwave technologies). This exploration entails an understanding of the way artists have initiated developments in digital technology. In addition to online communities and net cultures, we explore the key concepts of telepresence, appropriation, agency and aesthetics. At the chapter's end, we conclude by returning to 'internet art' as a concept and movement. What was once a form of 'new media' existing at the fringes of the mainstream art world is increasingly becoming an accepted part of global arts practices, reflecting the evolution and maturation of internet-based technologies in the broader society. In preparation for Chapter 8, we also note the methods that museums and galleries have evolved for displaying, promoting and preserving works of internet art. The artists included in case studies are Australian code poet Mez Breeze, Slovenian ASCII-based net art pioneer Vuk Cosic, American new media artist Golan Levin, American designer Joshua Davis and Russian experimental filmmaker and internet artist Olia Lialina. Featured projects include *jodi.org* (1995–), *äda'web* (1994–8), *7–11* (1997–9) and *VNS Matrix* (1991–7).

WHAT IS INTERNET ART?

Known also as online art, browser art, net.art, network art or net art, internet art makes use of and integrates into works the 'participatory, connective and dynamic' features intrinsic to online environments in general (Ippolito 2002: 485). These terms are usually used interchangeably. Josephine Bosma in her book *Nettitudes* (2011) defines net art simply as 'art based in or on Internet cultures' (24). In 2002, Tilman Baumgärtel offered this definition:

> Net art addresses its own medium; it deals with the specific conditions the Internet offers. It explores the possibilities that arise from its taking place within this electronic network and is therefore 'Net specific'. Net art plays with the protocols of the Internet, with its technical peculiarities. It puts known or undiscovered errors within the system to its own use. It deals creatively with software and with the rules software follows in order to work.

It only has any meaning at all within its medium, the Internet. (cited in Corby 2006: 2)

Corby acknowledges that network art includes technologically complex works but also works in which technology is not a necessary condition, such as print books and performances (2006: 2). While the web is the primary medium for many net artists, other practitioners exploit various forms of digital media or employ a combination of platforms: email, instant messaging (IM), streaming, text-based environments (MUDs or Multi-User Domains), three-dimensional environments (VRML), video-conferencing (CU-SeeMe), image files (JPEG, TIFF), audio files (MP3, WAV) and video files (MPEG, WMV). As a result, internet art encompasses a broad and dynamic range of email, multimedia and software-based projects, as well as online, offline and ICT (information and communications technology) driven works. As we will see, early internet artworks challenged conventional museum practices organized around the curation of art objects.

The majority of internet artworks come into existence only in connection with an 'online community' (Preece 2000) – a concept that is essential to understanding the processes of development and dissemination of net art. Bosma's sprawling declaration on the importance of 'net cultures' to internet art is almost a text-based artwork in itself:

> Net cultures are the basis, the means and the source of net art. They are *not* predominantly technological. They involve various academic communities, news sites, financial trading, gaming communities, hacker groups, online shops, web logs (blogs), software and hardware developers, social network sites, dating sites, porn producers and porn audiences, media activists, institutional and independent cultural platforms and anything else happening that could be disseminated via the Net. (Bosma 2011: 25)

The production, distribution and marketing of net art through 'net cultures' or 'online communities' allow practitioners to reach massive global audiences while circumventing the mainstream distribution channels associated with galleries and museums (Ippolito 2002). In particular, long-term web-based projects are often coordinated by online communities dispersed across the globe, but also across a variety of online and offline digital environments and software applications. These participatory and connective aspects of digital media influence the very production of internet artworks and enhance the public's capacity to interact with them. In order to introduce the possibilities and varieties of internet art, we proceed next to a case study of 'codework' – the appropriation of web-based protocols and programming languages for the devising of artworks. Codework provides an excellent example of how artists engage with and manipulate internet technologies – a general theme throughout this chapter.

Case Study 6.1
Codework

In 2001, the American poet and cyberspace theorist Alan Sondheim coined the term 'codework' to describe text-based digital art that appropriates computer languages for reasons other than formal coding functions. Codework websites, such as jodi.org, demonstrate, in Sondheim's words, 'the computer stirring into the text' (cited in Funkhouser 2007: 257) through the subversion of programming conventions and web navigational norms. Designed by Joan Heemskerk (b. 1968) and Dirk Paesmans (b. 1965), jodi.org resists the aesthetics of mainstream websites through its ironic misuse of language, symbols and iconography. Pulsing green code confronts the user venturing into the idiosyncratically URL'd portal (archived as wwwwwwwww.jodi.org), disorienting navigation and stimulating the experience of panic. Strategically, jodi.org exploits HTML errors: 'The blinking page throbbed obscenely in the browser window, one glitch thus compounding the other' (Reas and Fry 2007: 565). Clicking in flashing areas on the screen, a user is transported to a menu of net art experiences. These include Betalab in which sprawling code and other graphics lead the user to execute a program (posing as a possible viral threat) known as GOODTIMES.exe. Code-based works, such as jodi.org, capitalize on programming miscues, including 'excessive graphics, animations, unconventional design (including unclear navigational principles, drawing links that reach dead or unlikely ends' (Funkhouser 2007: 257). As another significant practitioner of codework, Mez Breeze is an Australian multimedia net artist who works under a number of aliases and avatars, including Mez and netwurker. Her unique hybrid language, which she terms 'mezangelle', is a synthesis of natural English language and formal computer code that blurs the distinction between the real and the digital through the interplay between online and offline works. Her recent book of code poetry, *Human Readable Messages*, is a collection of her mezangelle writings since 2003 (Breeze 2012).

INTERACTIVITY, AGENCY AND COMMUNITY: THEORETICAL CONSIDERATIONS

In his short article 'Ten Myths of Internet Art' (2002), artist and archivist Jon Ippolito attempts to dispel some of the misconceptions surrounding internet art nearly a decade after its birth in the 1990s. Movements towards democratizing practices in the creative arts – including the open exchange of concepts and data between artists and the public – galvanized the appearance of internet art nearly two decades ago as a distinct area of digital art (Ippolito 2002: 487). As former curator at the Guggenheim Museum and a practising artist in his own right, Ippolito's perspective on the emergence of net art carries weight: 'the online art community has developed almost entirely outside the purview of galleries, auction houses, and printed art magazines' (Ippolito 2002: 486). The nature of the market economy is reflected by the high cost of purchasing traditional works of art. Galleries inherently exclude certain audiences, including those not able to travel to its physical location or pay admission fees. Furthermore, the iconic standing of analogue objects means that the very definition of art is deeply intertwined with physical works, such as sculptures and paintings. Internet art counters these sorts of limitations. Open-source platforms and freely accessible academic research inspired practitioners, 'posting art and criticism with no promise of reward but the opportunity to contribute to a new artmaking paradigm' (Ippolito 2002: 487). The internet artmaking paradigm, sketched by Ippolito, continues to reflect an ethic of the democratization of art and its processes of production. It involves the viewer in its ongoing creation (see Chapter 1).

Reflection

Ippolito describes the second of the ten myths as 'Internet art is only appreciated by an arcane sub-culture' (2002: 486). Considering that Ippolito wrote this just 10 years after the inception of internet art, do you think the myth is still valid? How has net art become integrated into mainstream society? What does the term 'internet art' mean to you, your friends or your family?

In order to examine Ippolito's arguments conceptually, the media theory and concepts of Marshall McLuhan help to frame internet art, especially as a democratic movement. Indeed, in our media-saturated world, many of McLuhan's predictions from 50 years ago are ringing loudly true. His prescient notion of the 'global village' (McLuhan 1964: 93) prefigured online communities and their importance to net art practices. In the 1960s, McLuhan began to analyse 'the social transformations wrought by the new technologies of information and communication' (Gere 2006: 17). McLuhan's book *Understanding Media* (1964) contains the much-quoted dictum 'the medium is the message', that is, 'the personal and social consequences of any medium – that is of any extension of ourselves – result from the new scale that is introduced into our affairs by each extension of ourselves, or by any new technology' (McLuhan 1964: 7). In other words, different forms of media – television, radio, telephony, telegraphy, photography – configure human experience in new ways, ultimately fostering agency and interconnection for users, appreciators and partici- pants (Greene 2004: 21). For example, photography has now become an expressive medium used globally – not just by photographers or visual artists – in connection to social media communities (see Chapters 3 and 9). Moreover, his observation that 'the "content" of any medium is always another medium' (McLuhan 1964: 8) underlies the crossing-over of data that is central to different forms of internet art.

The interpretation of cyberspace as a democratic environment can be attributed, in large part, to McLuhan's 'rhetoric of subjective experience, feedback and choice' (Greene 2004: 21). For McLuhan, 'the next medium, whatever it is – it may be the extension of consciousness – will include television as its content, not as its environment, and will transform television into an art form' (McLuhan 1964). This statement foreshadowed the emergence of the internet and world wide web through the social transformation set in motion by an 'art form'. Remarkably, he seems to predict the emergence of internet art from television technology. The internet has become a relatively new interactive phenomenon based on older televisual devices. For example, the computer monitor is a development of the television screen. The 7–11 list community is an example of an experimental net art work that manifests McLuhan's notions through the creative application of the e-list convention. The project, especially when first conceived, also blurs the boundary between a functional communication portal and a conceptual work of art. Founded in 1997 by Vuk Cosic, British artist Heath Bunting (b. 1966), Russian artist Alexei Shulgin (b. 1963), German artist Udo Noll and jodi.org (discussed in Case Study 6.1), 7–11 was 'the first international mailing list dedicated entirely to experiments in net.art' (Bazzichelli 2008: 101). Cosic defected from the Nettime and Telepolis mailing lists in search of an open, unmoderated platform in which to experiment and satirize.

Initially a reaction to mainstream exhibition venues and to the non-interactive mailing lists of the mid-1990s internet art scene, 7–11 became a virtual locus for net art experimentation. The project evolved into a collaborative email artwork 'in which the dynamics and possibilities of the mailing list format were explored' (Bosma 2011: 156). 7–11 involved unconventional uses of internet technology in which the 'administration tool, including subscriptions, header and footer variables, and moderation rules, was world read-writable by any web surfer' (Reas and Fry 2007: 563). The project radically experimented with the acceptable uses of an emerging communications technology. A virtual persona named Keiko Suzuki – credited as author of the fictional *Classics of Net.Art* books series devised by Cosic as an online spoof – played the role of list mediator. As a female persona in the male-dominated net art movement, Keiko became an icon for cyberfeminism. 7–11 'was not about posts but about the ways of using the list almost like with other net art – not so much about particular pieces but about new ways of working. We were doing research, not development' (Cosic cited in Bosma 2011: 156). In other words, as they creatively redefined mailing lists and other platforms, early internet artists considered themselves to be artistic, technological and social researchers at the same time.

Reflection

Email list-based projects show the diversity of works and practices included within the term 'internet art'. When should something as commonplace as an email list or web portal become a work of art?

Additionally, many net.art theorists argue that internet works, such as mailing lists, cause the democratization of art. In what ways does internet art democratize the production and consumption of art? How does analogue fail to do this? In what ways does internet art possibly inhibit or, at least, fail to realize the ideal of democratization?

In addition to McLuhan, another key theorist for understanding internet art is French philosopher Jean Baudrillard. His seminal treatise *Simulacra and Simulation* (1981) distinguishes between these two concepts: a simulation refers to the representation of something in the real world, whereas a simulacrum is a copy without an original (also see Chapter 9 on hyperreality). Baudrillard foregrounds the tension between the 'real' (things, people, emotions, ideas, etc.) and the 'virtual' (computer representations, gaming environments, Disneyland experiences, etc.). He also suggests the importance of context (physical settings, political moods, artistic trends, etc.) in interpreting an artwork. His writings initiated interest in hyperreality and simulationist approaches to art, found in artworks that use gaming or virtual reality (VR) platforms (Greene 2004: 26; and further explored in Chapter 9). With the power of duplication made possible by simple CTRL-C keystrokes and file copy commands, techniques of data appropriation (i.e. basing a new work on the use of another project's data) and plagiarism have become integral to internet art practices (Greene 2004: 27). Baudrillard's simulacra–simulation binary calls into question the nature of the real in relation to 'telepresence', which is the virtual experience of being transported between spaces through the aid of a telecommunications apparatus (see Chapter 2). In other words, telecommunications devices, such as mobile phones and the internet, have the capacity to take us somewhere virtually while we remain stationary in a place, for example, behind a keyboard or with mobile phones firm against our ears.

Explored by internet artists, telepresence can be defined as 'a sense of "being there" during a mediated experience [in] highly immersive virtual reality systems' (Bracken and Botta 2010: 41). Interactive internet installation artist Eduardo Kac defines 'telepresence art' as 'a new art form generated in the intersection among telecommunications, computers, and robotics' (Kac 2005: 127). Telepresence art is an outgrowth of telecommunciations art, such as the experimental mail art of the 1970s and 1980s in which artists used the postal system, including letters and mailboxes, as a basis for conceptual artworks (see Chapter 2). It can also integrate internet technologies, as Ed Bennett and Kac's telepresence piece *Ornitorrinco in Eden* (1994) makes clear (see Figure 6.1). The work involved a range of media, including telerobotics, landline and mobile telephony, and videoconferencing (CU-SeeMe). Via the internet, anonymous participants could decide their own robotic movements through the remote physical spaces of installations set up in Seattle, Chicago and Lexington, selecting what they would see through the eye of the telerobot named Ornitorrinco (Kac 2005: 78). With the use of mirrors and lighting, participants could see themselves as the telerobot while they navigated a 'teleparadise of obsolescence', including magnetic tapes and circuit boards (Kac 2005: 157–60). As Kac states, 'one of the main issues raised by this piece is the cultural need for the Internet to become more of a shared social space and less of an information-delivery system' (Kac 2005: 160).

Ornitorrinco in Eden is a prominent example of Nicolas Bourriaud's conceptualization of art and aesthetics outlined in his book *Relational Aesthetics* (2002). His focus is on the relationships between actants, collective meaning-making and collaborative arts practices. Attempting to define the uniqueness of 1990s European art, Bourriaud's book is regarded as the definitive articulation of the collective intentions of much work during this period. Bourriaud outlines a new set of criteria for understanding the art of the 1990s, particularly through his application of internet terminology – such as 'user friendliness' and 'interactivity' (Bishop 2007). Bourriaud's definition of a 'relational arts practice' is that which considers 'the realm of human interactions and its social context, rather than the assertion of an independent and *private* symbolic space' (Bourriaud 2002). He means that an artwork is not produced by an isolated artist but rather by complex social interactions. Relational practices aim to 'establish intersubjective encounters that *literally* take place – in the artist's production of the work, or in the viewer's reception of it' [emphasis in original] (Bishop 2007). As the meaning of the work is decided collectively – in the case of net art, as part of a net culture or online community – the practice of relational aesthetics is contingent on the environment and the audience, both virtual and physical.

The appropriation of free software and the use of email lists by internet artists and collectives, such as äda'web and Rhizome.org, reflect Bourriaud's aesthetics (see Case Study 6.2). In 1994, curator Benjamin Weil and British arts patron John Borthwick

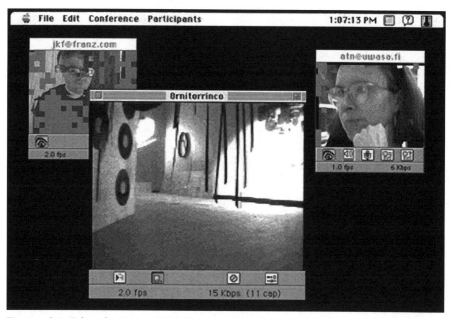

Figure 6.1 Eduardo Kac and Ed Bennett, *Ornitorrinco in Eden*, 1994. Screenshot. Image courtesy of the artist.

founded äda'web as one of the first internet art initiatives to curate (i.e. select) works for inclusion. Before shutting down in 1998, äda'web developed around multiple projects and collaborations as 'a research and development platform, a digital foundry, and a journey', becoming one of the first online curatorial initiatives to support the work of internet artists (Dewdney and Ride 2006: 63). A visit to äda'web (http://www.adaweb.com) reveals some of the same aesthetic techniques also used by jodi.org: dysfunctional navigational tools, geometric code-based graphics and pulsating neon green text reminiscent of 1980s electronic interfaces.

Case Study 6.2
Rhizome.org

Not by coincidence, the most cited thinker in Bourriaud's *Relational Aesthetics* is Félix Guattari, who along with Gilles Deleuze theorized the 'rhizome', a term from plant science which refers to a high level of interconnection and interactivity. In their book *A Thousand Plateaus* (1987), Deleuze (1925–95) and Guattari (1930–92) used the biological term 'rhizome' as a metaphor for networks, practices and ways of thinking that challenge traditional philosophical hierarchies, such as mind over body, thought over intuition, and vision over the other senses (see Chapter 2). The rhizome 'has no beginning or end; it is always in the middle, between things, interbeing, *intermezzo*. The tree is filiation, but the rhizome is alliance, uniquely alliance' (Deleuze and Guattari 1987: 27). As a symbol for alliances of various kinds, the rhizome counters the growth-dominated metaphors of modernity (e.g. found in notions of economic expansion and globalization) by 'burrowing through substance, fragmenting into simultaneous sprouts, moving with a certain stealth, powerful in its dispersion ... [destabilizing] the conventions of origins and endings' (Kaplan 1996: 87). The theory of the rhizome in relation to the media and internet describes the networked aspects of digital technologies. The rhizome symbolizes networks and collaborations. One of the most famous online examples of collaboration and interaction has been conceived of as both an artwork and public resource. Like äda'web, Rhizome.org (or *Rhizome*) is an internet artwork existing as a network of projects and users rather than a transportable object of art. It is a discussion forum and portal to new media artworks, but also can be viewed as an artwork in itself. Founded in 1996 as a democratic platform, Rhizome.org was initiated by the American artist Mark Tribe (b. 1966) 'as a mailing list, text archive and database, for and about art' (Bosma 2006: 32). Indeed, Tribe considers Rhizome.org a 'social sculpture' in the sensed that Joseph Beuys regarded certain arts practices as composed of 'discursive social materials, i.e. conversation' (Bosma 2006: 33). Rhizome.org is an interconnected environment involving viewers, curators, critics and artists. It facilitates open discussions and includes an unmoderated email list. Eventually Rhizome.org became a non-profit body in order to stay alive. Its website now reads: 'Rhizome is dedicated to the creation, presentation, preservation, and critique of emerging artistic practices that engage technology. Through open platforms for exchange and collaboration, our website serves to encourage and expand the communities around these practices' (Rhizome.org 2013).

PERFORMANCE, CHANCE AND INNOVATION: A BRIEF HISTORY OF INTERNET ART

In this section, we consider the history of internet art and the major art-historical and social moments that have influenced its emergence. Bourriaud's notion of relational aesthetics helps us to understand how internet art circumvents the traditional view of art productions as the independent and transportable objects of a '*private* symbolic space'. As the offspring of mail, computer, video, television and telematic art, internet art exhibits both participatory and conceptual approaches to art (explained in Chapter 2). Inspired by artistic developments in response to World War I and reflecting some of the techniques of experimental or avant-garde art, internet artists continue to challenge the predominance of the object of art, as well as the practices of artistic production in an evermore digitally networked world.

As we noted in the last section through various practitioners and projects, such as Kac's *Ornitorrinco in Eden*, internet artists focus on audience interactivity, information networks and the unorthodox application of digital technologies – exploiting randomness in their works while shifting away from modes of pictorial representation common to mainstream arts practices (Greene 2004: 10). Rather than being oriented towards discrete manifestations (paintings, photographs, sculptures or books), internet artists aim for user-specific, open-ended and technologically based creative processes as – in themselves – works of art, albeit ones with fluid boundaries and, often, never reaching a conclusion.

Internet artists tend to be inspired by the works of Dada, the international movement originating in Zurich in 1916 in response to the sociopolitical climate of World War I. As described in Chapters 2 and 4, the French Dada artist Marcel Duchamp, considered the founder of conceptual art, is a noteworthy figure within the historical roots of internet art. Duchamp as a conceptual artist, and Dada as his broader art-historical context, influenced the twentieth-century movement away from pictorialism in artistic practices (Greene 2004: 20). With fondness, net art innovator Vuk Cosic wrote that internet artists are 'Duchamp's ideal children' (cited in Greene 2004: 97), indicating the affection many digital artists maintain for his work even today. In 1916, Duchamp sent four postcards with meaningless (though syntactically plausible) writing to his neighbour in perhaps the first invocation of 'mail art' (Gere 2006: 15) – a movement which continued through the 1970s using 'the mail system as a medium' (Osthoff 2005: 263).

Moreover, Duchamp's unfinished work *The Bride Stripped Bare by Her Bachelors, Even*, commonly known as the *Large Glass* (1915–23), revealed Duchamp's preoccupation with the emerging technologies of radio and wireless telegraphy through graphical allusions to antennae and electrical condensers (Hughes 2004: 128). Other artists of Duchamp's period also engaged inventively with communication technologies, creating precedents for the emergence of internet art. For instance, in 1922, shortly after World War I, Bauhaus-based Hungarian painter and photographer László Moholy-Nagy (1895–1946) produced the first artwork, *Telephone*, to exploit the telephone system, specifically 'to communicate directions for the making of enamel tiles' (Goggin 2006: 199) through the new medium.

Other important influences on the evolution of 1990s net art include Fluxus, happenings and EAT (Experiments in Art and Technology). Coined in 1961 by American artist George Maciunas (1931–78), Fluxus comprised the performances and experiments of an international group of artists, poets and musicians most prominently including Allan Kaprow (1927–2006), Robert Watts (1923–88), George Brecht (1926–2008) and Yoko Ono (b. 1933). As Owen Smith comments, 'through their work and activities, these artists have actualized a network-based paradigm of creative engagement [through] collectivity, art, creative production, and distribution' (Smith 2005: 117). Central to understanding Fluxus are notions of 'performativity, process, play, networked culture, and communal artistic practices' (Smith 2005: 117), including creative strategies such as the unpredictable execution of instructions by audiences (see Chapter 2). Early Fluxus artists employed the postal system (especially postcards) and telecommunications media extensively to exchange ideas between practitioners dispersed across the globe (see Case Study 6.3). Proposed two years earlier to Fluxus by performance art pioneer Allan Kaprow, the term 'happening', explored in Chapter 4, refers to site-specific artistic events that entail the dissolution of the division between performance and spectator, between audience and participants. Kaprow's *Calling* (1965) consisted of a selection of New York City sites (where activities were conducted on a Saturday) and a rural site at a New Jersey farm (on a Sunday). In both environments, performers agreed on their collective patterns of behaviours, calls and responses both in advance of and during these distinctively open-ended performances (Kaye 2000). The work began with three people waiting at different places in New York City. The driver of a passing car called to each of the performers, who then entered their respective cars and were wrapped in aluminium foil and muslin, stuffed into rubbish bins on the streets and transported to Grand Central Station for display. The themes of calling, being called and being held captive continued in the woods of New York the following day in a comparable fashion.

Case Study 6.3
Eternal Network

In 1968, French Fluxus artist Robert Filliou (1926–87) and American conceptual artist George Brecht (1926–2008) coined the term 'Eternal Network' to refer to the different connections between art and life. Critics attribute the term specifically to Filliou's use of the postal system to produce artworks, including poems in the form of postcards and letters (Gere 2006: 16). However, Filliou preferred his neologism to the more fashionable 'the avant-garde' in characterizing the international associations of artists, poets and engineers corresponding with one another through various techniques. He presents a further elaboration of the collaborative, process-based concept of 'Eternal Network' in the following poem titled 'Research' (1970):

There is always someone asleep and someone awake
someone dreaming asleep, someone dreaming awake
someone eating, someone hungry
someone fighting, someone loving
someone making money, someone broke
someone traveling, someone staying put
someone helping, someone hindering
someone enjoying, someone suffering
someone indifferent
someone starting, someone stopping
The Network is Eternal (Everlasting)
(cited in Voyce 2013: 210)

Filliou's 'Art's Birthday' is an example of an Eternal Network project involving 'local and global telepathic exchanges and performances' (Drinkall 2011: 48). 'Telepathic' referred to the worldwide transmission of information between networks in which communication could happen instantaneously without face-to-face exchange. In 1963, Filliou chose 17 January as the millionth birthday of art, declaring somewhat facetiously that art did not exist before this date – which still forms the basis for performances and celebrations commemorating the birth of art around the world. Like Duchamp, Filliou explored telepathic practices through artist networks and mail art. As an affiliate of Fluxus, American collagist and pop artist Ray Johnson (1927–95) also became associated with mail art – known as postal or correspondence art – through his appropriation of letters and faxes, as part of the global network exalted by Filliou and later forming the basis for many internet artworks. As Reed comments in his book *Assimilate: A Critical History of Industrial Music*, mail art 'takes the epistolary act as its artistic locus. Mail art might be a handmade collage postcard sent to a friend, or a single-printing fanzine of cryptic phrases passed through the post to a dozen recipients from one to the next, or it might be mass mailings of doll parts to entire streets of strangers' (Reed 2013: 111).

Another important influence on internet art was E.A.T., a group formed in 1966 by Bell Labs engineer Billy Kluver (1927–2004), painter Robert Rauschenberg (1925–2008), theatre artist Robert Whitman (b. 1935) and electrical engineer Fred Waldhauer (1927–93). Convinced of the importance of truly equitable collaborations between artists and engineers, E.A.T. worked with seminal artists of the 1960s and 1970s, including John Cage, Andy Warhol (1928–87) and Jasper Johns (b. 1930) (Bijvoet 1990: 27) to produce a variety of artworks. An example of an E.A.T. project was the Pepsi Pavilion at the 1970 Expo in Japan, including a massive geodesic dome designed by a team of engineers and artists, and a fog sculpture by Fujiko Nakaya (b. 1933). In the 1950s and 1960s, John Cage's work particularly engaged with notions of interactivity, chance and multimedia through new forms of electronics, as evidenced by his silent piano work *4'33"* (1952) – which consisted of Cage sitting 'silently' at the piano for four minutes and thirty three seconds and came to influence Fluxus artists interested in 'process, interaction and performance' (Gere 2006: 16; see also Chapters 2 and 5).

In addition to mail art and early electronic art found in E.A.T., computer art – defined generally as any artwork that uses a computer in its production, exhibition and storage – is a precursor of internet art. French artist Vera Molnar (b. 1924), American computer artist Charles Csuri and German-born digital artist Manfred Mohr (b. 1938) are regarded as pioneers of computer art, explored in Chapter 3. In particular, Csuri was one of the first professional artists to begin using a computer

Figure 6.2 Roy Ascott, *La Plissure du Texte* (1993). Photograph of performance. Image courtesy of the artist.

for creative purposes. His work *Sine Curve Man*, a rendering of a man's face using algorithmic programming, won first prize in the Computer Art Contest (1967) – a predecessor of the prestigious Prix Ars Electronica inaugurated in 1987. Later in the 1960s, the first computer art exhibitions were held in the USA and Germany. The height of early computer art coincided with the exhibitions *The Machine as Seen at the End of the Mechanical Age* (MOMA 1968) and *Cybernetic Serendipity* (ICA, London 1968).

In the early 1960s, artists such as Roy Ascott (b. 1934) developed technology-based installations merging computers, video and satellites as well as theories of telematics, or what would later be referred to collectively as ICT. Ascott is known for his development of telematics, defined as 'computer-mediated communications networking between geographically dispersed individuals and institutions ... and between the human mind and artificial systems of intelligence and perception' (Shanken 2003: 1). The telematic combination of computers and communications technology is evident in Ascott's *La Plissure du Texte* (1983) – a collaborative work that went online through the software ARTEX (Artists' Electronic Exchange Network) all day for 12 days straight, enabling artists to create a collective fairy tale (Gere 2006: 19) (see Figure 6.2).

Internet art is also indebted to video, satellite and television art. During the 1970s and 1980s, video and cable television – integrated in certain instances with fax and satellite technologies – became more widely used by artists. These emerging media enhanced themes of interactivity, networks and data transfer. In particular, television art stimulated broader interest in artworks based in mass media. Like conceptual art, these forms of media-based art called into question the status ascribed to art objects, such as paintings and sculptures, and introduced unpredictability and chance as creative elements (Gere 2006). Precedents in video and television art, especially Paik's work, contributed to internet art's evolution. Paik's *Participation TV* (1963), *Magnet TV* (1965), *Silent TV* (1969), *The Selling of New York* (1972) and *TV Buddha* (1974) transfigured the television from a commercial broadcast medium to a platform for interactive, participatory and conceptual discovery. *Participation TV* enabled spectators to create abstract televisuals by external means – specifically by talking into a microphone hooked up to the television (Morley 2007: 284). Paik's work makes use of televisual distortion and appropriates the medium for artistic purposes – strategies which would later become fundamental to internet artists. The distortion of television signals through creative practices helped to elicit the latent possibilities of the technology.

Telecommunications artists from the 1960s used fax machines and satellites to produce globally networked works of art, as a conceptual forerunner of internet art (Corby 2006: 4). Artworks of the 1970s exploited developments in videography, video games, computer-generated special effects and satellites, demonstrating the increasing integration of art and technology during this time. In particular, Paik and others made use of early portable video technology, explored in Chapters 2 and 3. In *TV Buddha*, an eighteenth-century statue of Buddha placed on a table 'regarded' its own image broadcast on a television set through the use of a closed-circuit video camera: 'the statue sits there, in both animate and frozen time, contemplating itself as spectators contemplate the contemplation of contemplation' (Ran 2009: 188–9). Furthermore, in the later 1970s, Sherrie Rabinowitz and Kit Galloway produced *Satellite Arts Project* (1977), using satellites and television to devise a work of dance (also see Chapter 2). Their project *Electronic Café* (1984) has been described as a 'telecollaboration' (Gere 2006: 18).

These artists and works provided the foundation for the birth of internet art as a hybridization of artistic modernism, the avant-garde (or the Eternal Network in Filliou's terms) and emerging media platforms (Gere 2006: 13). The 1970s stimulated an interest in post-industrial economies based on information networks (Gere 2006). Gere goes on to trace the history of internet art to the development of communications technologies, such as telephones, in the late 1800s and early 1900s. Nagy's *Telephone* works, Cage's use of radios and Johnson's mail art – along with the first applications of media technologies in video, television, satellite and cybernetic art – drew attention to the potential ramifications of new technologies for human experience and creative production. By the late 1980s, Tim Berners-Lee would propose the world wide web as a global, post-industrial hypertext experiment (Greene 2004: 214). By the mid-1990s, international artists started to meet virtually on the list Nettime to explore the potential of the world wide web as an artistic medium and collaborative mechanism (Bosma 2011: 126). Later in the decade, key exhibitions of net art occurred with *documenta X* (1997) and *Net Condition* (1999). During these years, German media critic Tilman Baumgärtel wrote some of the first critical commentaries on net art, including *New Materials Towards Net Art* (2001), bringing heightened critical attention to internet art.

Reflection

One way in which we can appreciate the history of internet art is to think of the internet as both a technological and social creature that enables a variety of 'online communities' and 'net cultures'. Can you think of any examples, artistic or otherwise? How do these online communities foster a sense of inclusiveness for users? What are the ways in which one participates or interacts? What forms of etiquette are important to the communities?

BROWSING, CODING AND NETWORKING: THE TECHNOLOGY OF INTERNET ART

Technological developments have enabled internet art to mature into a global phenomenon. With the further development of internet technologies, 'net art' was first brought into circulation by critics such as German artist Pit Schultz (Bosma 2011: 29). Vuk Cosic (b. 1966) is a pioneer of internet art who in 1994 adopted the world wide web as a medium and devised the term 'net art' to characterize the practices of an emerging group of artists. His early works were comparable to the mail art of Ray Johnson. He mailed images to other artists and to his network, but he later began to develop web-based projects. As his first initiative, *Net.art per se* parodied a CNN site in commemorating 'Net.art per se', a meeting of internet artists and commentators in Trieste, Italy in 1996 (see http://www.ljudmila.org/naps/home.htm). As the first example of internet art to appropriate a mainstream website, *Net.art per se* reflects many characteristics typical of the movement, including parody, scepticism towards mass media technologies and the appropriation of web protocols. Indeed, the term 'net art' was 'found' serendipitously by Cosic in a scrambled email message containing undecipherable ASCII – the code used by computers to translate English characters to a series of numbers (Greene 2004: 214).

The history of internet art is, therefore, one of performance, chance and innovation. As we have seen in this chapter, internet art bears a lineage to its precursors – briefly outlined in this section – in media-based art that mobilized the transmission of ideas between spectators, artists and online communities. As with its media art forerunners, internet art developed outside the conventional auspices of galleries, print-based art magazines and auction houses (Ippolito 2002: 486). Employed as a technological and sociocultural mechanism, the internet makes possible the introduction of audience feedback into net art works. Hence, having outlined the art-historical influences, in this section, we survey the technological innovations that have precipitated internet art – including graphical web browsing, developments in programming languages and the rise of social media platforms. Indeed, the trajectory of internet art from its media-based precursors (mail, telephone, television and satellite art, as discussed in the previous section) is connected intrinsically to the emergence of new technologies. However, internet artists have also influenced the emergence of certain digital technologies.

Following World War II, developments in computing and information systems provided the context for avant-garde art practices (Gere 2006). During the 1950s, multimedia experimentation and audience participation served as methodological precedents for the internet arts practices of the late twentieth century. In 1969, the Cold War initiative ARPANET went online and was later decommissioned in 1989. As a predecessor of the internet of today, ARPANET was a supercomputer network created by the USA Department of Defense's Advanced Research Projects Agency (ARPA). Including an early version of email, it allowed researchers in different places to communicate with one another and created an information network that would survive if any one part were destroyed (Morley 2009: 102). The disruption of American communication networks was a monumental concern during the Cold War era. Further hardware and software developments in the 1980s led to the world wide web in the early 1990s.

One of the major technological factors in the advent of internet art was the development of user-friendly interfaces, particularly between 1994–6. A graphical user interface (GUI, pronounced 'gooey') combines text and graphics to facilitate the use of software in navigating the internet. In contrast, non-GUI browsers, such as Lynx, are text-only. The most popular graphical web browsers used today include Netscape Navigator, Internet Explorer, Mozilla Firefox and Google Chrome. However, Mosaic is an important predecessor to these browsers. Initially released in 1993 by the University of Illinois, Mosaic became the first browser of its kind to facilitate the arrangement of images and text on a single page (Bainbridge 2004: 456). With the increasing accessibility of web browsers, the general public began to refer to the internet as 'the web' (Kac 2005: 61). When these user-friendly graphical browsers became available in the mid-1990s, numerous artists took advantage of the technology with intense excitement, as noted, producing work in the name of 'net art' (Gere 2006: 21). Kac observes that artists have since employed the internet as 'a means of storing, distributing, and accessing digital information [as well as] a social space, a conflation of medium and exhibition venue' (Kac 2005: 60).

Motivated by the free software movement, in 1997 art critic Matthew Fuller, artist Simon Pope and programmer Colin Green, working under the label of I/O/D, began to devise a web browser for artists (Greene 2004: 84). Eventually known as Web Stalker (1997–8), the browser was an alternative to Netscape Navigator and Internet Explorer – both designed to serve corporate rather than aesthetic purposes. The new graphical interface highlighted the relationships between websites through 'web neighbourhoods' (Greene 2004: 85), allowing the user to visualize and access web content differently. Web Stalker utilizes the 'latent structure' of the internet: 'the user opens a Web address, then watches as the *Stalker* spits back the HTML source for that address. In a parallel window the Web Stalker exhaustively maps each page linked from that URL, exponentially enlarging the group of scanned pages and finally pushing an entire set of interlinked pages to the user. The pages are mapped in a deep, complex hypertextual relation' (Galloway 2004: 218). Web Stalker is an example of technological innovation by internet artists working in collaboration with programmers.

Developments in computer programming languages also facilitated the emergence of net art. In many ways, internet art has paralleled the growth of programming languages, including text-only HTML, Macromedia languages, Javascript, Java, Perl and PHP (Reas and Fry 2007: 565). In 1989, Tim Berners-Lee (b. 1955), a British scientist at CERN in Switzerland, formulated Hypertext Markup Language (HTML), enabling users to communicate and exchange information through the internet (Poole 2005: 15). More specifically, HTML made text and images available to viewers with suitable software and allowed the creation of links between documents (Gere 2006: 20). Between 1995–2000, the net art scene affiliated with Bunting, Shulgin and Lialina coded in browser-based languages, such as HTML, with Javascript in order to implement more complex processes, such as those involving algorithms (Reas and Fry 2007: 564). However, the bare-bones text-only format was characteristic of projects of this period, highlighted by wwwwwwwww. jodi.org.

The emergence of internet art coincided with the birth of the internet as coding became more sophisticated. By 1995, artists were responsible for 8 per cent of all websites, suggesting the crucial contribution of early internet artists to the development of digital technologies (Ippolito 2002: 485). In fact, internet artists overtly exploited programming protocols, often subverting the normal uses of coding languages. Olia Lialina's project *Agatha Appears* (1997) is a digital story of a romance between a 'sys admin' (or systems administrator, someone who maintains and administers computers) and Agatha, a young woman from a small village (Bosma 2011: 97). Agatha skips from server to server, as her narrative unfolds through the URL (uniform resource locator) of each web page. For example:

1. http://www.here.ru/agatha/cant_stay_anymore.htm
2. http://www.altx.com/agatha/starts_new_life.html
3. http://www.distopia.com/agatha/travels.html
4. http://www2.arnes.si/~ljintima3/agatha/travels_a_lot.html
   (Greene 2004: 103)

The address bars above, thus, are central to the artwork and act to distribute the story across the web, suggesting that in online environments name and location are synonymous. Other parts of the narrative are revealed via error screens and floating text (Greene 2004: 104). *Agatha Appears* is an example of an internet artwork that manipulates programming conventions, but does so in order to convey a poetic narrative. In fact, Lialina's extensive use of URLs and address bars reflects her mistrust of a web feature added to browsers in 1998, which embedded content from websites into a host website without exhibiting the code of the original sources (Bosma 2011: 97). In its creative use of networks to tell a story, the work can also be read as a criticism of the Cold War military origins of the internet, now appropriated for creative purposes. The social critique of technology is also evident in Case Study 6.4 on VNS Matrix.

Case Study 6.4
VNS Matrix

Formed in 1991 in Australia, the VNS Matrix collective consisted of Josephine Starrs (b. 1955), Francesca da Rimini (who also went by the pseudonym Doll Yoko) (b. 1966), Julianne Pierce (b. 1963) and Virginia Barratt (b. 1959). Until about 1997 when they disbanded, VNS Matrix challenged the gendered hierarchies of emerging technologies, providing an important voice for women artists using the internet to create work. *Cyberfeminist Manifesto for the 21st Century* (1992) introduced the term 'cyberfeminism' into popular vocabulary as a response to the male domination of the internet. Their *Manifesto* was inspired by feminist scholar Donna Haraway's essay 'A Cyborg Manifesto' (1985) published later in her book *Simians, Cyborgs, and Women: The Reinvention of Nature* (1991). The VNS Matrix *Manifesto* celebrates the creativity of women 'in a reversal of the concept of the male genius' (Mey 2007: 156). VNS Matrix was known for its arts-based feminist activism and gender satire, encapsulated in their phrase 'the clitoris is a direct line to the matrix' (cited in Schaffer 1999). One of their key works was *All New Gen* (1993), a participatory computer art installation based at the Experimental Art Foundation Gallery in Adelaide, Australia. In this parody of a computer game, players encountered an eclectic and highly ironic environment in which they first needed to identify their gender from the options 'male', 'female' or 'neither' — the first two choices triggering a loop that exits the unknowing user from the game. The protagonist, All New Gen, is a female persona out to get Big Daddy Mainframe. The exhibition space uses light boxes, animations, video, poster art and telephone lines, as well as a 'bonding box' room complete with foam flooring, a bottle of sake and computer access to a pornographic video of female bondage (Schaffer 1999). An interactive CD called 'Bad Code' accompanied the exhibition, making possible a broader base of users.

The next horizon of internet art relates to the uptake of social networking platforms, mobile phone and gaming technologies, such as apps, GPS (global positioning system) software, augmented reality, virtual spaces and programming advances, including HTML5 (also see Chapter 9). This exciting new direction for art and technology reflects internet art's continuing engagement with emerging technologies. Through these integrations, the boundary between internet art and other forms of digital art is increasingly becoming indistinct (as evident in Case Study 6.5, on the following page). For example, Joshua Davis (b. 1971) is an American designer and digital artist known for his use of emerging internet applications and coding novelties. Influenced by American abstract expressionist Jackson Pollock, Davis is regarded as a pioneer of Flash-based art, as outlined in his book *Flash to the Core: An Interactive Sketchbook* (2002). Adobe Flash or Macromedia Flash is a multimedia software for creating graphics and animation. However, his latest use of HTML5 language in *The Endless Mural*, an 'interactive, collaborative art website', is an example of a contemporary digital artist using novel internet technologies to produce participatory art (http://www.endlessmural.com). The work enables users to easily create artworks as part of an ongoing, online public mural. As the fifth revision of Tim Berners-Lee's original HTML from 1989, HTML5 more fully integrates multimedia and improves user readability. As one of the first online art projects to use HTML5, *The Endless Mural* produces a gesture-based environment (pointing, clicking or swiping across the page) in which randomly selected motifs are mapped to patterns drawn by the user. Images and source code are downloadable, foregrounding the customization of web environments that dominates the internet today. The work of Davis offers another example of the potential of the internet to democratize art, in the sense outlined in Chapter 1.

Case Study 6.5
Golan Levin

Golan Levin (b. 1972) is an artist-engineer once affiliated with the Massachusetts Institute of Technology (MIT) Media Lab's Aesthetics and Computation Group. Levin is known for developing software tools to facilitate the 'real-time manipulation of computer graphics and audio' (Salter 2010: 178). His works *Environmental Suite* (1998–2000), *Scribble* (2000), *Dialtones: A Telesymphony* (2001) (discussed in Chapter 9) and *Messe de Voce* (2005) demonstrate the ways that digital art boundaries are becoming more indistinct. For *Environmental Suite*, Levin created code 'that enabled a performer to treat image and sound in a highly abstract, textual manner that gave fluid life to digital floating lines, skeins, blobs, and tendrils, all in real time' (Salter 2010: 178) (see Figure 6.3). Levin's more recent installation work employs iPhone and robotic technologies to make art that is 'expressive potential of the new tools we have' (TED 2009). Interactive and immersive bodily experience defines *Interstitial Fragment Processor* (2008) in which participants explore the negative shapes formed around their bodies. Furthermore, the creative agency of participants is central to the work *Opto-Isolator* (2007) as one robotic eye in a black box blinks in response to the viewer's blinking.

This chapter has considered the democratizing of art through the internet and associated technologies. As we have seen through case studies and other examples, net artworks are neither restricted to museum or gallery locations nor to the internet itself. Internet art contains elements of conceptual, participatory and performance art, while crossing between many technological platforms, theoretical positions and web environments. Indeed, the internet itself has evolved far beyond the web of its formative years, and internet art is testimony to this. The way in which artists exploit the internet reveals the hidden potentials of technology, continually redefining human relationships to computers, robotics and digital inventions. Yet, the democratizing potential of internet art poses challenges to the conservation of the digital artworks themselves, as Chapter 8 goes on to explore. For example, in 1999, the Guggenheim Museum launched the Variable Media Initiative in an effort to preserve performative and media-based works (The Solomon R. Guggenheim Foundation 2013). The project allows the translation of the artwork into a different

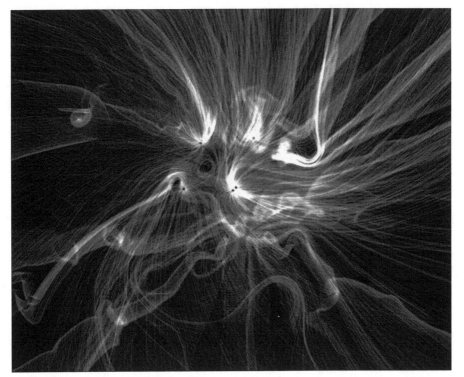

Figure 6.3. Golan Levin, *Environmental Suite* (1998–2000). Photograph of performance. Image courtesy of the artist.

medium once its original medium becomes obsolete. Included in the initiative is Paik's *TV Garden* (1974), among many others. Therefore, while internet art redefines the creation of art in today's world through enhanced agency, interactivity, collaboration and online–offline flows, the conservation approaches used to keep it alive also themselves help to redefine museum practices (discussion continued in Chapter 8).

Reflection

For a moment, we encourage you to think like an internet artist. Using your phone and any apps you might have available, briefly outline your plans for an artwork that can incorporate an app of your choice. How would the artwork involve a network of artists, viewers and participants? What kinds of concepts would inform the work?

Chapter Summary

This chapter has discussed internet art from theoretical, historical and technological perspectives. The case studies and other examples demonstrate the spectrum of practices and works that fall within the category. Internet art is an exciting area of digital arts to study because it is constantly evolving in parallel to the digital innovations of our times.

- Internet artists make use of web-based, offline and other technologies, but they also influence the very direction in which those technologies develop, as Joshua Davis' work *The Endless Mural* suggests.
- Internet art requires a digital community or net culture in order to be produced and sustained.
- The defining features of internet art are audience participation, artist networks, open-endedness, satire and social commentary, and innovation in coding and programming.
- The most common theories used to analyse internet art as a movement, as well as individual works of internet art, are the global village of McLuhan, the simulacra of Baudrillard, the relational aesthetics of Bourriaud and the rhizome of Deleuze and Guattari.
- The major influences on the emergence of internet art are Dada, Fluxus and conceptual art, as well as preinternet media-based movements, such as mail, television, satellite and other art-forms based in communications technologies.
- Developments in graphical web browsing, programming languages and social media platforms continually impact the evolution of internet art, themes which we will further develop in Chapter 9.

7 I WANT IT NOW: FINDING, DOWNLOADING AND DISTRIBUTING DIGITAL ART

In Chapter 6, we discussed the role of the internet and other new media in the production of art. Although a tool for creating works, the internet also provides an increasingly important means for locating and distributing digital art and digitized versions of traditional artworks, such as paintings. Chapter 7 focuses on the growth of internet technologies for arts distribution, as well as the manner in which novel technologies have reconfigured the relationship between the production and consumption of art. In particular, we explore the internet's impact on the emergence of global, interactive audiences for digital arts. The wider adoption of internet-based technologies for arts production, consumption and distribution includes the exemplary case of peer-to-peer file sharing – revolutionizing the way in which artists deliver music, video and graphics to their audiences. Peer-to-peer sharing also raises the issue of access to art in the public domain. The rise of internet technologies, in many instances, has resulted in the erosion of some traditional, non-internet or print-based forms of distribution. In this context, we return to the debate about the democratization of art through digital practices – a central theme in our discussion of internet art in the previous chapter.

Chapter 7 contains three sections. The first section presents theoretical perspectives that can be leveraged to understand the distribution of art in digital environments. In order to theorize the distribution of digital art further, we return briefly to Jean Baudrillard's 'simulacra' (1981), explored also in Chapters 6 and 9, and German critic Walter Benjamin's essay 'The Work of Art in the Age of Mechanical Reproduction' (originally published in 1936). Benjamin's analysis of the reproduction of art and Baudrillard's three orders of simulacra offer theoretical perspectives for thinking about digital art in relation to 'copy and paste' culture. Moreover, the key concepts we address include 'the database' and 'metadata' as cultural and artistic forms

(Manovich 2001a, 2003), the distinction between 'free' and 'permission' culture in the digital era (Lessig 2004), the notion of the 'prosumer' as a creative consumer (Kotler 2010) and the 'folksonomy' as a participatory structure for categorizing data in the digital commons (Yi 2008). Together, these concepts provide a critical framework for understanding the production, categorization, distribution and accessibility of digital art. The second section sketches the crucial historical moments in the evolution of digital arts distribution since the early 1990s, specifically the emergence of peer-to-peer (P2P) file sharing (and related issues of content piracy), Web 2.0 interactivity and Creative Commons licensing. Web 2.0 social networks have spurred the development of mainstream free market commerce in digital data, supported also by advances in Creative Commons-based access to artworks. The third section highlights key technological developments influencing digital arts access and distribution, returning again to peer-to-peer file-sharing software but also outlining high-quality audio, video and image file formats and digital compression technologies, also explored in Chapter 5.

In this chapter, through various artists, projects and new media developments, we underscore the most significant factors that have enhanced or diminished user access to digital artworks. As Chapter 6 reminded us, the internet is an audiovisual medium in its own right, one used to create art as well as new markets and modes of distribution. In some cases, consumers and users drive technological innovation towards novel forms of distribution and access to digital works. While a cause of legal concern for some companies, institutions and copyright-holders, illegal P2P file sharing – exemplified by Napster – has promoted direct links between artists and their global online audiences. Such technological innovations have also triggered the development of frameworks for copyright and definitions of intellectual property in digital environments. The four case studies featured in this chapter include Napster and online music piracy, Flickr as 'the world's photo album', the use of YouTube by leading art museums and Video Data Bank as the premier archive for video-based art. Project examples consist of DeviantART, Facebook, Myspace, SoundCloud and textz.com. Mark Amerika, interactive media artist George Legrady (b. 1950), German photographer Thomas Ruff (b. 1958), contemporary artist Alexei Shulgin (b. 1963), German artist Sebastian Luetgert (b. 1969), Russian internet artist Olia Lialina (b. 1971) and internet artists Eva and Franco Mattes (b. 1976) are the practitioners featured in this chapter.

FINDING AND FILE SHARING: CREATIVE CULTURE IN THE DIGITAL ERA

This section presents key theoretical perspectives that enable us to think contextually and analytically about the finding, downloading and distribution of digital art. First, new media theorist and computer scientist Lev Manovich's commentary on the narrative role of the database in the digital era provides an opportunity to sketch out examples of digital artworks that exploit the functionality of the database through tags, keywords and other forms of metadata. While a medium for creating digital art, the database is also an essential means of categorization and distribution. Second, writer and futurist Alvin Toffler's portmanteau 'prosumer' raises questions over the production and consumption of art while also pointing to the creative digital consumer as increasingly the norm. Third, political activist and co-founder of Creative Commons Lawrence Lessig's distinction between 'free' and 'permission' culture presents a framework for the broader consideration of copyright and intellectual property in terms of digital art. The work of Jean Baudrillard and Walter Benjamin furnish theoretical cornerstones to our discussion. In particular, Baudrillard's three orders of simulacra and Benjamin's analysis of the reproduction of artworks provide critical concepts for approaching the relationship between 'copy and paste' culture and the methods of digital artists. Finally, throughout the section, we revisit the argument that the production and consumption of digital art involves the democratization of artistic practices, a theme discussed in Chapter 1.

The rapid distribution of digital artworks – photography, music, images, video and multimedia projects – through search and download functions foregrounds the authenticity and duplicability of works. As mentioned in Chapter 3, in his seminal essay 'The Work of Art in the Age of Mechanical Reproduction', German theorist and critic Walter Benjamin (1892–1940) examines the relationship between technology, art and 'cultural reproduction' (Kellner and Durham 2006: xviii). In particular, he conceptualizes the impact of capitalistic methods of producing and reproducing art. For Benjamin, the reproduction of an artwork results in the loss of the original's aura or 'its presence in time and space, its unique existence at the place where it happens to be' (Benjamin 2006: 20). 'Aura' refers to the work's authenticity, originality, uniqueness and presence. However, rather than a largely negative historical evolution, the decline of the aura has resulted in a more discriminating public able to discern critically between cultural manifestations. Benjamin comments:

> In principle a work of art has always been reproducible. Man-made [*sic*] artifacts could always be imitated by men. Replicas were made by pupils in practice of their craft, by masters for diffusing their works, and finally, by third parties in the pursuit of gain. Mechanical reproduction of a work of

art, however, represents something new. Historically, it advanced intermittently and in leaps at long intervals, but with accelerated intensity. (Benjamin 2006: 19)

Technical reproduction results in a multitude of copies and the loss of the authority of the aura. Mechanical copies are not dependent on the original (to the degree that a manual reproduction would be). Instead, mechanical reproduction transports a representation of the original object (e.g. a tree in a photograph) into new domains, such as the print media of magazines and newspapers (Hullot-Kentor 2003). The techniques of computerized reproduction – copying, cutting, pasting, clicking, dragging and dropping – raise questions about the aura of digital artworks and whether Benjamin's critique is relevant to the digital era.

As we saw in Chapter 6, Jean Baudrillard's theory of simulacra provides a perspective for further considering the proliferation of digital works, particularly images, as well as the relationship between an artistic object and the reality it represents. A simulacrum is a copy for which there is no original. As a theoretical framework, the three orders of simulacra outlined by Baudrillard allow us to comprehend the visual representation of the world over time, as further explored in Chapter 9. In *Symbolic Exchange and Death* (1993), Baudrillard proposes three orders of simulacra in order to characterize the various ways artistic objects have been produced and distributed historically (Toffoletti 2011: 17). The evolution of the first-order simulacrum begins during the Renaissance to the Industrial Revolution period and predates the economic or aesthetic value of images. During this time, artistic objects were indeed valued, but for sacred purposes, according to Baudrillard. The Industrial Revolution stimulated the rise of the second-order simulacrum in which mass production altered the value of objects. Images shifted from ritualistic to aesthetic value according to commercial demands and accrued 'meaning relative to a capitalist economy of value exchange' (Toffoletti 2011: 21). Baudrillard argues that industrial-scale reproduction interferes with the relationship between the artistic object (including images) and the reality represented; objects (such as trees) come to be understood in relation to their multiple copies (images of trees) rather than to the actual world (a forest). The third-order simulacrum marks the emergence of 'hyperreality' and 'simulation', triggered by consumer culture, mass media and communication technologies (Toffoletti 2011: 24; also see Chapter 9). Examples of third-order hyperreality include brands, advertising, icons, graphics and labels in which images proliferate without concrete connections to real-world phenomena.

The duplicability of digital artworks is, in part, a function of databases. Databases are fundamental to all aspects of finding, downloading and distributing work. In his book *The Language of New Media*, Lev Manovich describes the database as the epicentre of creative processes for the new media age (Manovich 2001a: 218–43). According to Manovich, the database is both a cultural form and technological apparatus or a 'structured collection of data … organized for fast search and retrieval by a computer' (218). The database is the digital correlate of existing forms of narrative, specifically the novel and cinema (Manovich 2001a: 218). However, it is also the 'natural enemy' of these forms. Key differences between the database and the literary or cinematic narrative bring to light the exact nature of database technologies. As an unordered domain, the database impels users – including digital artists – to create, rather than merely interpret or accept, meaning in the world:

> As a cultural form, the database represents the world as a list of items, and it refuses to order this list. In contrast, a narrative creates a cause-and-effect trajectory of seemingly unordered items [events]. Therefore, database and narrative are natural enemies. Competing for the same territory of human culture, each claims an exclusive right to make meaning out of the world. (Manovich 2001a: 225)

Moreover, new media favours the algorithm-like behaviours intrinsic to the database (e.g. executing a number of tactics in a gaming environment in order to advance to the next level). Advocating digital arts practices that engage the database as a mode of cultural expression, Manovich (2001: 219) calls for a 'poetics, aesthetics, and ethics' of the database.

As an exemplar, Olia Lialina's *Anna Karenin Goes to Paradise* (1994–6) (http://www.teleportacia.org/anna) is an internet-based narrative work underpinned by the database functionality of the search engine (see Figure 7.1). The comedic net art project contains references to the vintage pre-Google search engines Yahoo (1995–), AltaVista (1995–2011) and Magellan (1995–2001). Based on Leo Tolstoy's classic novel *Anna Karenina* (1878), Lialina's reinterpretation of the themes of love and adultery hinges on three prearranged search terms: 'love', 'train' and 'paradise'.

With the humour and irony representative of early internet art or net art (Chapter 6), Lialina reconfigures the narrative structure of the source text through Anna's newfound 'dialogue' with search engines. Instead of finding human affection, the famous protagonist falls deeply in love with a train (Deseriis 2012). In light of Manovich's theory of new media narratives, *Anna Karenin Goes to Paradise* can be viewed as the semi-ordered middle ground between database anti-narrative and the cause-and-effect narrative structure of literature and film. Lialina's net art project subverts the narrative authority of literary works, here represented by the source material of the novel.

Other digital artworks and artists make explicit use of the database form as a medium for creative expression. A notable project was *textz.com* (2002) – 'an open archive of sometimes closed works of authorship' (Greene 2004: 189). Founded by Sebastian Luetgert, the project was an open-access 'warez' database of texts. 'Warez' is a corruption of the word 'wares'. The term refers to infringing copies of copyrighted works – predominantly computer software, music and video. In the case of *textz.com*, illegal content included texts from different sources and genres, such as fictional works, theoretical treatises, song lyrics and political manifestos. The copy-protection mechanisms of warez files have been inactivated or 'cracked'. They are,

Figure 7.1 Olia Lialina, *Anna Karenin Goes to Paradise* (1994–6). Screenshot of internet artwork. Image courtesy of the artist.

therefore, distributed in breach of copyright and without royalties or reproduction fees returning to the creators or publishers. Organized warez collectives like *textz. com* source the illicit materials – which are then released into the public domain in violation of copyright law. According to the website Monoskop, texts were sourced in a number of ways: 'submitted by the authors themselves, supplied to the *textz.com* database by various online collaborators as freely circulating texts on the Net, or they were scanned in from printed media page by page, processed via a text recognition program, and transformed into ASCII files' (Monoskop 2013).

Whereas the *textz.com* project depended on an internet platform for its meaning, other database-oriented digital artworks exist offline, such as the installations of George Legrady. In the view of Manovich, Legrady has engaged intensively with the artistic possibilities of databases and metadata. Legrady's works include *The Anecdoted Archive* (1994), *[the clearing]* (1994), *Slippery Traces* (1996), *Tracing* (1998) and, more recently, *Pockets Full of Memories* (2003–6). Legrady develops site-specific and interactive installations drawing upon algorithms. Commissioned for the Centre Pompidou Museum of Modern Art in Paris, *Pockets Full of Memories* was a partici-patory installation that involved a data collection kiosk and addressed notions of the archive, memory and audience involvement in the production of digital works (see Figure 7.2). Legrady involved the audience in the development of the database, 'inviting them to scan their personal possessions and then to ponder the concept of a communal archive and the way in which collective memory functions' (Wands 2006: 165). Participants took digital photos of objects, then labelled the properties of the images with keywords or tags. This kind of user-generated data expanded over the exhibition's duration. The collection of semantic descriptions became the basis for the artist's generation of images and patterns through a 'Kohonen self-organizing map algorithm' (Greenberg 2007: 18). A self-organizing map (SOM) or a Kohonen map (named for Finnish professor Teuvo Kohonen) makes possible the visualization of complex data. In *Pockets Full of Memories*, the data consisted of keywords and tags – or what is known as 'metadata'. Manovich (2003: 13) characterizes metadata as 'data about data: keywords assigned to an image in a media database, a number of words in a text file, the type of codec used to compress an audio file'. Metadata allows 'computers to "see" and retrieve data, move it from place to place, compress it and expand it, connect data with other data' (Manovich 2003: 13). Legrady's digital artworks creatively work with metadata, resulting in visualizations based on the tags and keywords assigned to photos by participants in the installation.

Legrady's *Pockets Full of Memories* evidences the breaking down of the division between producer and consumer – symbolizing the capacity of digital technologies (e.g. images, databases, metadata) to democratize the creation and distribution of art. Legrady's viewers were active participants in and contributors to the installation; they had unique roles. *Pockets* also shows how digital art practices can catalyze a

Figure 7.2 George Legrady, *Pockets Full of Memories* (2003–6). Photograph of installation. Image courtesy of the artist.

shift from the creator's absolute control of the art object to a joint responsibility for the artwork that is negotiated between creator and participant. The distribution of internet-based works – beyond the constraints of place and venue – contributes to a process-based and networked form of art linked to democratic ideals and notions of 'the commons' explored later in this chapter. Internet artworks, such as *Anna Karenin Goes to Paradise*, exist in the highly visible online public sphere. The content of the project is available to any viewer at any time and from anywhere. Furthermore, digital artworks – including those now based on Web 2.0 technologies – depend on the agency of users to generate metadata and navigate an installation (*Pockets Full of Memories*), locate and upload warez (*textz.com*) or take on the role of central participant, as evident in Ed Bennett and Eduardo Kac's *Ornitorrinco in Eden* (1994) (see Chapter 6). Explored in mail artist Chuck Welch's (b. 1948) landmark book *Eternal Network: A Mail Art Anthology* (1995), email art often incorporates notions of user agency towards the democratization of art through digital practices. Importantly, the digital artwork and its manner of distribution are inseparable, in such a case.

The practices of finding, downloading and distributing point to the relationship between the consumption and production of digital art. In Legrady's *Pockets Full of Memories*, for example, the viewer (consumer) is also a participant (producer) of the installation. In many other examples, digital artists are more fully both consumers and producers of artwork. In the 1980s, Alvin Toffler (b. 1928) and Heidi Toffler (b. 1929) attempted to reconfigure the consumer–producer binary by formulating the concept of the 'prosumer' – a term describing a creative consumer who engages in both consumption and production. In *The Third Wave* (1980), Alvin Toffler attributes the emergence of 'the consumer' to the Industrial Revolution (1760–1840) or what he refers to as the 'second wave'. Whereas the 'first wave' involved prosumptive agricultural societies, the 'third wave' of modern times is characterized by deindustrialization, in his opinion. Toffler asserted that the prosumer would continue to serve a vital role in the context of our Information Age knowledge economies (Kotler 2010: 51–2). Echoing Toffler, in the early 1990s, artist and design theorist Stephen Wilson distinguished between creators (authors, directors, composers) and consumers (readers, listeners, viewers). For Wilson, interactive media experiences, particularly those made possible by the digital arts, 'break down this distinction by providing authoring opportunities to the consumer' (Wilson 1993: 'What Is Interactive Media').

Reflection

Consider three digital artworks – referenced in this book or elsewhere – in terms of production and consumption. In what ways do these works provide 'authoring opportunities to the consumer'? Do they embody the democratization of art through digital technologies? Do you think it is possible to be either a consumer or producer, or has the 'prosumer' become the norm for art in the digital world?

The breakdown of the consumer/author distinction has led to the profusion of media-based work, broader notions of creativity and higher degrees of public access to artwork. However, since its inception, the internet has triggered debates over copyright and intellectual property in online environments. One of the most vocal advocates for new models of copyright is American law scholar and political activist Lawrence Lessig (b. 1961). In *Free Culture* (2004), Lessig draws a distinction between 'free' and 'permission' culture. The adjective 'free', for Lessig, relates to 'free speech', 'free markets', 'free trade', 'free enterprise', 'free will' and 'free elections' or, in other words, the dimension of a society that 'supports and protects creators and innovators' (xiv). A free culture advocates for the value of intellectual property rights, but only in defence of both the creator and future follow-on creators. For Lessig, free culture is maintained 'by limiting the reach of those rights, to guarantee that follow-on creators and innovators remain *as free as possible* from the control of the past [emphasis in original]' (xiv). In contrast to a free culture, a 'permission' culture, as Lessig further describes, is 'a culture in which creators get to create only with the permission of the powerful, or of creators from the past' (xiv). In his view, permission culture weakens creativity, burdens innovation and increases costs related to the constant need for the expertise of lawyers and expensive legal processes (Lessig 2004: 173, 192).

How does access to digital art relate to Lessig's notion of free and permission culture? Sharing and collaborating are significant elements in the production of digital artworks. For example, the projects *life_sharing* and *Frequency Clock* call attention to the practice of sharing within a free culture as an underlying premise. *Life_sharing* (2000–3) was commissioned by the Walker Art Center (WAC) and founded by Eva and Franco Mattes, who are also known as 0100101110101101.ORG. *Life_sharing* is a variant of the term 'file sharing' (Walker Art Center n.d.). The project utilized emerging file-sharing software – which, for the first time in the digital age, allowed users to exchange the contents of their hard-drives. 0100101110101101. ORG made the files on their server publicly available through the WAC website. The artists granted users free, unchecked permission to 'rummage through archives, search for texts or files they're interested in, check the software, watch the "live" evolution of projects and even read' the artists' email (Walker Art Center n.d.). The metaphors of the archive and database central to *life_sharing* foreground the tension between the public and the private – as well as access to digital artworks generally – through complete, uncensored admittance to the artist's private virtual life (Grzinic 2011: 155). Clearly, *life_sharing* reflects the ethos of Lessig's notion of 'free culture', ensuring that 'follow-on creators and innovators remain *as free as possible*'. As a similar example from digital sound art, Honor Harger and Adam Hyde of the Australian collective Radioqualia founded the global participatory FM network *Frequency Clock* (1998–2003) as 'a geographically dispersed independent network of Net radio stations, broadcasting on autonomously owned FM transmitters'. The aims of *Frequency Clock* included 'the incorporation of more open systems for determining content [making possible] the abatement of centralized program administration' (Harger and Hyde cited in Lovink 2003: 146) (also see http://soundcloud.com/radioqualia).

Works such as *life_sharing* and *Frequency Clock* defy conventional models of copyright and intellectual property. As Lessig suggests, the finding, downloading and distributing of digital art bring to the fore debates over free and permission culture – specifically in relation to digital copyright and intellectual property online. These productions used open P2P software as an integral part of the process of design and distribution (Greene 2004: 189). Digital arts practices – including the use of P2P networks and cut-and-paste protocols – inherently run against the grain of the copyright conventions of a 'permission' culture. New models, represented by Creative Commons licensing discussed in the next section, have been developed in response. In general, copyright grants the owner of a work – who may not necessarily be the creator – exclusive permission to publish, manage and alter the work, as well as total control over copies or derivatives of the original. Importantly, the reach of copyright reflects the spectrum of rights granted to the creator under law (Lessig 2004: 136). Intellectual property (IP) is a generic legal term for intangible assets, including copyright, patents, trademarks, trade secrets and design rights (Cornish 2004: 1). Intellectual property law grants owners rights to these assets. As Lessig argues, the internet and other forms of digital technology have fostered a 'cut and paste culture' (Lessig 2004: 105). However, rather than being questionable practices, cutting, pasting and other forms of duplication are essential to the digital arts and the maintenance of the digital commons – a concept explained in more detail later in this chapter.

Reflection

As a digital artist, how would you manage copyright to your artwork? Would you allow 'follow-on' creations from the public? How might you maintain creative control over your work in a free culture?

Online communities are essential to the digital arts and the maintenance of an ethos of sharing. For example, DeviantART (or deviantART) is a web portal and social network dedicated to the sharing of artworks and ideas (http://www.deviantart.com). Founded in 2000 by Scott Jarkoff, Matthew Stephens and Angelo Sotira, DeviantART provides a platform for artists to display, discuss and share their productions. The website allows artists to exchange digital duplications of traditional works, as well as online and digital works. The left-hand side of the homepage contains a list of categories, including digital art, traditional art, photography, literature, film and animation, motion books, cartoons and comics, fan art and community projects. By 2009, nearly 11 million artists, writers and viewers had become members of the community. By late 2010, DeviantART received 100,000 new submissions each day (McHaney 2011: 44). As of 2013, it is now billed as the 'world's largest online art community' with 261 million artworks from over 27 million artists and contributors (deviantART 2013). Social media interfaces through Twitter, Facebook, Tumblr and Google have expanded the capacity of DeviantART for user interactivity and exchange. Users have the option to post comments about artworks and respond to polls on a variety of art-related topics. The ways in which you can access DeviantART works range from open and browsable to very specific and targeted.

As the DeviantART example suggests, the 'free culture' capacity to create art in relation to online communities and by manipulating the commands 'copy', 'paste', 'send' and 'print' leads to the discussion over the originality of digital artworks. Digital artist Bruce Wands observes that 'some artists choose to print only a single

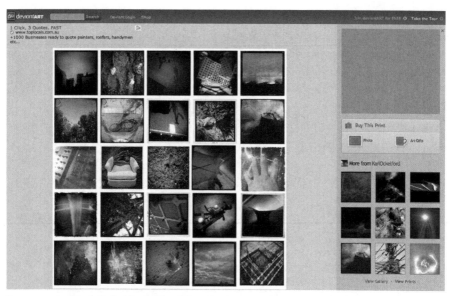

Figure 7.3. Karl Ockelford, *DeviantART* (2013). Ongoing, photograph of personal page. Image courtesy of the artist.

original of a work; many issue limited editions; and others produce open editions. Some artists even provide a copy of the digital file in case an original print should become damaged or faded' (Wands 2006: 34). As we have seen through a number of examples and case studies, many digital artworks are derivative and rely extensively on source material, such as novels, emails, news feeds and photos. In his extended poem 'Source Material Everywhere' (republished in *Remix the Book* [2011]), American author and artist Mark Amerika reflects on the relationship between source material and artistic meaning, as well as the identity of a digital artist as a 'remixologist':

> As we have already acknowledged
> the remixologist *is* a novelty generator
> one who performs in the immediate present
> as a way of establishing the mysterious resonance of
> social relatedness within the context of
> a fluctuating currency in the always-emergent market
> a market that is fueled by this same sense of novelty

(Amerika 2011: 17)

DOWNLOADING THE COMMONS: THE HISTORY OF DIGITAL ARTS DISTRIBUTION

You paint a landscape. Your work is displayed as part of a gallery exhibition. A viewer purchases a print of your landscape. You compose a song. You perform the song at a venue. Listeners purchase a CD copy of your music. You write a poem. The poem is published in an anthology. Your admirers buy print copies of the book. Traditional (that is non-digital) works of art are distributed in these ways. Such forms of art are accessed through galleries, exhibition halls and performance spaces. However, the digital era has shifted the fundamental structure of arts distribution, bringing to light a variety of issues surrounding copyright, intellectual property, access and originality, as we briefly discussed in the previous section. As early as 1936, French poet and philosopher Paul Valéry (1871–1945) in his book *Aesthetics* predicted that images and sounds would become plentifully available to the public. This section examines some of the developments leading to the cornucopia of digital material we know today. Featured events include the emergence of netcasting, P2P sharing, Web 2.0 technologies and Creative Commons licensing. Interactivity and user participation define these historical landmarks. The notion of a 'folksonomy' is explored in the context of Case Study 7.2 on Flickr as the 'world's photo album'.

Between 1997–9, new online platforms and formats emerged for music distribution, effectively blurring the distinction between the internet and mainstream or non-internet-based forms of broadcasting (Greene 2004: 110). In particular, these platforms set the stage for a proliferation of experimental music and micro-radio initiatives. Online broadcasters or 'netcasters' populated the internet with new stations, set up quickly and simply with encoders and servers. Notable early art radio websites, including Heath Bunting's *Radio 90* (1999) and Radioqualia's *Frequency Clock* (1998–2003), enabled users to program play lists (Greene 2004: 110). Online broadcasting took advantage of developments in the MP3 (MPEG-1 or MPEG-2 Audio Layer III compression) as a compact format for distributing audio. These kinds of digital technologies provided new ways of sharing and customizing music recordings.

Emerging technologies triggered the growth of alternative radio communities broadcasting through the internet, but also provoked debates about regulation and copyright. In response to questions surrounding sharing and authorship, Alexei Shulgin's *386 DX* (1998–2005) was perhaps the world's first cyberpunk rock band. *386 DX* actually refers to a computer that uses text-to-speech software to play songs by popular artists. In 1998, Shulgin delivered real-time rock performances using a 386dx processor computer and Windows 3.1 operating system (386 DX 1998) (see http://www.easylife.org/386dx/). The project included versions of popular songs like *California Dreaming, House of the Rising Sun, Smells like Teen Spirit* and *Purple*

Haze 'performed by 386 DX / 4Mb RAM / EGA / 40 Mb HD [with] synchronized text-to-speech and midi synthesis' (1998). *386 DX* demonstrated the increasing acceptability of reinterpreting popular music through digital audio platforms. In the context of distribution, we now turn to the revolutionary example of Napster (Case Study 7.1).

Case Study 7.1
Napster and Online Music Piracy

Another example of Lessig's concept of free culture is Napster. In 1999, Shawn Fanning, a 19-year-old university student, launched Napster – a digital music company and real-time platform that enabled computer users to exchange MP3 music recordings through its peer-to-peer file-sharing software MusicShare (Ferrell and Hartline 2008: 373). Napster is the precursor to many peer-to-peer file-sharing formats (Ramey 2003: 253), discussed later in this chapter. The project was groundbreaking because it granted users access to the music files on the computers of its members. Napster members were able to search according to artist or song and then download MP3s to their computers. As the third section of this chapter explains, MP3s are digital formats that compress a sound structure into a relatively small file (Ramey 2003: 253). Napster combined the technological innovation of file sharing with community and social features. The platform included a search engine, file-sharing capability without the need for a central server and IRC (Internet Relay Chat) for synchronous chatting among users. Other features of the Napster forum included instant messaging and user-generated bookmarks. During the height of its popularity, Napster was estimated to have between 26 and 70 million subscribers.

In 2000, Napster was taken to court by the Recording Industry Association of America (RIAA) on behalf of key music companies Sony Music, BMG and Warner Music Group (Ferrell and Hartline 2008: 374). Also during 2000, the heavy metal band Metallica accused Napster of copyright violation and racketeering, leading to the landmark lawsuit *Metallica et al. v. Napster, Inc.* Copyright became the central issue of the Napster legal debate as the company was eventually found liable for violation. In many ways, the Napster controversy initiated the discussion of intellectual property and the internet. When the company was sued for copyright violation by various parties including Metallica, digital rights became a contested issue, opening the way ahead for pioneering work by Lawrence Lessig and others on Creative Commons licensing. On a technological level, the Napster platform made possible the exchange of copyrighted material between users. Rather than hosting files, the Napster server optimized the MP3 search function, streamlining the transfer of files directly between the computers of Napster users. Although the company benefitted from the copyright infringements of its users, it never charged fees for the content it enabled users to access (Lessig 2004: 34, 60). Later acquired by the American software company Roxio and the digital music service Rhapsody, Napster has now become an online music store, effectively shedding its controversial identity as a rogue peer-to-peer sharing platform.

One of the principal historical events influencing the finding, downloading and distributing of digital art was the emergence of P2P technologies about ten years after the introduction of the world wide web. As the Napster example demonstrates, P2P networking enables the sharing of resources between computers. In 1969, formative P2P concepts were proposed by Steve Crocker, co-founder of the ARPANET protocols that would serve as the basis for the internet. Some precursors of P2P include Usenet (1979) and FidoNet (1984). For example, Usenet was created by computer scientists Tom Truscott and Jim Ellis as a democratic platform. Usenet aimed to enhance public access to digital resources and 'to remedy the inequities in the distribution of computer tools' (Pfaffenberger 2003: 24). It was designed as the 'poor man's ARPANET' through software innovation and 'bottom-up democracy' (Pfaffenberger 2003: 24). By 1984, nearly 1,000 sites were participating in Usenet through newsgroups that enabled users to retrieve and post messages.

Designed by Tom Jennings in 1983 and made public in 1984, FidoNet supported email and bulletin board systems (BBS) in a similarly democratic fashion. Both Usenet and FidoNet provided the groundwork for later P2P evolutions that would decentralize the distribution of information through the use of 'peers' or network nodes, reflecting Toffler's notion of the prosumer explored earlier in this chapter. P2P networks differ from client-server paradigms of information technology in which servers control the flow of data to clients. Hence, P2P epitomizes the ethos of Web 2.0 interactivity, in which the division between the consumption and production of art becomes indistinct.

In most P2P networks, a user has digital media files to exchange with other users. These files are categorized according to title, artist, date and format. The files are then downloaded from the peer to the local hard drive of another user. Following the Napster controversy, Gnutella (or GNUtella) (2000), BitTorrent (2001) and FastTrack (2003) were released as second-generation P2P protocols lacking central directories. All file transfers and searches occurred through users or 'peers'. Founded by Justin Frankel and Tom Pepper, Gnutella is a 'distributed search' protocol in which every 'peer' acts as both a user and server (Taylor 2005: 102). Ian Taylor (2005: 181) in *From P2P to Web Services and Grids* observes that Gnutella 'provided a mechanism that offered a much more tolerant structure, where no single entity could be isolated to bring down the entire network'. Gnutella demonstrates the evolution of P2P file-sharing platforms.

Computer programmer Bram Cohen developed BitTorrent in 2001 as a P2P service lacking search functionality. The open source BitTorrent software uses a strategy known as 'swarming' to circulate large digital files, such as video, between users simultaneously (Werbach 2008: 102–3). Swarming divides massive files into smaller chunks, which are then reassembled from different locations simultaneously when downloaded, thereby enhancing ease of access to digital content. The BitTorrent approach avoids the common P2P problem of 'free riding' where a peer uses the file-sharing platform but without contributing content back to other peers (Buford et al. 2009: 1–3). Despite such technological breakthroughs in the history of digital distribution, P2P sharing has become synonymous with content piracy.

Furthermore, P2P networks are often weighed down by spyware, malware and corrupted content.

The emergence of Web 2.0 technologies has also affected the distribution of digital art. The term 'Web 2.0' connotes the evolution of the world wide web towards more interactive and dynamic services. In 2004, Dale Dougherty, a vice-president of O'Reilly Media, first used the term 'Web 2.0'. His essay 'What is Web 2.0: Design Patterns and Business Models for the Next Generation of Software' (2004) further outlines the scope and capabilities of Web 2.0 technologies. Web 2.0 comprises blogs, wikis, podcasts and social networks as well as the free circulation of information via email, instant messaging and RSS (Really Simple Syndication) feeds. All of these technologies underpin a socially interactive online environment where users can contribute to and influence information in the public sphere. Web 2.0 has been marked by the rapid growth of the social media and content-sharing platforms YouTube, Facebook and Flickr – all of which began as small start-up businesses in the early 2000s. Web 2.0 is both a technological and social movement. Its key ideals include social participation, user interactivity and online community (see Chapters 6 and 9). More specifically, O'Reilly proposed seven principles of Web 2.0, including rich user experiences through friendly interfaces and collective intelligence harnessed through social media (Anderson 2012: 1–9).

Reflection

How do Web 2.0 technologies differ from P2P sharing structures? In what ways has Web 2.0 increased access to and distribution of digital art in the last ten years? How might Web 2.0 propel digital arts practices into new directions?

Creative Commons (CC) licensing exemplifies the principles of participation and democratization explored throughout this book in relation to digital art. In 2001, Lawrence Lessig, Hal Abelson and Eric Eldred founded Creative Commons in partnership with the Center for the Public Domain and Stanford University. The CC project aimed 'to develop a rich repository of high-quality works in a variety of media, and to promote an ethos of sharing, public education, and creative inter-activity' (cited in Lee, J-A. 2012: 37). As a not-for-profit US-based organization, Creative Commons facilitates the free, public and legal use of creative works through a variety of fair use licensing agreements (Creative Commons 2010). The CC initiative was the outcome of debates over internet copyright – pointing to the need for a convenient legal standard to provide creators a way to grant public rights to use their online content. Before CC licensing emerged, an internet user would need to identify and make contact with the rights-holder for a digital artwork in order to request permission. In some cases, prohibitively expensive transaction fees would have been required before reproduction, modification or redistribution of a work could go forward legally. As Lessig comments:

> By developing a free set of licenses that people can attach to their content, Creative Commons aims to mark a range of content that can easily, and reliably, be built upon. These tags are then linked to machine-readable versions of the license that enable computers automatically to identify content that can easily be shared. These three expressions together – a legal license, a human-readable description, and machine-readable tags – constitute a Creative Commons license.
>
> (Lessig 2004: 282–3)

According to digital commons theorists, the CC strategy operates on both legal and social levels (Abelson et al. 2012).

On a legal level, CC licenses permit the distribution and use of works within fair use conditions. The licenses supply creators an infrastructure for giving users permission to access, copy, edit, distribute and remix their works. Different forms of Creative Commons licensing attract different conditions of use. Attribution, Public Domain Dedication, Founder's Copyright and No Derivative Works are categories of CC licensing. For example, an Attribution category grants conditional permission to use a work with proper attribution given to the creator and with no derivative works or commercial gain to the public. Through a Public Domain Dedication, the creator surrenders complete rights to the work, whereas Founder's Copyright permits the creator to retain copyright over the work for a fourteen-year period (Ratliff 2009: 52). On a social level, CC initially attempted to influence digital platforms to reduce transaction costs for works given public rights by their creators.

As a social mechanism, Creative Commons refers to the growing reservoir of public domain content as a 'digital commons'. Indeed, 'the commons' is a crucial notion across studies of culture, law, economics, philosophy, literature, history and landscape. Anthropologist Donald Nonini defines the commons broadly as 'the great variety of natural, physical, social, intellectual, and cultural resources that make human survival possible … those assemblages and ensembles of resources that human beings hold in common or in trust to use on behalf of themselves, other living beings, and past and future generations of human beings' (Nonini 2007: 1). The term 'digital commons' could be described as the digital content held in common or in trust, providing a cultural resource and facilitating the legal distribution of intangible digital assets.

Since its founding, Creative Commons licensing has grown exponentially and has transformed the digital copyright environment through its ethos of sharing and interactivity. In 2002, CC released its first copyright licenses – known as Version

1.0 – to the public domain. Version 2.0 appeared in 2004 with nearly five million licensed works being available by the end of the year. In 2008, the American industrial band Nine Inch Nails (NIN) released the album *Ghosts I–IV* under the CC scheme, demonstrating the influence of new licensing standards on the mainstream music industry. By 2009, approximately 350 million Creative Commons licensed works were publicly available – a 700 per cent explosion since 2004. By 2011, Flickr reported 200 million photos licensed within its repository under CC guidelines (Creative Commons 2010).

Reflection

The pioneers of Creative Commons promoted the values of exchange, interactivity and open access to digital content. But is the digital commons freely available to all internet users across the globe? What factors could restrict public access to artworks distributed through Creative Commons schemes?

Case Study 7.2
Flickr as 'the World's Photo Album'

Co-founded in 2004 by Caterina Fake and Stewart Butterfield of the company Ludicorp, Flickr is an online image and video hosting and sharing community that was acquired by Yahoo! for $35 million in 2005. Flickr is now considered one of the first and most successful Web 2.0 platforms. Flickr began as a feature in Ludicorp's *Game Neverending* – an online role-playing platform based on social interaction. Ludicorp was a small game development company started in 2002 by Fake. By 2003, the company identified a need for a browser-based photosharing platform. Flickr integrates Web 2.0 functions, such as social networking and community open APIs (Application Programming Interfaces), as well as tagging and algorithms that optimize a range of content. Flickr users can create profiles, upload photos and chat to one another. An article in the English newspaper *The Telegraph* calls Flickr 'the world's photo album' as well as the premier website for exchanging photos (Telegraph Media Group 2013). In 2011, Flickr had 51 million members and 80 million different users, as well as 6 billion images – a 3 billion increase in content since 2009.

The way in which images are located on Flickr demonstrates the use of innovative socially based technologies. Dedicated users sort Flickr content for the benefit of the public. 'Tags' are search terms that describe the contents of an image, whereas 'geotags' are marked on a map to indicate the place where the photos were taken. Themed groups of images are also available for categorizing Flickr content (Fake 2007). Flickr makes use of a 'folksonomy' approach to image categorization. Developed by information architect Thomas Vander Wal, a folksonomy is a non-hierarchical 'informal, collaborative taxonomy' (Telegraph Media Group 2013). More specifically, a folksonomy is a 'collective set of keywords used by participants ... more keywords can be assigned by more people to the same digital resource' (Yi 2008: 322). Yi further defines a folksonomy as a vocabulary developed by systems users or information consumers, created collaboratively and growing as more users take part. In a folksonomy, the suite of tags assigned to a digital resource is

DISTRIBUTING THE DIGITAL: THE IMPACT OF KEY TECHNOLOGIES

Finding and downloading are closely related to distribution. This section outlines some of the key technologies that have impacted the distribution of artworks. We begin with a brief overview of digital compression technologies, including lossy and lossless standards. Explored in Chapter 5, the psychoacoustic process of perceptual coding has been the basis for the evolution of ubiquitous file formats (JPEG, MP3, MPEG) through digital compression. SoundCloud is an exemplary model of an audio-sharing platform using social media to facilitate the distribution of sound files. Case Study 7.3 highlights the emergence of YouTube in the context of video compression. The increasing use of YouTube as a platform by major art museums demonstrates a dialogue between mainstream and digital arts practices that has become gradually more commonplace. The chapter ends with Case Study 7.4 on the Video Data Bank project.

As one of the most influential technologies in the digital age, compression has significantly increased the accessibility of digital artworks. 'Compression' refers to the process by which complex data is converted into compact and readily downloadable forms. Compression reduces file sizes before they are transferred or stored in media. Certain kinds of compression involve the removal of redundant data components, while all forms utilize decompression algorithms (Pu 2006: 1–2). As discussed in Chapter 5, there are two principal classes of compression: lossy and lossless. Lossy compression formats – for example, JPEG, MP3 and MPEG-4 – reduce quality but enhance the storage and delivery speed of a file, making it possible for websites such as YouTube to deliver high-quality and easily accessible video streaming (Kratochvil 2013: 48). Lossy compression shrinks file sizes by permanently erasing extraneous information. Most lossy audio file formats, including MP3s and MP4 (.mp4 or .m4a), employ a process known as 'perceptual encoding' (discussed below) to reduce file sizes with minimal impacts on overall quality (Hosken 2011: 81–2).

By comparison, lossless compression is less efficient and was designed initially for text (e.g. ZIP files). For example, developed in 1952, Huffman coding was the first modern compression algorithm to use the lossless structure. For audio,

Huffman coding increases compression by substituting shorter codes for recurring sound patterns – particularly applicable to most musical compositions, in which patterns are easily identifiable (Fries and Fries 2005: 174). The advantage of lossless compression is that the original data structure (i.e. before compression) can be restored. In other words, the decompressed data is identical to the original uncompressed data. A resurgence of interest in lossless compression technologies during the last 20 years has paralleled the proliferation of digital file formats, including text, video, audio and graphics, where it is essential that compressed and decompressed data remain the same (Sayood 2003: xix).

The image file formats PNG (Portable Network Graphics) and GIF (Graphics Interchange Format) support lossless data compression, whereas other file formats, such as JPEG-2000, employ both lossy and lossless standards. For digital audio, lossless and lossy compression allow the distribution of a smaller quantity of audio data at a faster rate of transfer. Advantages of audio compression also include extended playing time, 'miniaturization' (equal playing time with smaller hardware), reduced storage density (involving less maintenance of equipment), reduced bandwidth, more efficient transmission and better signal quality in relation to bandwidth (Watkinson 2001: 275).

Case Study 7.3
YouTube and Art Museums

Audio compression technology forms the basis of online multimedia platforms such as YouTube. Former employees of the e-commerce portal PayPal, Chad Hurley, Steve Chen and Jawed Karim, launched the YouTube website in June 2005. Through the YouTube initiative, they aimed to foster the global exchange of online video. With little technical knowledge of file-sharing protocols, YouTube users can upload and access streaming video from around the world. Moreover, video can be embedded into other websites through YouTube's URLs and HTML codes, promoting interactivity and exchange between users. In 2006, Google purchased YouTube for US$1.65 billion. Shortly after the acquisition, YouTube became one of the most visited websites in the world. Co-founder Jawed Karim attributes the success of the project to four features: 'video recommendations via the "related videos" list, an email link to enable video sharing, comments (and other social networking functionality), and an embeddable video player' (Burgess and Green 2009: 2).

Exemplary of online participatory culture, YouTube embodies the ideals of Web 2.0, chiefly the value of user-driven innovation (Burgess and Green 2009: 2). Along with other social networking sites, including Myspace and Flickr, YouTube provides a space for digital art and fosters linkages between artists. In this context, art museums worldwide have been using YouTube to promote, support and provide a medium for the creation of art. For example, the Museum of Modern Art (MoMA) began posting videos to YouTube in 2007, featuring speakers who had given real-time lectures at MoMA (http://www.youtube.com/user/MoMAvideos). Moreover, the Guggenheim Museum's project *YouTube Play* (2010) solicited videos of any genre from around the world. The competition aimed to showcase the internet as a catalyst and disseminator of digital media, such as online video. In other words, *YouTube Play* foregrounded the relationship between emerging technologies and creativity. For example, *Birds on the Wires* (2009) by Brazilian artist Jarbas Agnelli (b. 1963) is an audiovisual orchestration evoking the connections between birds and sound through images of music notation and overhead power lines set against the sky (see Chapter 5 on digital music).

Closely related to compression technologies, the introduction of new file formats has moulded the evolution of digital art and its distribution. In 1991, the Fraunhofer Institute in Germany pioneered the MP3 digital audio compression format (Wands 2006: 211). The MP3 has now become the most common medium in the world for distributing recorded sound. Media theorist Jonathan Sterne in *MP3: The Meaning of a Format* observes that 'more recordings exist and circulate in MP3 format than in all other audio formats combined. A single file on a single network may be available simultaneously in dozens of countries, without regard for local laws, policies, or licensing agreements' (Sterne 2012: 1). The compactness of MP3 file sizes explains their popularity. MP3s are typically 10 per cent of the original file size of other audio formats, including WAV (Waveform Audio File Format). The condensed MP3 structure makes use of compression – which streamlines the audio file through the removal of superfluous segments. MP3 technologies maximize the quality of digital recordings in relation to the complexities of human hearing, while maintaining relatively small file sizes.

Audio compression technologies take into account the normal range of human hearing. As Chapter 5 explored, the psychoacoustic process known as 'perceptual encoding' (also known as 'perceptual coding') discards redundant and irrelevant components of the audio signal that the human ear does not perceive (Sterne 2012: 2). This process also minimizes or avoids losses in sound quality at the same time. 'Psychoacoustics' refers to the scientific and psychological study of acoustic phenomena – an important framework for compression technologies (for further reading, see Howard and Angus 2012). 'Encoding' refers to the conversion of uncompressed digital audio data to a compressed format. Finally, a 'CODEC' refers to the mathematical process for encoding and decoding information.

Perceptual encoding employs lossy compression, but is used by MPEG (Moving Picture Experts Group) files and other formats – in conjunction with lossless compression – to reduce the audio file size further. Since 1989, the MPEG has been developed by the International Organization for Standardization (ISO). The goal of the organization was to develop a standard for audio and video compression for use in CD-ROM applications. The committee has since released MPEG-1, MPEG-2, MPEG-4 and MPEG-4 AVC or H.264. Despite technological advances, such as the MPEG format, variability between the hearing of listeners and the quality of acoustic environments (e.g. the introduction of background noise) mean that perceptual encoding and consequently, digital file formats are not always efficient. The efficiency of file formats is a crucial consideration for the themes of exchange, distribution and access covered in this chapter. Of course, digital arts audiences do not want corrupted files, just as 'live' audiences do not want imperfect real-time performances. It is a matter of quality control.

Compression technologies underpin the widespread availability of digital music, as evident on audio portals like SoundCloud. Created by Alex Ljung and Eric Wahlforss in Berlin, Germany in 2007, SoundCloud (http://soundcloud.com/) is an online platform that allows sound artists to record and distribute audio. By November 2011, SoundCloud's user base reached eight million (Santos 2012:241). Ljung and Wahlforss originally envisioned an audio-sharing service comparable to Flickr for photography and Vimeo for video. SoundCloud is a highly interactive audio distribution service. Designed to integrate Twitter, Facebook and other social media, SoundCloud makes it possible for users to follow the activities of one another as members of a global audio community. It also incorporates the use of waveforms that track member comments across segments of the audio, creating what is known as 'timed comments'. User feedback is uniquely referenced to specific parts of an audio track. SoundCloud also allows the use of widgets and apps. Newly uploaded tracks can be tweeted via widgets placed on the personal websites of users. Finally, the SoundCloud API enables users to upload and download audio files with their smartphones.

Digital compression technologies have also inspired a number of artists and works. German photographer Thomas Ruff (b. 1958) engages with JPEG compression, particularly the erasure of data through lossy compression. Ruff's works critically interpret the notion of 'artifacts' – data errors resulting from the discarding of information through compression algorithms. His oversize photography book *jpegs* (2009), published by the Aperture Foundation with commentary by curator Bennett Simpson, features a series of online JPEGs – downloaded from the internet and enlarged, resulting in pronounced pixelation. The series calls attention to the inconsistencies and imperfections of digital technologies, exemplified by compression errors. Cataclysmic sites, ruined landscapes and uncanny places feature in Ruff's works (Lee, P. 2012: 103). Like Ruff, American artist Jason Salavon (b. 1970) also makes use of compression algorithms. In particular, Salavon's *Every Playboy Centerfold* (2002) exploits the creative potential of image compression. Salavon sourced *Playboy* magazine centrefolds, beginning in the 1960s, compressing them digitally into a single image roughly resembling a woman. The outcome is a 'shroud-like' feminine figure composed of blurry colours (Salavon and Hill 2004: 14). Salavon's work represents the synthesis of visual data through the overlaying and arranging of the original imagery, in the form of *Playboy* centrefolds.

Figure 7.4 Jason Salavon, *Playboy Centerfold* (2002). Photograph of artwork. Image courtesy of the artist.

Case Study 7.4
Video Data Bank

Video Data Bank (VDB) is the premier platform and archive for digital and analogue video work by contemporary artists. Founded in 1974 by Kate Horsfield and Lyn Blumenthal at the School of the Art Institute of Chicago (SAIC), VDB is now the leading resource for video created by and featuring contemporary practitioners. The project was co-founded at the beginning of the video arts movement when Horsfield and Blumenthal began recording interviews with female artists (see Juhasz 2001). The history of VDB is linked to the larger feminist arts movement and is hence a precursor to cyberfeminism, discussed in Chapter 6. VDB comprises an impressive collection of work by 550 artists across 5,500 video art files. It is a national and international video art distribution service that promotes understanding of the genre. One of the aims of VDB is to forward the preservation of historically momentous video artworks, both analogue and digital, as well as writings about video art. VDB publishes *Surveying the First Decade: Video Art and Alternative Media in the US 1968–1980*, a 17-hour compilation of experimental video. First released in 1995, the two-volume compilation surveys the history of experimental video art, including 68 titles by 60 artists classified according to the following genres: conceptual, performance-based, feminist, image-processed, documentary and community-based works (Video Data Bank 2013). For more information, see http://www.vdb.org.

The finding, downloading and distributing of digital art are complex processes that integrate digital technologies with artistic practices. While traditional access to art takes place in galleries, museums, theatres and other physical venues, digital access occurs through file-sharing services and other platforms. For both analogue and digital art forms, quality (of audio, video and still images) is the most important consideration. Chapter 8 will extend the the concepts of exchange, interactivity and community to the preservation of digital art.

Chapter Summary

This chapter has discussed the finding, downloading and distributing of digital art through a number of case studies and key examples bridging art and technology. As exemplified by P2P file sharing, the distribution of digital art is underpinned by democratic, interactive and participatory ideals. The development of distribution channels has paralleled the emergence of digital technologies and social media platforms.

- A theoretical approach to digital arts distribution taken in this chapter encompasses four major concepts: Manovich's argument that the database is the centre of digital creativity, Lessig's distinction between free and permission culture, Toffler's notion of the prosumer as a creative consumer, and Vander Wal's concept of the folksonomy as a non-hierarchical user-driven way to categorize different forms of data (e.g. images) in the public domain.
- Benjamin's reflections on the reproduction of art and Baudrillard's three orders of simulacra provide theoretical lenses for analysing digital art in terms of its duplication in the context of our 'copy and paste' culture.
- Creative Commons licensing reflects debates over copyright and intellectual property in the digital era.
- The emergence of Web 2.0 technologies and peer-to-peer (P2P) file sharing have facilitated access to digital artworks extensively.
- Compression technologies, including lossy and lossless forms, underpin the proliferation of file formats for digital video, audio and graphics, including JPEGs, MP3s and MPEG-4s.
- The democratization of art through digital interventions is exemplified in the theory, history and technology of distribution.

8 WAYS OF BELONGING: ARCHIVING, PRESERVING AND REMEMBERING DIGITAL ART

How do – and will – we remember the digital arts? How should we safeguard twenty-first-century digital arts heritage for future generations – a heritage that remains intrinsically connected to mutable, impermanent and fragile technologies? And how have digital practices inspired and – in many instances – necessitated new strategies for archiving and preserving art? Whereas Chapter 7 addressed issues of distribution and access, this chapter investigates the preservation of digital artworks for the benefit of future creators, participants and viewers. As we have seen thus far in this book, digital practices have precipitated remarkable changes in the global accessibility of art. However, the digital revolution has also radically influenced the archiving, preserving and remembering of art. This chapter focuses on how creators and conservators negotiate the preservation of variable media artworks when interoperability and enhanced access increasingly inform the design of digital archives. Indeed, the continuously shifting technological landscape – marked by the centrality of digital technologies to everyday life – problematizes the preservation of digital art through mainstream museological paradigms.

Despite the critical role that technologies play in recording, transmission and preservation, digital artworks are highly ephemeral and prove difficult to conserve through conventional approaches. Software develops bugs and degrades, hardware is superseded by new models, and internet sites fall into disrepair or go offline when the server space is no longer supported. In the light of these challenges, the aim of Chapter 8 is to emphasize the impact of digital arts practices on traditional approaches to preserving art, including phases of acquisition, collection and archiving. Mark Tribe of Rhizome.org describes four methods of digital arts preservation: documentation (including screen grabs and artist statements), migration (applying recent technologies, such as new file formats, to artworks), emulation (using software to allow works to function on new platforms) and recreation (remaking the artwork for new technologies) (Wands 2006: 206). We foreground innovative models of archiving that have pioneered these methods – most notably the Variable Media Questionnaire (VMQ) – to encompass the changing relationships between conservators, creators, technicians, participants, audiences and technologies. In this chapter, we outline the array of conceptual and technical challenges that conservators encounter when working with digital productions. One of the primary archival considerations is the complexity of interactive, participatory and process-based works – which generally resist an object-centred approach to conservation and tend to involve multimedia components and distributed authorship. The fact that media can be fragile and become obsolete – a process that new media theorists refer to as 'technological obsolescence' (Ippolito 2003a: 47) – requires forward-looking solutions to digital arts preservation. The chapter also discusses the importance of metadata in archival systems – as well as the broader correlation between preservation and technological infrastructures – in terms of promoting public access to content over networks. The preservation of digital art has transformed the role of libraries, museums and galleries from that of collection and curation to that of co-production and co-creation, ensuring the long-term viability of works through the active management of change over time. In sum, collaborative interaction between conservators and creators will continue to transform digital arts preservation.

Following the structure of previous chapters, Chapter 8 opens with key theoretical perspectives on the realities of digital arts preservation and the changing role of the archive. Some theorists maintain that digital arts preservation is more broadly a matter of preserving digital heritage and memory. For others, the archive is not an inert repository for storing objects or artefacts, but rather a site for the production of social values and, therefore, an indispensable component of a 'cultural economy'. Other concepts that can assist us in understanding the unique challenges of digital preservation include performativity, tacit knowledge, acceptable loss and crowdsourcing. We then outline the emergence of models of digital arts preservation, specifically DOCAM (Documentation and Conservation of the Media Arts Heritage), MANS (Media Arts Notation System), PADS (Performance Art Documentation Structure) and CMCM (Capturing Unstable Media Conceptual Model). These models use notation systems and 'scoring' protocols to facilitate the re-creation or re-performance of digital artworks by future conservators, curators and artists. The final section of Chapter 8 explains a suite of technologies central to digital preservation. Archival interoperability is achieved through the use of metaservers, the MPEG-21 Multimedia Framework and XML (Extensible Markup Language) technologies.

Four case studies illustrate the content of the chapter and include the preservation of the seminal internet artwork *net.flag* (2002) (Case Study 8.1), the VMN (Variable

Media Network) as the leading exemplar for preserving digital and new media artworks (Case Study 8.2), UbuWeb as an open-access repository of avant-garde art (Case Study 8.3) and Janet Cohen, Keith Frank and Jon Ippolito's *The Unreliable Archivist* (1998) (Case Study 8.4), a net art creation that calls into question the authority of archives and the role of the archivist through the use of irony, humour and absurdity. Featured works and artists referred to in the discussion include *net.flag* by Mark Napier (b. 1961), *The Erl King* (1982–5) by Grahame Weinbren (b. 1947) and Roberta Friedman, *I Never Done Enough Weird Stuff* (1996) by Richard Layzell (b. 1949), the Internet Archive (1996–) founded by Brewster Kahle (b. 1960) and the *etoy* collective's *Mission Eternity* (2005–).

THE IDEA OF LIVENESS: PRESERVATION AS THEORY AND CONTINGENCY

In this section, we consider the place of 'the archive' in the production of cultural meaning and values, as well as the particular conservation realities faced by digital arts conservators. We will see how German-Russian philosopher Boris Groys' notion of the 'cultural economy' provides a way of thinking about the fundamental place of the archive in culture. Digital theorist Rick Prelinger characterizes the 'accessible archive' as necessitating a community of users, whereas conservation theorist Vivian van Saaze advocates the principles of change, intervention and production in archive management. Moreover, German media theorist Wolfgang Ernst theorizes digital memory as 'working memory' that crosses between the hardware-based memory of computers and the cultural memory of human users. Echoing van Saaze's principles, Josephine Bosma identifies technological obsolescence and the decline of audience participation as some of the multiple factors that jeopardize the preservation of variable media productions. Furthermore, media theorist Philip Auslander conceptualizes digital arts preservation through the notion of performativity in which highly ephemeral creations must be re-performed regularly to retain their value, meaning and impact. In these terms, performativity becomes an essential component of digital arts conservation plans. This section includes Case Study 8.1 of Mark Napier's *net. flag* (2002) and also explores ideas of crowdsourcing, tacit knowledge and acceptable loss in relation to digital arts preservation.

In describing the role of the archive broadly in Western history, culture and society, Boris Groys proposes the term 'cultural economy' as 'the exchange that takes place between the archive of cultural values and the profane space outside this archive' (Groys 2012: 1). By definition, an archive preserves immaterial (digital) or material (artefactual) items of cultural importance. Conversely, it excludes things that are irrelevant or have no value, relegating these items to the 'profane' world that exists outside of the archive's ambit. Most importantly, the boundaries of the cultural archive are fluid and changing. Things in the profane space can become valued while those in the archive can become irrelevant or ignored over time (Groys 2012: 1–2). For Groys, the determination of what is significant and, therefore, to be included in an archive (what he terms the 'New') and what is irrelevant and, therefore, to be excluded (what he calls the 'Old' or 'noncollected reality') is a matter of power and politics. Being more than a representational system or mechanical structure, the archive actively furnishes the groundwork for the future manifestation of historical, cultural and artistic forms:

> The function of the archive cannot consist merely of illustrating or repre-senting history or of holding fast to the memories of history the way in which this history took place 'in reality.' Rather, the archive constitutes the prerequisite for something like history to emerge in the first place, because only if the archive is already there are we able to compare the New with the Old [...] The archive is a machine for the production of memories, a machine that fabricates history out of the material of noncollected reality. (Groys 2012: 3)

An archive, in the view of Groys, operates according to an internal logic, attracting material that contributes to its coherence and expands its reach. In its capacity to establish and preserve the 'New', the archive is an arbiter of cultural value and an actant in the course of history. ('Actant' is a term that comes from the actor-network theory [ANT] of French philosopher Bruno Latour, explored later in this chapter; the term here refers to a institutional actor, including people and inanimate things.) In short, the flow of content in and out of an archive does not only mirror shifting societal values (i.e. an item in the profane world is judged of value and included in the archive). Rather, the multi-dimensional movement between the profane and the archive is part of a cultural economy's fabric. In Groys' terms, the archive is a living repository (although he prefers the term 'machine') for future creative production; by inference, the archival space is something like a sacred place.

Like Groys, Rick Prelinger theorizes the act of archiving as a crucial mode of cultural production. For Prelinger, an 'accessible archive' is one in which preser-vation and access are not static concepts. An archive should engage a network of users, creators and conservators. Mirroring Thomas Vander Wal's concept of a folksonomy outlined in Chapter 7, Prelinger advocates the work of citizen archivists and community members. For both Groys and Prelinger, archival work is that of a 'cultural producer', facilitating the production of new works from archival materials without inducing unnecessary anxiety over copyright and other regulations that stifle creativity (Prelinger 2009: 173). A 'sandbox' model of the archive would make available a testing environment in which artists could experiment with archival material. As such, Prelinger's ethos of the archive is comparable to Lawrence Lessig's articulation of 'free culture' (Chapter 7), in which innovation, creativity and risk are nurtured rather than quashed by legal structures. As a 'new folk art', archiving is 'widely practised and has unconsciously become integrated into a great many people's lives, potentially transforming a necessity into a work of art' (Goldsmith 2011a on the work of Prelinger).

In this spirit of providing open access to archival information, the Internet Archive (IA) (http://www.archive.org) is a massive digital repository founded in 1996 by American computer scientist Brewster Kahle. In addition to preserving texts, audio, video and software, the IA includes a service called Wayback Machine that archives websites and grants users access to previous web content as it appeared originally. As of 2012, the IA contained ten petabytes of data with the Wayback Machine archives accounting for two petabytes or 20 per cent of the total. (A petabyte is equivalent to one quadrillion bytes of data [Claypoole and Payton 2012: 9].) The IA also holds about 5,000 digital files of films and footage from the Prelinger Archives, founded in 1983 as a traditional, site-based archive in New York City (Internet Archive 2013).

Another key precept in the literature of digital arts preservation is digital memory. Put in broad terms, the practice of digital memory involves cultural heritage preservation through digital approaches. Wolfgang Ernst theorizes the interface of memory and new media. In the digital era, cultural memory is intimately connected to the technical memory of computers as part of an active, integrated process that Ernst calls 'working memory' (Parikka and Ernst 2013). However, the problem is that, while memory can be individual, collective or institutional, the notion of digital memory is often conflated with data storage. In contrast, for Ernst, digital memory is a dynamic form of cultural memory that emerges through human use of social media and participation in 'everyday media environments' (Parikka and Ernst 2013: 16). Digital memory comprises the storage capacities of devices, the structure of archives and the faculty of human memory – in both individual and collective modes. Without a doubt, the boundary between the storage of data (a technical, digital matter) and the practice of operating the storage device (a cultural, habitual one) has become evermore indistinct. In a similar sense, Bosma (2011: 177) describes 'the archive of the real' as the amalgamation of archival technologies, new media sources and oral memories transmitted through the internet. As the preservation of cultural memory, the archiving of digital artworks requires traditional materials (e.g. documents) in conjunction with multimedia (e.g. audio and video) (Bosma 2011: 188). The cultural memory work of media scholars like Wolfgang Ernst and Josephine Bosma protects against the 'digital dark ages' in which data loss has multiple, negative implications for technology and society (Bosma 2011: 185).

Reflection

Wolfgang Ernst's concept of 'working memory' relates the memory capacity of machines to the human ability to remember. Can you think of some ways in which how you remembered something that you encountered through a medium (including some part of the internet, or a particular device) was influenced by the nature of the medium or how you used the medium? Can you think of ways in which digital artists could make use of memory – their memories, those of others and those of devices?

In order to appreciate the difficulties negotiated by digital archives, it is important to have a sense of traditional approaches to arts preservation. On the whole, mainstream strategies strive to keep intact the original state of an object of art through the control of its environment and the exclusion of certain influences, most prominently human interaction (see, for example, Richmond 2012). An object is typically protected from deleterious external variables – including light, heat, vibration and physical wear from handling by people. However, museological practices and basic definitions of what constitutes an archive have been transformed and expanded by the special demands of digital preservation. As Bosma points out, digital artworks require that archives evolve beyond 'specific locations (museum archives) and the on-site conservators' (Bosma 2011: 179). Moreover, digital artworks often create meaning only in reference to a technologically based environment and a community of users participating actively in the production of the work over time (for example, see Mark Napier's *net.flag*, Case Study 8.1). As a consequence, software obsolescence, diminished technological support or failure to engage an audience might compromise the long-term evolution of digital artworks (Bosma 2011: 165). Hence, conservators must become intimately acquainted with the design and ethos of ephemeral works to ensure their longevity: 'to preserve art that is produced using unstable media, or to restage any process- or time-based works, it is necessary to know the artist's intent and work process' (Bosma 2011: 171).

Case Study 8.1
Mark Napier and the Flag of the Internet

Mark Napier (b. 1961) is a software developer and one of the pioneers of net art (Chapter 6). His project *net. flag* (2002) is exemplary of early internet art, particularly for the work's interactive and participatory aspects. Acquired by the Guggenheim Museum for their permanent collection, *net.flag* confronts themes of national identity and nationalistic allegiance (see http://webart.guggenheim.org/netflag/). The Guggenheim acquired net art (consisting of the software and the continuously changing content) on the condition that the work would 'always be on view' (Napier cited in Dietz 2005: 88). Napier's request reflects a simple yet profound inversion of the norms of mainstream acquisition where most art objects (paintings, photographs, sculptures or installation pieces) could not be made publicly available at all times. In its ever-shifting content, *net.flag* expresses how the internet has radically transformed human identity by dissolving the physical borders between nations. The profusion of interactive platforms – more recently manifested as social media – ensure that content is accessible on a round-the-clock basis. In Napier's work, the flag as a relatively stable symbol of nationhood is supplanted by the flag as a constantly changing form – one evolving in response to the input of internet users:

> *Net.flag* explores the flag as an emblem of territorial identity by appropriating the visual language of international flags. An online software interface makes this language of shapes and colours available to anyone with web access. The visitor to *net.flag* not only views the flag but can change it in a moment to reflect their own nationalist, political, apolitical or territorial agenda. The resulting flag is both an emblem and a micro territory in its own right; a place for confrontation, assertion, communication and play. (Napier n.d.)

Some media art commentators acknowledge the artwork as 'an emblem for the internet as a new territory, one composed by people from various geographical regions and ideologies' (Ippolito 2003b: 109).

Fulfilling Napier's initial request, the Guggenheim archive of the sole copy of *net.flag* makes the work available to anyone at any time over the internet. An unregistered visitor to the website can devise a new internet flag in real time by manipulating preset motifs, including stars, colour fields and shapes. *Net.flag* employs Java programming to enable users to construct a flag as *the* flag of the internet (until another user decides to modify it). For Napier, the Java applet programming and the computer operating system only support the existence of the artwork – which is, instead, an algorithm built on the infrastructure making possible a high standard of user interactivity. The recognizable symbols of countries meld within each new flag, subverting the primacy of any single nation's identity. Users select the 'change the net.flag' option from the right side of the webpage. There are also columns for 'anatomy of the flag' and 'flags of the web'. A 'statistics' navigation bar provides a summary of the 'elements' appearing in the internet flags. For example, the red stripes of the United States flag appear 6,226 times and the cross of the Greek flag shows up 5,366 times in different flags. The countries with the highest frequencies of their visual motifs across all flags include the US (7 per cent), Australia (5 per cent), Greece (5 per cent), Argentina (2 per cent) and Ghana (1 per cent). The top-ranking elements include unity, valour, purity, peace and harmony. The work also includes a 'browse history', summarizing the overall symbolic dimensions of the current flag. In terms of preservation, *net.art* exhibits all four behaviours of the Variable Media Questionnaire to be explored in Case Study 8.2. It is interactive, duplicated, encoded and networked and, therefore, one of the earliest and most important examples of the archiving of internet art by a major institution.

The *net.flag* case study suggests the kinds of negotiations that transpire between a creator (Napier) and the archiving organization (the Guggenheim). Web-based works – such as Napier's internet flag – encode preservation principles inherently in their design and delivery, but such works do require regular maintenance and creative infusion. Moreover, practical concerns – particularly about web hosting and website obsolescence – impact the long-term success of preservation strategies. On a related note, Boris Groys addresses the importance of dialogue between conservators and artists during the preservation process. He characterizes the conservator as a co-creator, interpreter, conductor, director or active interpreter of a digital artwork (Bosma 2011: 169–70). For example, works of browser or code art (explored in Chapter 6) require that the conservator makes crucial decisions about their reconstruction or re-enactment. The preservation of code necessitates that the conservator becomes – to an extent – a creator who re-enacts the code. While some conservation strategies draw from analogue approaches to minimize impacts, other strategies use publicly accessible archival formats in order to encourage public contribution to the content, structure and meaning of a digital work (Bosma 2011: 166). With prescience, artist communities such as *etoy* embed a preservation mechanism in the very design of works through public domain or open-source approaches, community-based contribution and other techniques that promote interactivity (Bosma 2011: 175). An international collective founded in Zurich in 1990, *etoy* consists of media theorists, coders, architects and engineers (Petrović-Šteger 2011: 146). Their long-term project *Mission Eternity* (2005–) highlights issues of cultural memory, memorializes the death of loved ones and rethinks the notion of the afterlife through the digital traces left by participants facing death. The ethos of the project is that people leave behind their physical selves as well as voluminous amounts of information about their lives – both of which constitute how the living remember the dead (Petrović-Šteger 2011: 147). A 'multi-modal post-mortem activity plan' includes the *Arcanum Capsule*, an interactive 'digital portrait' of subjects who have passed on (Petrović-Šteger 2011: 147). The portrait preserves the digital signatures of participants, including photos, voice recordings, biodata and social network mappings.

Performativity is another key principle for understanding the preservation of digital artworks. Artworks face obsolescence and death; like people in ill health, their ability to perform declines and must be restored or reinvigorated in order to persist into the future. For the *etoy* collective, human death, like art, is a kind of performance recorded and re-enacted over a body of dispersed materials, even after the mortal body has perished. Similarly, recordings must be reactivated or re-performed to be experienced in the present, that is, to avoid obsolescence. As a consequence of its very nature, digital art is performative in two senses. First, its forms and styles on the whole must be experienced interactively in real time. Second, many classic works of digital art have become extremely difficult to access or re-create and, accordingly, must be re-performed as part of a conservation plan. As we have seen through a number of other works, digital art profoundly redefines notions of documentation, conservation and the archive in terms of performativity. For example, as Philip Auslander and others have observed, it is ironic that most people came to know the first-generation performance artists of the 1960s and 1970s through photographic documentation of their performances. Auslander argues that the idea of 'liveness' is itself dependent on the possibility that a performance can be recorded in some way (Auslander 2006). In sum, documentation and archiving are themselves performative in that they reflect 'an artist's aesthetic project or sensibility ... for which we are the present audience' (Auslander 2006: 9). In this respect, the Variable Media Network model (Case Study 8.2) designates 'performance' as a part of the conservation process 'whenever the re-creators have to re-enact original instructions in a new context' (Ippolito 2003a: 48–9).

In his essay 'Learning from Mario' (2010), Jon Ippolito considers the 'crowdsourced' model of preservation – common in gaming in which, for example, companies promote game design competitions and monitor the games created by players – as an alternative to the centralized approaches of mainstream preservation. Crowdsourcing is a significant feature of participatory culture in the digital era. It is a problem-solving approach that enables an institution to acquire content, services or concepts through the efforts of a large group, community or 'crowd'. However, in contrast to what are called commons-based online projects, such as Wikipedia, that offer users a shared platform to work collaboratively, crowdsourcing is initiated and managed from beginning to end by a company, organization, organizers or other initiating institution (Brabham 2013b: 120–1). Coined in 2006 by Jeff Howe of *Wired* magazine, crowdsourcing:

> represents the act of a company or institution taking a function once performed by employees and outsourcing it to an undefined (and generally large) network of people in the form of an open call ... The crucial prerequisite is the use of the open call format and the large network of potential laborers. (Howe cited in Brabham 2013b: 120)

In crowdsourcing, creative production occurs at the interface between the public (the crowd) and the managing party (the institution). This combination of 'bottom-up, open creation by the crowd' and top-down management by the organization characterizes crowdsourcing as a creative, although not entirely collaborative, approach (Brabham 2013a: xxi). For digital art preservation, crowdsourcing can draw from the skills of amateur archivists and members of the public who might contribute their memories or experiences of an artwork. This mode of operating calls into question the role of centralized repositories that have limited public participation and access. As an exemplary initiative, the VMQ (Case Study 8.2) captures quantitative and qualitative information about digital artworks, including recorded interviews with creators, programmers and artists. Whereas the first two versions of VMQ were stand-alone systems, the most recent version is internet-based, allowing the public to register their opinions about the work – and, thus, take part in the crowdsourcing approach to digital art preservation (Ippolito 2010).

In outlining the challenges of digital preservation, Ippolito provides the example of *The Erl King*, a collaboration between experimental filmmaker Grahame Weinbren (b. 1947) and Roberta Friedman (see Figure 8.1). Using multimedia features that invited participants to interrupt the production at any time, *The Erl King* was one of the first works of interactive video art or 'narrative cinema' of the 1980s. It was based on two major texts: Johann Wolfgang von Goethe's poem 'Der Erlkönig' (1782) and a dream analysed by Austrian psychoanalyst Sigmund Freud (1856–1939). The technological components of the project included PASCAL code that integrated information from a SMC-70 computer, a custom-built video switcher and three laser disk players. The

Figure 8.1 Roberta Friedman and Grahame Weinbren, *The Erl King* (1982–5). Photograph of artwork. Image courtesy of the artists.

PASCAL controlled the loading of graphics, text, video and audio files. In 2003, Ippolito and Guggenheim curator John Hanhardt proposed *The Erl King* as a pilot study of media art preservation using the VMN model. The work's hardware was 20 years old at the time. As a result, the conservators chose 'emulation' in which a newer computer impersonates the original, allowing the execution of the source code and reproduction of the intended user experience, including the periods of lag or delay during which different components communicated in the original version. In general, emulation entails the replacement of outmoded or multi-component hardware through programming. Weinbren and Friedman worked with a VMN software engineer to develop a new platform for the code on a single computer using the Java programming language. The platform mimics the video switcher, the graphics cache and laser disk players to guarantee the correct timing and sequencing of the work as first set out by the artists. The emulation process required programming in delay – such as disk search time – to imitate the user experience of the original work based on new technologies of the 1980s (Weinbren n.d.).

The Erl King is evidence of how digital arts preservation requires a variety of living, non-living and mechanical actants. For Vivian van Saaze, 'continuous intervention' should be the core principle pursued by museums and other conservators to preserve new media works – those that defy the notion of art as consisting of material objects only. Following the actor-network theory of Bruno Latour and others, van Saaze identifies a 'collective of actants' involved in the conservation of ephemeral works. Digital art conservation requires the dynamic interplay of actants: 'materials, humans, spaces, spatial arrangements, procedures and protocols' (Van Saaze 2009: 21). Human and non-human actants also include the building, its administration, technicians, curator, conservator, director and artist. The acceptance of notions of 'change, intervention and production' in arts conservation contrasts starkly to the 'hands-off or minimalist intervention approach of traditional conservation ethics' (Van Saaze 2009: 21). In order for conservation practices to accommodate digital works, the concept of change should be linked to productivity and potentiality rather than loss or damage. Indeed, traditional conservation discourses assume the fixed identity of the artwork – as an entity that must be controlled physically and conceptually in order for conservation to succeed. However, the restoration of a work back to its original state does need not to be the guiding ethic in all cases; works such as Napier's *net.flag* exist only because they have changed. The context of a digital artwork is complex and consists of 'tacit knowledge' – sensory and conceptual information, including artistic purpose, sociocultural meanings and the practices involved in re-creating the work (MacDonald 2009: 61). Examples of tacit knowledge include patterns of audience movement through the artwork's venue, environmental variables (e.g. sunlight, wind, temperature, etc.) that affect the interpretation of the work, or greater political circumstances that influence the audience's reception of the work.

Reflection

In addition to sensory information, the creator's intent and broader cultural meanings, can you think of other kinds of tacit knowledge that could be considered during the preservation of digital artworks? How might these forms of tacit knowledge be identified and documented? How might they affect the re-creation or re-performance of the work by curators, conservators or other artists? You can select an artwork from any chapter in reflecting on these questions.

The final, core theoretical and ethical issue surrounding the preservation of digital artworks addressed in this chapter is 'acceptable loss' (Harvey 2012: 76). As the literature of digital heritage shows, what is considered acceptable loss varies considerably and depends on creators, conservators, technicians and users. Theorists of digital archiving agree that loss of content and functionality is unavoidable and that acceptable loss should generally be factored into conservation strategies. However, a 2003 joint report on digital archiving and preservation by the US National Science Foundation and the EU-based DELOS Network of Excellence on Digital Libraries asks: 'How can we measure what loss is acceptable? What tools can be developed to inform future users about the relationship between the original digital entity [artwork] and what they [users, viewers, participants] receive in response to a query?' (cited in Harvey 2012: 76). Moreover, according to the UNESCO *Guidelines for the Preservation of Digital Heritage* (2003), there are two major axioms of digital preservation, the first of which definitively rules out access as acceptable loss: 'digital materials cannot be said to be preserved if access is lost' and 'digital preservation must address threats to all layers of the digital object: physical, logical, conceptual and essential' (UNESCO 2003: 21).

Digital art further redefines traditional conservation paradigms by accepting transformation, degradation and, in some instances, loss. Regarded as negative attributes to be avoided in the conservation of most traditional, object-oriented artworks (e.g. paintings, sculptures, furniture), transformation and degradation are often acknowledged by digital artists or even incorporated into digital works (Bosma 2011: 171). However, excessive loss can permanently alter the original intention of the artist. Areas of acceptable loss can include the physical deterioration of the work itself; the decline of the media used to record the work; the obsolescence of technologies originally employed to execute or access the artwork; or the loss of the concepts that underpinned the artist's intentions in making the work (Bosma 2011: 171). To avoid the distortion of the project and to ensure an ethical conservation plan, acceptable loss needs to be delineated clearly in relation to digital artworks because many of these works rely on original conceptual aims (Stringari 2003). In particular, loss can occur when restoration or re-creation is based solely on what is documented about the work – to the exclusion of unknown, undocumented or discarded tacit dimensions of the work. As with digital arts conservation generally, the management of acceptable loss is most optimal in dialogue with the artist and conservators, helping to safeguard the conservation process from misinterpretation and the 'loss' of elements of the work through misidentification. Indeed, one of the goals of the VMN is to identify the acceptable range of loss through documented interactions between artists, technicians, audience members and conservators (Case Study 8.2).

Reflection

The question of how much loss is acceptable loss continues to attract the attention of digital arts conservators. Select one artwork presented in any chapter of this book and identify a few areas of possible loss if the work were to be archived or preserved. Putting on your conservator's hat, which of those areas of loss would be more acceptable than others? And why?

SCORING THE WORK: DIGITAL ARTS PRESERVATION THROUGH NOTATION SYSTEMS

In the previous section, we outlined the principal theoretical issues affecting the preservation of digital artworks. This section examines key initiatives in the history of digital and media arts preservation, most notably the Capturing Unstable Media Conceptual Model (CMCM) (2003), the Documentation and Conservation of the Media Arts Heritage (DOCAM) (2005), the Media Arts Notation System (MANS) (2007) and the Performance Art Documentation Structure (PADS) (2008). The purpose of this section is to provide an overview of the history of notation systems in the preservation of digital artworks. Appearing after the year 2000, these four systems operate according to notation structures that generate a 'score' of the work through the use of descriptive metadata. Curator Richard Rinehart (2004b: 3) defines a score as 'the clearest type of description that compiles formalised (systematic) discrete elements into documents that aid in the re-performance or re-creation of works of art'. The section includes Case Study 8.2 on the VMN, featured because its principles form the basis of other notation systems for preserving digital artworks. The section concludes with Case Study 8.3 of UbuWeb as the repository of avant-garde art, demonstrating the concept of the 'gift economy' to free online archives. The preservation of digital art through scoring systems and open-access repositories is moreover a matter of digital heritage protection necessitating the collaborative efforts of a number of parties. As Josephine Bosma (2011: 173) argues, the preservation of digital art demands 'structural changes' within and between organizations to make possible extended collaborations with external partners in the long-term interest of artworks.

One of the first digital arts preservation strategies was the Capturing Unstable Media Conceptual Model (CMCM) (2003), developed at the V2_Organisation, an interdisciplinary centre for art and media technology in Rotterdam, the Netherlands (Fauconnier and Frommé 2004). The central aims of the initiative were archival interoperability and the development of an 'ontology' that could be used to describe relationships between the facets of an electronic or unstable media artwork. The CMCM recognized the challenges of determining the original state of an artwork and, therefore, sought to document processes, contexts, materials, practices, collaborations and user interactions. Archival interoperability allowed individual institutions to input data on specific artworks, assembling a broader snapshot of the perspectives of external curators, critics and conservators. An 'ontology' resulted from a focus on considering artworks as processes rather than fixed entities and the attendant shift from object-oriented models of art preservation to process-oriented approaches. The CMCM documentation methodology recorded various interactions between software, hardware and networks through the creation of metadata and the use of interviews about user exchanges, user numbers, intensities of interactions between users, physical contexts and sensory modes.

The DOCAM Research Alliance was founded in Montreal in 2005 by the Daniel Langlois Foundation for Art, Science and Technology. DOCAM (Documentation and Conservation of the Media Arts Heritage) develops and implements models for digital arts preservation through the ethos of heritage protection. Most significantly, the DOCAM framework involves documentation throughout an artwork's lifecycle, building in crucial preservation strategies from the inception of the work. DOCAM conservators record the perspectives of contributors, generating a graphic representation of the relationships between items of documentation and producers, as well as the phases, iterations and components of the work (Daniel Langlois Foundation 2013). The framework builds a hierarchical description, ensuring the completeness of documents, agents and sources and safeguarding the distinctive nature of digital artworks through this lifecycle approach. An artwork's lifecycle spans creation, dissemination, critical reception and custody – the latter phrase including aspects of cataloguing, curating and conserving. The hierarchical scheme is used by music cataloguing systems (such as the Functional Requirements for Bibliographic Records or FRBR) and distinguishes between the terms 'work', 'expression', 'manifestation' and 'item'. 'Work' is 'a distinct intellectual or artistic creation'; 'expression' is 'the intellectual or artistic realization of the work'; 'manifestation' is 'the physical embodiment of an expression of a work'; and 'item' is 'an exemplar of a manifestation' (Iseminger 2012: 46). The documentation process begins with artists and collaborators, then broadens to include conservators, curators and critics. It includes the installation, preservation and restoration of the works based on the belief that, in many cases, documentation survives the original work and its creator. Documentation comprises a range of materials such as animation files, acquisition reports, bibliographies, copyright agreements, critical essays, exhibition leaflets, screen captures and technical booklets. The DOCAM framework reflects three attributes of digital artworks: (a) they are based in technology through the use of devices that are often developed or modified by the artist; (b) they produce a range of effects related to light, sound, movement and other behaviours; and (c) they are variable over time, especially as we have seen with participatory internet-based works such as Napier's *net.flag* (Case Study 8.1).

Case Study 8.2
Variable Media Network

Initially developed by curator, artist and theorist Jon Ippolito, the Variable Media Questionnaire (VMQ) (2000) is the forerunner of the DOCAM, PADS (Performance Art Documentation Structure) and MANS (Media Arts Notation System) frameworks (see Figure 8.2). The VMQ evolved out of the broader efforts of the Variable Media Network (VMN), an initiative of the Forging the Future consortium devoted to digital curation. More specifically, the VMQ emerged from the Guggenheim Museum's preservation of video and conceptual art (Wands 2006: 206–7). There are now first, second and third generation questionnaires – designed by Ippolito at the Guggenheim Museum (2000), curator Alain Depocas at the Langlois Foundation (2003) and programmer John Bell at the Still Water research centre at the University of Maine (USA) (2010), respectively. The VMQ allows creators and users to develop guidelines for 'translating their works into new media once the original medium has expired' (Forging the Future n.d.). Creators identify the most appropriate method for translating their works, including storage, emulation, migration or reinterpretation, or, in Bruce Wands' analogous terms, documentation, emulation, migration and recreation (Wands 2006: 206). The VMQ requests that creators – rather than archivists, critics or new media experts – outline the mechanical components and conceptual dimensions of a work that are essential to preserving or recreating it. The Variable Media Network requires that decisions concerning the preservation of unstable artworks be made when the work is acquired by a holder (Stringari 2003). The VMQ produces a narrative of the life of a work, relying 'on the sharing of stories and individual experiences told by artists and related participants in the creation, exhibition and collection of art' (Hanhardt 2003: 8). The narrative also serves as a 'score or documentation form for unstable works of art' (Bosma 2011: 171). Notation systems, such as the VMQ, describe a work and provide the basis for its recreation or re-enactment.

Ippolito's essay 'Accommodating the Unpredictable' (2003a) outlines the philosophy and approach of the VMQ shortly after the second version was released. Building on the knowledge artists have about their works, 'the variable-media approach asks creators to play the central role in deciding how their work should evolve over time, with archivists and technicians offering choices rather than prescribing them' (Ippolito 2003a). On a case-by-case basis, the VMQ identifies 'behaviours' or 'medium-independent, mutually-compatible descriptions of each artwork', documenting crucial factors such as installation space, lighting requirements and the ratio of elements (sound, wind, visual features). In VMQ terms, 'performance' refers to the re-creation or re-enactment of the work in a new setting using the work-specific protocols developed by the VMQ in conversation with the artist. 'Reinterpretation' is a major strategy used in the VMQ to address the technological obsolescence of the work's hardware or software components. The VMQ categorizes works as reproduced, duplicated, interactive, encoded and networked.

'Reproduced' refers to a work that diminishes in quality when copied to a medium such as video and audio. 'Duplicated' works can be replicated identically through programming, such as Java applets, or event-based sequences, evident in Felix Gonzalez-Torres' *Untitled (Public Opinion)* (1991) in which a massive spillage of candy occupies the floor space. Indeed, Napier's *net.flag* (Case Study 8.1) falls into this category as well as the next two. 'Interactive' works require that the artist decide whether traces of previous participants or visitors should be erased or preserved in future incarnations of the work. 'Encoded' pieces involve programming and are often accessed through networks, thus becoming 'networked' artworks that require some form of networking (e.g. through the internet or mobile phone system). Weinbren's *The Erl King*, discussed in the previous section, is an example of an interactive video and networked digital creation. Furthermore, the VMQ defines the 'migration' of an artwork as the upgrading of its medium to a current standard. VMQ3 allows artists to compare the perspectives on their works presented by curators, conservators, technicians and artist assistants (see the next section for a brief discussion of the latest version). Based on the VMQ, conservators Caitlin Jones and Lizzie Muller used four processes to document media art: artist interviews, audience interviews, data structure scoring and access points identification (Jones and Muller 2008).

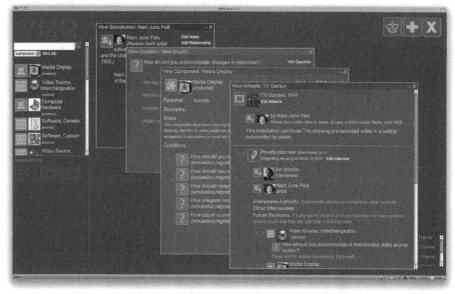

Figure 8.2 John Bell (lead developer), Jon Ippolito (architect), *Variable Media Questionnaire* (2000) (shown: v3.0, 2010). Interactive networked code. Image courtesy of Jon Ippolito.

Extending the VMQ model, other digital art preservation strategies make use of notation systems for scoring. Established by American curator and digital artist Richard Rinehart, the MANS is a conceptual framework for preserving digital and related media works (Rinehart 2007). The MANS is one of the first formal notation systems for preserving digital art. Rinehart's approach to preservation responds to the 'ephemeral, documentary, technical and multi-part' nature of digital creations, as well as their 'performative' 'behaviour-centric' and 'variable' qualities (Rinehart 2007: 181). Just as a musical composition can be 're-created' across a variety of instruments while still being recognized as the original, digital art is comparably variable. In Rinehart's system, the structure of an artwork is preserved and re-created through the use of a score (Bosma 2011: 172). The score preserves the interrelationships between the work as a whole and its technical components. The process takes into account the relationships between creators and users, instances of distributed authorship and the nuances of open-ended digital arts projects (Rinehart 2007: 185). MANS notation captures enough detail to result in a record of the artwork in conjunction with relevant descriptive metadata. Moreover, the model implements tags or what are referred to as 'behaviours', developed by the Variable Media Network (Case Study 8.2). These include works that are 'contained' (no additional infrastructure required); 'installed' (specific to spaces, sites or placements); 'performed' (process-oriented); 'reproduced' (involving a loss of quality when recorded); 'duplicated' (in which the copy and the original are indistinguishable); 'encoded' (requiring the interpretation of computer code); and 'networked' (present in more than one physical location) (Rinehart 2004a: 2–3).

Developed by curator Paul Clarke, the Performance Art Documentation Structure (PADS) is a similar notation system designed to record the components of a performance work – including, for example, audiovisual material, interviews and objects (Gray 2008). The PADS model presents a notation system of value to performance art researchers and one which characterizes the relationships between components of a work. In addition to capturing technical information, PADS records the parties involved in identifying an artwork's constituent parts – creators, users, curators, conservators or audience members. The process foregrounds the importance of interviews with artists, curators, technicians, audience members and archive users in formulating a score. The PADS draws extensively from the Variable Media Network model, while addressing the specific challenges of performance art preservation. Like the VMN and Rinehart's MANS, the PADS model avoids categorizing works by media type (for example, painting or sculpture) and instead applies behavioural tags, such as those mentioned above. An 'interoperable' system results from the use of common metadata usage. The MPEG-21 metadata framework (explored technically in the next section of this chapter) allows the distribution of performance art scores between archives.

The first work selected to receive a PADS scoring was *I Never Done Enough Weird Stuff* (1996) by British performance, installation and video artist Richard Layzell (see Figure 8.3). The original performance involved an eclectic combination of 'weird' bodily gestures (e.g. choking movements), objects (e.g. pilates balls) and garments (e.g. floor dusters). The scoring began with a series of interviews with Layzell from the perspectives of curator (focused on context and influences) and conservator (highlighting the specifics of the work). The process identified the key elements as objects, garments, roles, space, location, audiovisuals, electronics and gestures. For example, the score, as it appears on the STARS (Semantic Tools for Screen Arts Research) archive, lists 'torch' as one of the component objects. An interview with the artist reveals the provenance of the object data: 'Richard's torch was a small, black Maglite, a novel item at the time as the brand was largely unknown in the UK. It was used in several performances as an "antidote" to theatrical lighting...It is hidden in Richard's inside pocket for much of the performance' (STARS 2013).

Figure 8.3 Richard Layzell, *I Never Done Enough Weird Stuff* (1996). Photograph of performance. Image courtesy of the artist.

Reflection

We have seen how different actors such as individual artists, artist collectives, curators, conservators and technicians can work together to preserve digital artworks. Can you anticipate any problems that could arise in collaboration between these different actors or issues that might come up?

Case Study 8.3
UbuWeb and the Repository of the Avant-Garde

Founded in 1996 by American poet Kenneth Goldsmith (b. 1961), UbuWeb (http://www.ubuweb.com) is a volunteer-based, curated collection of 'avant-garde' artworks, including sound art, visual works, film and poetry. Particularly focusing on obscure, out-of-print and small-run works, the archive is replete with 'the detritus and ephemera of great artists' (Goldsmith 2011b). Hosting over 7,500 artists and several thousand works, the digital archive has none of the embellishments of most websites – even non-commercial ones. The interface is 'flat' and 'cool', avoiding any 'illusionistic depth-of-space' (Goldsmith 2002: 2). UbuWeb uses no advertisement banners, institutional logos or donation-soliciting icons; its server space and bandwidth are donated by universities, as Goldsmith points out. UbuWeb is known for uploading sound and video files without seeking the permission of authors in an inversion of copyright protocol. This maverick approach to digital archiving has produced surprisingly affirmative responses:

> UbuWeb posts much of its content without permission; we rip full-length CDs into sound files; we scan as many books as we can get our hands on; we post essays as fast as we can OCR them. And not once have we been issued a cease and desist order. Instead, we receive glowing e-mails from artists, publishers and record labels finding their work on UbuWeb. (Goldsmith 2001)

In the mid-1990s, UbuWeb began with an emphasis on what is known variously as 'concrete', 'visual' or 'shape poetry'. Concrete poetry uses the arrangement of words visually on the page or screen to create an effect and convey meaning. Another early UbuWeb interest included 'found street poems', that is 'poems' in the form of street signs, advertisements, posters and graffiti. With the emergence of streaming audio technologies, UbuWeb later expanded its ambit to include sound poetry – created and performed through a combination of literary and musical techniques. When MP3s became available and bandwidth limits increased, UbuWeb began adding video artworks to its collection, becoming an ever-increasing 'repository for the "avant-garde"' (Goldsmith 2011a). The archive now houses over 2,500 full-length streaming and downloadable films and videos. Additionally, in 2005, UbuWeb acquired *The 365 Days Project* – a collection of rare audio works, including tracks by the Russian-American conductor and composer Nicolas Slonimsky (1894–1995). The archive has broadened to include 'ethnopoetic' audio works, including recordings of Inuit throat singing, as well as ethnopoetic visual poetry, such as Native American song pictures. /Ubu Editions is an open-access collection of PDFs on literature and poetry.

UbuWeb began as a poetry community with the common intention of revitalizing concrete poetry in the public domain. The project exemplifies the notion of a web-based 'gift economy', outlined below, through radical approaches to distribution and access. Moreover, the term 'nude media' describes the liberation of a digital file from its original context — including the UbuWeb platform itself — through P2P sharing systems (Goldsmith 2002: 4–5). Emancipated from the authority of the source or host, nude media create new networks of meaning. UbuWeb situates its archive of nude media squarely within a digital gift economy. In contrast to a commodity exchange or capitalistic model, a gift economy involves exchanges of goods, services and intellectual property, with reciprocity (rather than money) expected. Whereas a commodity market ascribes power to those with the most capital, a gift-based market recognizes the act of giving as a value that ensures social cohesion and cultural longevity (Hyde 1999). Early anthropological research into gift economies focused on the exchange networks of Native American and Canadian peoples. New media theorists have since used the term to signify the capital-free economies that underpin knowledge exchange in the information age (for an example, see Creative Commons licensing in Chapter 7). The longevity of UbuWeb is, in part, made possible through an ethic of making its variable media acquisitions available as gifts. For example, the Andy Warhol Audio Archive contains interviews with the artist from between 1965 and 1987, as well as audio recordings of contemporary Canadian filmmaker David Cronenberg reflecting on Warhol's evolution as an artist.

TOWARDS ARCHIVAL INTEROPERABILITY: ARTS PRESERVATION AND TECHNOLOGY

The previous section outlined the principal scoring systems for digital arts preservation, beginning with the VMQ first developed in the year 2000. As we have seen in Chapter 8 and elsewhere in this book, archival difficulties plague works of media art. For instance, tape degradation will impact works of video art and failure to use archival quality paper will compromise the longevity of digital photographs. Bruce Wands describes three technological factors to consider in the preservation of digital artworks: data storage, bandwidth and interactivity (Wands 2006: 33). In terms of the latter factor, Mark Napier's *net.flag* (Case Study 8.1) demonstrates that many digital artworks are lost when user interactivity diminishes or access becomes constrained by technological obsolescence. Additionally, as the original media becomes degraded or simply outdated, the dual processes of documentation and preservation are ever-more pressing. The truth is that forms of documentation can exist long after the work has been lost (Wands 2006: 33). Images of internet artworks, critical commentaries about installations or artist interviews about performative pieces are the strands of documentation coalesced by the notation systems we have discussed so far in this chapter.

Reflection

We just mentioned tape degradation and paper quality as factors that can affect the long-term survival of video and photographic artworks, respectively. Can you think of three to five other technical issues that would hasten the decline of a digital work if not addressed adequately by a preservation plan?

To a certain extent, the evolution of higher quality digital formats and increased bandwidth will continue to support data delivery, storage and, ultimately, arts preservation. Moreover, technological development – including high-definition video and multichannel audio – will contribute to preservation efforts by increasing the capacity and efficiency of media. In addition, high-speed computer infrastructures – such as National LambdaRail (NLR) in the US – have the potential to enhance the production and transmission of audiovisual works (Cisco Systems 2008). However, these technological strides alone will not ensure the future of the digital arts. In this respect, the continued refinement of notation systems is fundamental. Returning to the realities of 'technological obsolescence', this section deepens our focus on key technologies and technical issues negotiated by digital arts conservators. Specifically, we explore the concept of interoperability as an approach used by digital archivists to ensure the long-term viability of artworks through extended collaboration between repositories and institutions. How is archival interoperability achieved through the technologies of metaservers, MPEG-21 and XML? Metaservers, the MPEG-21 metadata framework and markup languages have been central to the interoperability of the VMQ, MANS and PADS notation systems.

First, the use of metaservers distributes digital arts preservation efforts across different individuals, parties and organizations. Building a more complete picture of the work, metaservers also heighten the accessibility of archival data, so information about digital artworks is not isolated from other networks or databases. Second, the MPEG-21 standard enhances multimedia access between artists and consumers across different networked platforms. Third, markup languages, such as XML, are employed to establish relationships between the components of an artwork. These languages also support user participation while making possible the recording of the human and non-human components of a work so it can be re-created or re-performed (MacDonald 2009: 63). In this section, we conclude by returning to the new role of art museums and galleries in digital arts preservation. Indeed, digital arts practices have transformed museums into places of creation, documentation, technical innovation and preservation with conservators and curators working cooperatively with artists, programmers and technicians (MacDonald 2009: 62).

Interoperability refers to a state of effective and integrated information exchange. The term often describes the technical compatibility between machines that makes communication and, hence, exchange (i.e. operations between devices) possible. In addition to archival interoperability, there are other forms, including technical, semantic, political, community, legal and international (Pelizzari 2012: 38). Interoperability realized through the use of a metaserver is a pivotal practice to the archival initiatives of the VMN. The second version of the Variable Media Questionnaire (VMQ2) offered partial flexibility, especially regarding the different components of a work that each required a unique, though interrelated, preservation plan. In contrast, the third version (VMQ3) (2010) (Case Study 8.2), designed by computer programmer John Bell, foregrounds flexibility by focusing on the relationships between parts of a work and manifests a higher level of interoperability. Bell's version is notable for its use of a metaserver, allowing communication about the artwork to happen across different systems and platforms. By uploading data to the metaserver, the third iteration of the questionnaire links the VMQ architecture to external schemes, such as The Pool. Developed by Jon Ippolito, Joline Blais and the Still Water Lab, The Pool is an online database for documenting the evolution of internet artworks through different stages – specifically 'intent', 'approach' and 'release'. The Pool includes descriptions and reviews of projects, as well as the relationships between projects in the database (Paul 2008: 174).

In order to foster interoperability, Bell deployed object-oriented programming (OOP) in which concepts are schematized as objects with attributes denoted in data fields. Additionally, VMQ3 makes use of open code programming, such as the open-source database management system MySQL and the programming languages PHP (Hypertext Preprocessor), HTML (HyperText Markup Language), CSS (Cascading Style Sheets) and JS (JavaScript) (Bell 2010). The metaserver searches for an artist's name and generates an identification list. It then returns a full record of all metadata related to the identification including titles of works, media and links to different forms of documentation. In this way, a metaserver operates as a data repository tracing the relationships within and between artworks. The metaserver offers a place of convergence between online databases, such as The Pool and any other information system accessible via the API (Application Programming Interface). Thus, the aim of preserving digital artworks by carefully delineating their changes is enhanced through the principle of interoperability in which the documentation performed by dispersed institutions can be integrated.

In 1999, the concept of the MPEG-21 standard or the MPEG-21 Multimedia Framework emerged within the MPEG community in an effort to develop approaches to intellectual property management in digital environments (Cox et al. 2006). Becoming a standard in 2003, MPEG-21 allows digital items to be declared and modified. Interoperability is one of the principal aims of the standard. MPEG-21 increases the exchange of multimedia resources between creators, users and providers across an array of networked devices. The development of MPEG-21, in part, signifies the blurring of the line between private individuals (users) and production companies (creators). The standard makes intelligent use of metadata to establish an environment for content exchange. Different domains of MPEG-21 metadata include production details; descriptions of the interactions between users and the content; descriptions of content exchange and optimization; and guidelines specifying the legal use of the material (Cox et al. 2006: 48). The main concept behind the framework is the 'digital item' (defined as any single multimedia file or a group of such files). The basis for transactions is a 'digital item declaration', which defines content using metadata about the owner, the media and the parameters of its possible distribution or modification according to copyright.

In addition to the MPEG-21 standard, markup languages, such as XML, are also essential to archival interoperability. Extensible Markup Language (XML) is used to exchange data across networks, to create data sets for transfer across mismatched systems and to enable data translation from one format to another. XML simplifies the process of data exchange between two or more applications – a core function for platform interoperability (Kahate 2009: 5). For instance, the Media Arts Notation System (MANS) uses a form of XML known as Digital Item Declaration Language (DIDL). This language allows the creation of more detailed descriptions about digital objects. Specifically, DIDL enables the pronouncement of a digital item through the specification of its metadata and the relationships between its metadata and other artworks (Salomoni and Mirri 2011: 28). The MANS produces a score of an artwork in three layers: the development of a conceptual model, the generation of a vocabulary to interpret the DIDL XML and the production of a score as its top layer, resulting in a record of the artwork for future re-creation or re-performance.

Interoperable technologies have been indispensable to the digitization of artworks in library collections. While the technological landscape shifts perpetually and ephemeral artworks slip into disrepair or decline, libraries ensure digital heritage continuity between generations of users and artists (Bosma 2011: 177). Moreover, the archives of libraries act as repositories of data but, at the same time, offer content for subsequent creators (Bosma 2011: 178). The archiving of artworks at libraries and institutes using notation systems and other methods of preservation reminds us that a work of art is both 'object and meme; it is an artist's work and a possible source of inspiration for other artists' (Bosma 2011: 178). Information theorist Prodromos Tsiavos recommends open-source frameworks for GLAMs, or galleries, libraries, archives and museums (Tsiavos 2011). Commitment to an open-source ethos ensures interoperability between library archives and those of other cultural heritage institutions, such as museums and galleries. Founded in 2002 by curator Timothy Murray at Cornell University, the Rose Goldsen Archive of New Media Art is one of the first library-based archives of digital art. The archive preserves artworks based on CD, DVD, video and the internet, and includes a collection of catalogues, monographs, design catalogues and other supporting materials.

Case Study 8.4
The Unreliable Archivist

Created by Janet Cohen, Keith Frank and Jon Ippolito, *The Unreliable Archivist* (1998) is an example of an early internet artwork that uses an established archive — äda'web — to critique the swiftly transforming role of the archivist in the digital era (http://www.walkerart.org/collections/artworks/the-unreliable-archivist) (see Figure 8.4). Now preserved by the Walker Art Center and originally designed for Netscape 4.07, the project began as a response to the archiving of äda'web (1995–8) by Benjamin Weil. *The Unreliable Archivist* interrogates the ethics of digital archiving through the use of a collections database-structured website that allows the user to disrupt or subvert the äda'web archive in unusual ways (Graham 2007: 102). For example, a user selects the style and layout of the website, and manipulates images taken from the äda'web collection of new media art. The reconfiguration of the äda'web archive is executed according to the categories 'language', 'image', 'style' and 'layout'. The user-determined metadata tags signal idiosyncratic departures from the usual archival categories: creator, title, date created and medium. Some of the interactive features are just plain absurd (Graham 2010: 167–8). Texts, videos and sound from äda'web are combined in unusual ways, allowing the user to 'alter this archetypal äda'web page to suite [sic] your preferences' (Walker Art Center 1998). Changing the category sliders gives the user the false appearance of choice.

Just how much should a collection change over time? What are the appropriate choices a user can make when participating in an artwork? What is the role of the conservator in the digital era? As a parody of the archival process, *The Unreliable Archivist* raises questions over how to preserve the dynamic, interactive qualities of many digital artworks. The work highlights some of the concerns of early new media archivists and queries the inherent limitations of archiving, particularly the condensing of complex projects into reductionistic metatags. Ippolito characterizes *The Unreliable Archivist* as 'parasite art' that requires a host to feed on (Dietz 1999). The project maps metadata about äda'web, exploring the dynamics between a host and a parasite in digital domains, specifically in terms of archival structure and content. Indeed, the discourse of interactivity can be utopian and misplaced, in the sense that the degree and nature of interaction is fixed by the artist. Access occurs on physical and conceptual levels with metadata providing a window into the intellectual mechanisms of an artwork. The archivist's role as the arbiter of interactivity, metadata and the ultimate fate of the artwork is one not to be taken lightly.

Figure 8.4 Janet Cohen, Keith Frank and Jon Ippolito, *The Unreliable Archivist* (1998) (shown: v2.0, 2013). Interactive networked code. Image courtesy of Jon Ippolito.

Chapter Summary

This chapter has discussed the archiving, preserving and remembering of digital art through a palette of concepts, artists, projects, notation systems and technologies. Digital practices have transformed the conventions of arts preservation. Unlike most traditional works of art, the archiving of digital artworks requires extensive, ongoing collaboration between artists, curators, conservators, technicians and users. In many instances, the preservation of a work necessitates a creative re-performance, which never identically reproduces the original work but instead produces an extension of the work as a time-based process.

- The democratization of art (e.g. increased access to art, an inclusive range of participants in arts production and involvement of multiple parties in conservation) through digital paradigms extends to community-based archival practices that necessitate the collaborative involvement of many stakeholders.
- Drawing from the work of Boris Groys and Rick Prelinger, theoretical perspectives on digital arts preservation regard the archive as a dynamic site of cultural values production.
- Conservators invoke performativity as a concept in which ephemeral works must be re-performed to retain their value, meaning and impact.
- Digital arts preservation intersects with notions of digital heritage and digital memory.

- Crowdsourcing, tacit knowledge and acceptable loss are three key issues explored in relation to preserving digital productions.
- Notation systems, such as the Variable Media Questionnaire, produce a score of an ephemeral work and provide a key to its re-creation or re-performance.
- While technological capacities inherently increase over time, the refinement of notation systems through enhanced archival interoperability and other strategies is essential to the long-term survival of digital artworks.

9 CONCLUSION: HYPERREALITY AND THE POSTDIGITAL ART OF THE FUTURE

Chapter 9 brings together the themes, frameworks and case studies in the book with an outlook towards the future. This chapter considers contemporary trends and potential directions for digital art in the coming years. While current aesthetic practice has deep roots in the history of modernity, the rise of digital culture and its ever-greater penetration into all facets of life – including in nations historically on the outskirts of European and North American technological centres – reflects both a new state of technology and a multitude of possibilities for culture and the arts. Since the 1990s, the employment of digital technologies as tools by artists has been regarded as unique enough to deserve the typologies 'digital art', 'new media art' and others outlined in Chapter 1. By most accounts, digital approaches are increasingly becoming more mainstream and closely integrated into creative practices of all kinds. Interactive technologies continue to grow into our everyday lives, particularly with regard to social media, gaming, virtual reality and wearable devices. Undoubtedly, there will come a moment in the near future when artists will have never experienced being alive without computers, mobile phones, social media and futuristic devices that most of us can now only imagine. However, as critics have observed, predicting the future of digital art is not a simple endeavour. It requires the consideration of the complex intersection of at least three trajectories: art, culture and technology (Wands 2006: 206). As this chapter argues, there are other values that artists consider, including justice, equality and freedom of expression.

We suggest that contemporary art will assimilate technology to the extent that the very premise of digital art could become banal, redundant or anachronistic. In comparable terms, theorist Roy Ascott has argued that 'the digital moment has passed' as interfaces between humans and machines disappear through wireless, mobile and multisensory devices that streamline the role of technologies in daily life (Ascott 2008: 47). Ascott argues that the impending symbiosis between humans and machines will encompass the wearing of computers or the containing of digital devices within our bodies, thereby reducing distance and physical barriers (i.e. interfaces) and bolstering the inescapability of technology on a day-to-day, moment-to-moment basis. Hence, in Ascott's view, the future of art lies in the engendering of productive alliances between the arts and sciences. He proposes the concept of 'moist-media' to characterize artworks of the past, present and future that exist (have existed or will exist) at the dynamic edge of the digital and biological domains. For Ascott, the digital realm has transformed human consciousness, perception and creative potential, as evident in his idea of 'cyberception' – an emerging human faculty that enables us to tap into a myriad of conscious and subconscious states not accessible through our normal five senses. In addition to science-art alliances and embodied forms of technology, the future of art will entail more intensive engagement with networks that cross between the virtual and the real – in which reality becomes ours to construct. The future of digital art will continue to reflect themes of connectivity, immersion, emergence, interaction and transformation through the increasing use of artistic technologies (Ascott 2008: 58).

Following Ascott's enticing assertion that the world is ours to construct, 'reality' is the core concept examined in this conclusion. We define reality as the domain of phenomena (e.g. buildings, trees, emotions, thoughts, sensations, etc.) available to human experience and perception as real time, material and embodied 'data'. We first return to the framework of Baudrillard's hyperreality (also discussed in Chapter 7), which signifies the blurring of the difference between what is real and what is artificial through the power of technology. In considering the future of digital art, it is imperative to contemplate reality in all possible forms. The greater frequency of artists adopting commonplace tools, such as mobile phones and geographical information software, we argue, is a continuance of the fascination artists have had with technology since Dadaism and before (Hope 2006: 42). Art will continue to merge with technology of the ongoing 'digital transition', involving the continued replacement of material objects (e.g. maps on paper) with electronic data (i.e. inter-active digital maps) that becomes immediately accessible over networks (Poole and Le-Phat Ho 2011: 5). We also address how the merging of art and technological innovation offers a potent mechanism for confronting the prevailing concerns of today's globalized world, including matters of personal privacy, social destabilization and ecological fragmentation.

To what extent can artists shape, augment and remake reality? How do digital artists engage with the pressing material realities – including social, cultural, political and environmental issues – of contemporary life? How do artists use new digital technologies in artworks that address the real problems of the world rather than merely reinforce the hyperreal scenarios, virtual preoccupations and fancy new gadgetries of the digital age? As an antidote to the dislocation (between mind and body, real and artificial) embedded in hyperreality, the possibility of a 'postdigital arts' and the humanization of technologies through art is explored again (Alexenberg 2011; Bolognini 2008; Cascone 2000). Through a number of artists and artworks, Chapter 9 invites students to think about how digital art employs interactive technologies to call attention to issues of disruption, privacy, surveillance, information control, social inequity and the deterioration of the natural foundation (i.e. water, soil, air, flora and fauna) on which all forms of reality depend.

REALITY AND HYPERREALITY IN DIGITAL ART

Whether through realism or abstraction, art has always engaged reality by bringing into focus the ways in which we regard the world around us. As we noted in Chapter 2, postmodernism contends that reality is not a single or static phenomenon – perceived as the same by all – but something that artists determine through the combination of technologies and aesthetic techniques. Postmodernists assert that we must consider a multititude of realities rather than a unified reality of any sort. The latter, for postmodernists, is an illusion. This pluralistic understanding of reality also holds true for art. Certain artworks maintain a sense of spatiotemporal continuity (in which time and space appear real to our ordinary perception) while at the same time representing reality in such a way that the concept of the real becomes questionable or hyperreal. The adjective 'hyperreal' (and the corresponding noun 'hyperreality') comes principally from the work of Jean Baudrillard to characterize an experience that is ostensibly not grounded in terra firma, but nevertheless becomes more believable than the reality we commonly accept (Kac 2005: 16; also see Chapter 7). Baudrillard articulates the concept in the chapter 'The Precession of Simulacra' in his book *Simulacra and Simulations* (1981), using Disneyland as a consummate study. Baudrillard believes that the manufactured façade of Disneyland (e.g. its houses and streets, as well as its animals) convinces people that it is a real place when, for him, it is an illusion of something real and a fake world in itself. The human imagination constructs Disneyland as a genuine reality, worth pursuing in real life back home. Moreover, the simulacrum of Disneyland depends on commercialism (e.g. buying tickets to enter) and order (e.g. standing in line). Other examples of simulacra used by Baudrillard include a manicured garden (simulacrum) in contrast to nature itself (referent); bodybuilders as hyperreal versions of ordinary human beings; and new buildings or objects designed to appear old or antique. The hyperreal, as described by Baudrillard, is a heightened situation that strikes us as somewhat artificial (e.g. the Main Street of Disneyland), but we nevertheless treat it as genuine (Paul 2003: 38). Hyperreality is also a mode of experience in the postmodern context that can seem more real than the everyday world we perceive through our senses, resulting in the absence of an original to which the constructed hyperreal refers (Toffoletti 2011: 25). Hyperreality can be considered a form of representing reality that goes beyond realism or abstraction through virtual experience. In semiotic terms, the concept is contingent on the wearing down of the distinction between the *sign* (the form or medium that represents a thing) and the *referent* (the actual content or the reality of the thing) (Kac 2005: 55).

As Chapter 7 demonstrated, digital technologies offer many examples of Baudrillard's theory of the simulacrum. They collapse the difference between the mediation of reality and the existence of the real as an actual thing (e.g. a tree, stone, building or person) once regarded as distinct from the form of mediation (e.g. a photographic image, a gaming environment or a disembodied voice on a social media website). Baudrillard argues, echoing Marshall McLuhan, that media (i.e. signs) are no longer distinguishable from content (i.e. referents). For example, digital photography as a medium makes possible the reconfiguration of visual reality and underscores the questionable truth of images (Paul 2003: 36; also see Chapter 3). For example, how often do we now doubt the real identity of a photograph by asking what has or has not been manipulated by image processing software? We might ask: Has a blue sky been added digitally to a photograph of a dark winter day? Indeed, the notion of artistic realism is closely connected to the history of photography in which a visual work is thought to represent the world truthfully, that is, as it can be known through the senses, emotions and intellect. Critics of the 1980s and 1990s stirred debates about the nature of digital imagery in contrast to analogue darkroom photography (Drucker 2009: 136). In sum, digital media have triggered the unravelling of the modernist notion of realism through the production of simulated modes of reality.

Telepresence becomes hyperreal under certain conditions. The medium (e.g. a digital interface or telerobotics system) and the real (e.g. the human body or a gallery space) can fuse together, allowing an artist or participant to alter the real world from a disembodied distance (Kac 2005: 141). Moreover, telepresence works become hyperreal when audiovisual content imparts such a powerful sensory effect that taste, touch, smell, proprioception and other senses are evoked in addition to vision and sound (Grau 2003: 275). Multisensoriality can be an important dimension of hyperreality for understanding immersive virtual reality (VR) environments and their rising importance in society and art.

Reflection

Can you give a few examples that might capture the experience of hyperreality in your daily life? What form of technology were you using, and how did the technology enable you to experience the world in ways that were otherwise impossible?

It is useful to think about hyperreality neither as a development of recent years nor as such an abrupt departure from modernist notions of truth. Indeed, Baudrillard is critical of hyperreality, seeing it as an artificial state of reality that he considers to underpin the superficiality of many aspects of popular culture. Consider, again, Disneyland as a self-contained reality or simulacrum of the outer world. However, other theorists and artists have a comparatively more positive outlook on the integration of technology, life and art, and on the possibility of multiple realities, in the postmodern sense. Roy Ascott uses the metaphor 'bye bye Baudrillard' to imply the uninhibited embracing of technology and the opening of deeper symbiosis between humans and machines, beyond the cynicism implicit in Baudrillard's philosophy of hyperreality. Seminal media artists of the twentieth century have made use of hyperreal elements in their works to invoke the possibility of truth in artistic representation through pre-digital and digital technologies. For example, the work of Peter Campus, a pioneer of video art, returns consistently to the theme of the hyperreal (also see Chapter 3). His video and photographic projects foreground the interrelationship between the referent and the sign – between nature and the media that represents (and supposedly enhances) it (Paul 2003: 44). Touching on matters of illusion and ethics, Campus' works indicate a much more long-standing interest in the 'dissolution of material reality' through media art (Falconer 2011: 402). His photographic experimentation focuses on the continuum between older darkroom and newer digital practices. It reminds us that debates over the truthfulness of analogue photography often disregard the variety of tools, such as multiple exposures and the manipulation of plates, used by early pre-digital photographers to achieve a desired visual effect (Drucker 2009: 136).

As an example of the above, *Three Transitions* (1973) is a series of theatrical yet reflexive self-portraits that explore perception as a limited gauge of reality (Museum of Modern Art 2006: 261). Campus deploys a host of technical tricks to produce visual illusions without digital accessories. Two cameras, facing opposite sides of a paper wall, film simultaneously. The artist slices through the paper, creating the impression he is cutting through his own back. The application of blue paint to his face is the basis for another self-portrait, which he superimposes onto similarly coloured paper before setting it on fire (Museum of Modern Art 2006: 261). The probing of perception's limits is further evident in Campus' colour photograph *Flutter* (1993) of a butterfly in grass, where the sense of space and depth in the image is hyperreal (Falconer 2011: 402). Similarly, *Mere* (1994) depicts an insect in a preternatural setting which, though believable, remains outside normal human experience and firmly in the mode of science fiction (Paul 2003: 44). Likewise, his digitally manipulated *Wild Leaves* (1995) experiments with the production of a sense of depth through the two-dimensional surface of a naturalistic image (Drucker 2009: 136).

HYPERREALITY AND POSTDIGITAL ART

In Baudrillard's view, hyperreality dehumanizes experience by dislodging us from the material basis of perception (e.g. actual trees, beaches or people), leading to the proliferation of floating signs without that basis. In contrast, postdigital art heralds a renewed interest in the human dimensions of art and technology, as well as the further integration of the digital and material realms on an everyday basis. Indeed, 'digital activism' and the social redefining of technology are prominent in postdigital practices. Artist and theorist Mark Tribe characterizes postdigital art as moving beyond a purely technical focus on such elements as two-dimensional pixelations, software code and digital animation to expressing – first and foremost – how technology moulds human perceptions, emotions and behaviours (Gartenfield 2008). Rather than prioritizing the technologies of software codes and hardware devices, postdigital art highlights 'the communication structure between the people involved' in the work (Bolognini 2008). In fact, artist Maurizio Bolognini revises the very notion of a digital device to encompass hardware, software and *the public* (Bolognini 2008). Postdigital artists see digital devices as enmeshed in social processes and patterns. For Bolognini, 'neo-technological art' (his preferred term for new media art) refers to a heterogeneous field that coalesces around the pillars of art, technology and *activism*, reinforcing the social dimension of the science–art alliance. New modes of participation offer a variety of possibilities for digital art in which there is a shift from weak modes of public interaction to stronger modes that promote democracy and public decision-making.

To be sure, digital art in the future will utilize participatory technologies and mobile communications to a greater extent. It is the pervasiveness of digital technology in our everyday lives that underpins the postdigital character of art. Bolognini argues that the shift to the postdigital occurs as practices go beyond early experimental phases and enter mainstream circulation. For example, software is now routinely used in art and design, making the notion of 'software art', including software-based art and programming aesthetics, somewhat outmoded (unless, of course, the history of the genre is being considered). For Bolognini, the first stage of 'neo-technological art' was marked by experimentation and research, followed by a period of 'diffusion' in which the distinction between media art and media technology collapses as works (and their associated technologies) reach larger audiences and more users. Moreover, 'generative art' (another post-media aesthetic in Manovich's terms; see Chapter 2) allows artists to set out the rules followed by devices that are designed to operate autonomously. Here, Bolognini distinguishes between 'device-oriented generative practices' (which use software in experimental ways aligned with early media art) and 'outcome-oriented generative practices' (which prioritize final products rather than creative processes and are aligned with the rather non-experimental diffusion phase mentioned above).

As these commentators put forward, postdigital art is concerned with understanding human behaviour, values and social interactions in response to the profusion of technologies. For other theorists, postdigital art also confronts the 'binary model of reality' that is inherent in digital technology, including the logic of zero/one, either/or, on/off. These theorists argue that the abstraction of the real world into binaries is a significant conceptual limitation of the digital paradigm, which 'insists on the reduction of continuous reality into discrete binary units' (Alexenberg 2011: 36). In other words, people think more in black and white (e.g. binary) terms than they did before, and have therefore lost sight of the ways that technologies are socially situated. As an interdisciplinary prospect, a postdigital future lies in a dynamic zone between the digital and material, the real and the constructed, the sign and the referent. Artist and critic Mel Alexenberg in *The Future of Art in the Postdigital Age* echoes the social emphasis of Mark Tribe and Maurizio Bolognini in defining postdigital art as:

> of or pertaining to art forms that address the humanization of digital technologies through interplay between digital, biological, cultural, and spiritual systems, between cyberspace and real space, between embodied media and mixed reality in social and physical communication, between high tech and high touch experiences, between visual, haptic, auditory, and kinesthetic media experiences, between virtual and augmented reality, between roots and globalization, between autoethnography and community narrative, and between web-enabled peer-produced wikiart and artworks created with alternative media through participation, interaction, and collaboration in which the role of the artist is redefined. (Alexenberg 2011: 10)

Postdigital art seeks a multisensory form of practice amplifying the qualities of immersion and collaboration – hallmarks of media art since the mid-twentieth century. Alexenberg's conceptualization of postdigital art also evokes Ascott's notion of 'moistmedia', described earlier and later in this chapter as the interplay of 'dry' pixels and 'wet' biomolecules or the fusion of technology, culture and biology through pervasive computing.

What do postdigital artworks look, sound and feel like? What aesthetic characteristics are typical of postdigital artistic practices? As described in Chapter 5, electronic composer Kim Cascone (2000) outlines the evolution of a 'postdigital aesthetic' in computer music. The failure or breakdown of technologies, in the form of glitches, bugs, application errors, system crashes, clipping, distortion and noise, has led to a new palette of creative possibilities for artists (Cascone 2000: 13). Composers incorporate technical errors into their works, producing interesting textures and novel sonic spaces, while also underscoring the fallibility of technology. Hence, postdigital electronic music is concerned with audio detritus and background effects – those aspects 'beyond the boundary of "normal" functions and uses of software' (Cascone 2000: 14). Cascone argues that the Italian Futurist movement, specifically the painter Luigi Russolo, and John Cage's 'silent' composition *4'33"* (1952) established the groundwork for the emergence of postdigital music and its emphasis on technical limitations and equipment breakdowns. Following Cascone's position, we maintain that postdigital art inverts the conventional applications of technology to forge new aesthetic vocabularies and social possibilities. The levelling of technology through exposing its imperfections results in a humanizing effect; machines, like humans, are not perfect.

Reflection

Early media artists were known for intentionally distorting the conventional uses of technology. Consider again, for example, Paik's *Magnet TV*, discussed in Chapter 2. How might the goals of postdigital practices differ? In what ways might postdigital art mark a renewal of pre-digital practices?

NEW TECHNOLOGICAL FRONTIERS AND THE FUTURE OF DIGITAL ART

As we have argued throughout this book, artists love experimenting with technology. History attests to this fact. This section outlines a number of emerging technologies adopted as tools and mediums by contemporary digital practitioners. Ubiquitous computing, wearable technology, gaming and MMORPG networked environments, social media, mobile telecommunications, open-source software and wiki platforms for generating open-ended, interactive and collaborative works will be considered. The artists and artworks included in this section collectively allude to a number of possible directions for digital art in the coming years. While conclusive predictions are impossible, artists will continue to devise novel modes of hybridizing technology and art. These include Yacov Sharir's use of computerized choreography in performances such as *Intelligent City* (2003), Ian Bogost's game poetry, Feng Mengbo's political game-based video work in *Long March Restart* (2009), the Twitter art of Man Bartlett and Brian Piana, Golan Levin's mobile phone musical composition *Dialtones: A Telesymphony* (2001–2) and Lauren McCarthy's wiki-based performance *Script* (2010).

UBIQUTIOUS COMPUTING AND WEARABLE TECHNOLOGY

The division between virtuality and physicality arguably dominates our perception of digital technology in our lives. Certainly, the binary division between the virtual and the physical also underpins Baudrillard's theory, since hyperreality is contingent on the severance of the sign from the referent, the digital from the material domain. Meanwhile, others have argued that since the internet revolution of the 1990s, the digital realm has been caught between two extremes: the virtuality of cyberspace (made possible by programming and software) and the tactile interaction with computer hardware that augments the physical capabilities of our bodies (Paul 2011: 105). However, the emergence of 'ubiquitous computing' (UbiCom), also known as 'pervasive computing', arguably challenges Baudrillard's doctrine of separation. The very ordinariness and taken-for-grantedness of computer processors in the day-to-day world and the instantaneous access to networks provided by mobile communications are signs of the fuller integration of society and technology (Paul 2011: 106). Ubiquitous ICTs make it possible for information to be available anywhere and at any time. Meanwhile, intuitive human interfaces and familiarity of usage mean that physical devices themselves become less and less noticeable (Poslad 2009). UbiCom comprises computers, printers, routers, phones, cameras, gaming consoles, home appliances and other devices that reflect the social influence of technology, making those technologies less visible. Moreover, new forms of UbiCom are light, compact and relatively unnoticeable. Such forms of embedded computing are designed to be self-sufficient and to execute specific tasks that obviate the need for the complete operating system of a personal computer or laptop (Poslad 2009). Indeed, UbiCom points to an impending moment in the course of technological progress when 'going online' will be a phrase of the past – when 'being online' will be a seamless part of everyday awareness and behaviour, not a special virtual experience separate from the offline world.

Wearable technology – also known as tech togs or fashion electronics – is a form of ubiquitous computing holding considerable promise in culture, society and art. Computer engineer Steve Mann, known for his work in computational photography and more recently for 'digital eye glasses', defines a wearable computer (or a WearComp) as 'a computer that is subsumed into the personal space of the user (wearer), controlled by the wearer, and has both operational and interactional constancy (i.e. is always on and always accessible)' (Mann 1998: 144). He enumerates the principal characteristics of WearComp as 'constant', 'unrestrictive to the user', 'unmonopolizing of user attention', 'observable by user', 'controllable by user', 'attentive to the environment' and 'communicative to others' (Mann 1998: 144–5). The growth of wearable technologies can be attributed to developments in computer processing power and miniaturization, leading to technologies that become embedded in life (Seymour 2008: 15). By 2018, the wearable computing market is estimated to grow to 485 million product shipments or more per annum – dramatic growth fuelled in part by major electronics corporations such as Apple (ABI Research 2013). It should be noted, however, that wearable technology is not a recent phenomenon. In 1961, mathematicians Edward Thorp (b. 1932) and Claude Shannon (1916–2001) developed the first wearable computer – a miniature, shoe-mounted analogue device with toe-operated switches that could predict the speed of a roulette wheel in a casino and transmit the results via radio to the user's earpiece. The device was further developed by the Eudaemons, a group of physics students based at the University of California in the 1970s, and later commercialized by Keith Taft, the pioneer of blackjack card counting computers (Randell 2008: 166). In 1981, Mann developed a back-mounted computer to manage photographic processes.

Artists have been making use of the expressive potential of ubiquitous computing and wearable technology since the early development of these mediums. In addition to *Dancing with the Virtual Dervish/Virtual Bodies* (1994) discussed in Chapter 3, *Intelligent City* (2003) was a collaboration between Yacov Sharir, dancer Wei Yei, dancer Sophia Lycouris, composer Stan Wijnans and others (also see Sharir 2008). The work involved wearable computing suits developed by the performers. Designed for hospitals, libraries and shopping centres, the project created visual projections in response to the movement of the public through common spaces. Furthermore, Sharir's *Automatic Body* used the computational method Particle Swarm Optimization (PSO) to convert human behaviours into sounds, images and movements. The project involved a cyber-suit that 'collected data from the wearer, including EEG information, talked to a "mothership" and returned, via radio-frequency communications, an image representing the data. You could move your eyes and the image would move, or extend an arm and the image would extend' (Sharir cited in Digital Cultures Lab 2005). On the whole, Sharir's performance works demonstrate the application of ubiquitous computing principles to digital art.

GAMING AND NETWORKED ENVIRONMENTS

Gaming offers new technological avenues for digital artists to explore, particularly vis-à-vis the creation of unprecedented modes of networked virtual realities. MMORPGs (Massively Multiplayer Online Role Playing Games) (pronounced 'mor-pegs'), such as *World of Warcraft*, represent the emergence of highly interactive and social incarnations of cyberspace. For participatory works, the social milieu of the network as a community of users becomes an important site of meaning (Flanagan 2011). In 1996, video game developer Richard Garriott coined the term 'MMORPG' to describe gaming platforms that had become sophisticated enough to accommodate several thousand players in one game. In the same year, *Meridian 59* (or *M59*) became the first real-time online role-playing game released commercially. Shortly after, Garriott released the role-playing fantasy game *Ultima Online* (1997–). The predecessors of MMORPGs were known as MUDs (Multiuser Domains), then commonly referred to as 'virtual worlds'. The original MUDs were interactive text-based environments combining real-time chatting and role-playing. Known also as 'multiuser dungeons', MUDs allowed the creation of virtual fantasy worlds in which users interacted through textual and visual tools that predate the complex user interfaces of MMORPGs (Khosrow-Pour 2007: 459).

A growing number of interdisciplinary digital artists move fluidly between traditional and digital art forms, incorporating gaming technology as a medium for creativity, innovation and commentary. While some practitioners identify themselves as video game artists, other digital artists work with gaming broadly in conjunction with a variety of new media. Indeed, networked gaming environments, such as MMORPGs, have been characterized as forms of interactive storytelling and performance (see, for example, Laurel 1993). Narrative elements are especially evident in the work of video game designer Ian Bogost, who merges the interactivity of games with the meditativeness of haiku poetry. *A Slow Year* (2010) comprises four games, each pertaining to one of the four seasons. Rather than being fantasy-driven and fast-paced, the work evokes contemplation and unhurried change. Described as 'game poems' or '1K machined haiku', *A Slow Year* was released in two editions: as a poetry chapbook with accompanying PC software and as an Atari emulator for Mac computers. Bogost designed the work for the Atari Video Computer System (Atari VCS) with each of the four games occupying a remarkably low (by today's standards) one kilobyte of memory. For Bogost, the technical constraints of the Atari VCS make possible a minimalist aesthetics and a reflexive ambience uncharacteristic of most contemporary gaming environments (Bogost n.d.). *Guru Meditation* is a Zen-based meditation game also intended for the Atari VCS but with an iPhone edition. *Cow Clicker* (2010) is a Facebook game similarly based on the ethos of slowing down in a world consumed by the immediacy of social media.

Other artists utilize gaming technology as a catalyst for political commentary and activism. For example, Feng Mengbo (b. 1966) is a Chinese painter and video artist whose work satirizes Chinese political figures through game-based art. *Game Over: Long March* (1994), acquired by the Museum of Modern Art (MoMA) in 2010, features animated Red Army soldiers alongside Western pop cultural icons, including Coca-Cola cans. The digital work builds upon a series of oil paintings Feng created in 1993. Moreover, his interactive CD-ROM-based work *Taking Mount Doom by Strategy* (1997) is based on the *Doom* video game and, like *Game Over*, makes reference to heroic personae of the Chinese Cultural Revolution. The name of the work is a condensation of *Doom* and the revolutionary opera *Taking Tiger Mountain by Strategy*, titled after an event during the Chinese Civil War involving a soldier masquerading as a bandit. Mengbo based his computer-generated film *Q3* (1999) on the video game *Quake III Arena* (or *Quake 3*) in which the artist himself plays the role of a CNN reporter who joins a rebellion of clones. For the installation

Q4U (2002), Mengbo customized the open-source code of *Quake 3* to convert all the game's characters into versions of himself. *Long March Restart* (2009) is a more recent game-based production by the artist and the last in his series *Game Over: Long March*. Mengbo's body of work confronts the history of Chinese politics through a cosmopolitan form of video art that incorporates and modifies gaming technology (Braester 2005: 202–3).

SOCIAL MEDIA

In addition to embracing ubiquitous computing and gaming technology, digital artists are poised to engage more intensively with social media as tools and mediums for expression. In general, social media comprise online networks (e.g. Facebook, Myspace and Tumblr), blogs, micro-blogs (e.g. Twitter), sharing sites (e.g. YouTube and Flickr), podcasts, wikis (e.g. Wikipedia and others explored later in this section) and widgets or apps such as those available for mobile phones (Poole and Le-Phat Ho 2011: 13). As the hallmark of Web 2.0, social media foster interactive dialogue and collaboration between artists and audiences, promoting the exchange of user-generated content (Poole and Le-Phat Ho 2011: 13; also see Chapter 7). There have been at least three impacts on arts production and access as a result of social media popularity: (a) the matching of audiences to artworks; (b) the development of mechanisms for creating art and sustaining communities of practice; and (c) the provision to arts organizations of a variety of tools for building broader public consciousness of digital art (Poole and Le-Phat Ho 2011: 4). The recent growth of social media parallels developments in hardware (e.g. personal computers, mobile phones and recording equipment), software (e.g. search engines and graphic manipulation) and networks (the internet and mobile telephony) (Poole and Le-Phat Ho 2011: 11).

As Chapters 2 and 6 suggest, the histories of participatory, conceptual and media art prove that there have always been artists who readily absorb emerging technologies into their practices. But how are contemporary digital artists responding to Web 2.0 technologies and social media interactivity? Again, the question relates to the critical distinction between digital technologies as tools and mediums, explained in Chapter 2. While a growing number of artists use social media as avenues for disseminating, selling and promoting their works, others, such as Brian Piana and Man Bartlett, draw on social media as the fundamental medium for artistic production. Media artist An Xiao Mina distinguishes between 'art on Twitter' and 'Twitter art': 'The former suggests the traditions of art [that] moved into Twitter, while the latter suggests art in which Twitter is seamlessly integrated' (Xiao 2010). With its emergence linked to the release of Facebook in 2004, 'social media art' is an expression that has gained currency to describe art that uses social media networks to stage works. As Xiao observes, the internet is not only a tool for marketing or locating art but a medium for its production and expression. Reflecting the democratic ideals of digital art, social media art is 'inherently social', 'conceptually rich' and broadly accessible to the public outside of mainstream gallery or museum settings in the art capitals of New York, London, Beijing and other cities (Xiao 2010). Like net art before it, social media art is available to anyone with online access.

Guthrie Lonergan's *Myspace Intro Playlist* (2006) is a curated assemblage of online video excerpts in which Myspace users introduce themselves to the internet. The work addresses issues of identity, privacy and sociality on Web 2.0 platforms. Lonergan extracted each Myspace introduction from the context of the user's whole video, highlighting the shared ways users attempt to construct online identities (New Museum of Contemporary Art 2009). In a similar fashion to *Twitter Hymn Book* (2012) cited in Chapter 5, Brian Piana's *Ellsworth Kelly Hacked My Twitter* (2009) translates the Twitter postings of users followed by the artist into fields of colour, producing a geometric grid that changes in real time depending on Twitter feeds. The concept is based on the grid paintings of Ellsworth Kelly, particularly *Colors for a Large Wall* (1951) (Piana 2009). Another notable artist who experiments with

Figure 9.1. Man Bartlett, *#24hEcho* (2010). Documentation of durational performance, photograph of performance. The Hostess Project, P. P. O.W. Gallery, New York. Image courtesy of the artist.

social media platforms is Man Bartlett. In the performance work *#24hEcho* (2010), based physically at the P. P. O.W. Gallery in New York City and virtually on Twitter, Bartlett recited a stream of Twitter feeds into a webcam over a twenty-four-hour period, requiring only 'a table, 12 glasses of water and the internet' (Bartlett 2010) (see Figure 9.1).

MOBILE TELECOMMUNICATIONS

Mobile telecommunications offer a dynamic example of ubiquitous computing with which most of us are familiar. As with social media, it is hard to imagine a world without mobile phones – a time in which phone access was limited to handsets, telephone lines and coin-operated payphones. In 2010, there were an estimated 5.4 billion mobile phones globally. But the history of mobile networks extends back to the late 1970s when AT&T established in Chicago the first analogue network of mobile phones. By 1979, NTT in Tokyo released a commercially automated mobile network, which in 1984 became the first national mobile network, covering the whole of Japan. In 1981 and 1982, the NMT (Nordic Mobile Telephone Group) introduced international roaming as a feature of its network. By 1992, the GSM (Global System for Mobile Communication) emerged as the European standard, including enhanced signal quality, stronger frequencies, greater potential for a larger subscriber base and the introduction of the SIM card (Balbi 2013: 216–17; for an introductory overview, see Green and Haddon 2009). Digital artists have been exploring mobile phones as mediums since the early days of the technology. We expect the utilization of mobile communications by artists to swell as the technology becomes omnipresent – enhancing audience interaction with artworks and contributing to the democratization of art through technology. Maurizio Bolognini's *Collective Intelligence Machines* (CIMs) (2000) series is an early mobile communications work that made use of networks to facilitate audience participation and to link installations in different geographical locations. The images created by the CIMs and projected onto public buildings were modified in real time by participants through SMS (short message service) data uploaded to the installation from their mobile phones. This form of art-based 'electronic democracy' is generative, interactive and public (Bolognini 2008).

Another seminal mobile communications work, Golan Levin's *Dialtones: A Telesymphony* (2001–2), was a collaborative performance in which sounds were produced through the orchestrated ringing of about 200 audience members' mobile phones. Described as a telesymphony performance, *Dialtones* included an interdisciplinary team of composers, engineers and software developers and premiered at the Brucknerhaus Auditorium in Austria as part of the Ars Electronica Festival (Hope 2006: 43). Merging symphony, conceptual artwork and social commentary, the performance highlighted the function of the mobile network as a community and artistic sphere. Each phone was registered at a web terminal and assigned a ring tone before the performance, with seating assignment varying to suit the desired outcomes of the artists. During the performance, the artists and engineers dialled crowd members using customized software that enabled up to 60 phones to go off simultaneously. Three movements, each about ten minutes long, demonstrated the aesthetic possibilities of a real time mobile communications performance. Different sound textures moved across the crowd. Visualizations of the musical structures were projected onto a screen via performer interfaces. The work foregrounded the pervasiveness of digital space made possible through wireless networks. The postdigital dimensions of the performance in Cascone's sense involved disturbance, disruption and noise – all of which tend not to be regarded as pleasing interjections into controlled concert spaces. The artists and engineers comment that 'by directing our attention to the unexplored musical potential of a ubiquitous modern appliance, *Dialtones* inverts our understandings of private sound, public space, electromagnetic etiquette and the fabric of the communications network which connects us' (Levin et al. 2003: 4).

OPEN-SOURCE AND WIKI PROJECTS

Another technology with significant capacity for growth, Open Source Software (OSS) also enables artists to customize software for generating works. OSS has been defined by the Open Source Initiative as software available freely on a non-exclusive commercial basis in which the source code is made available for the creation of derivative works. The principle of open modification, hence the availability of code, is central to OSS (St Laurent 2004: 8–9). Free and Open-Source Software (FOSS) is a similar term for software that is free and open-source, in contrast to proprietary software that is managed strictly by copyright and conceals its source code from users. A notable example of a digital artwork that uses OSS is *0xA* (2005–), an ongoing collaboration between musician Aymeric Mansoux, software artist Chun Lee and others. *0xA* experiments with musical interfaces for live performance through an online repository of codes, virtual instruments and algorithms (see Chapter 5 on digital music). The project has involved a variety of OSS, including Pure Data, an open-source platform designed initially for audio synthesis. Broken beats and glitches are part of the *0xA* aesthetic. Sound effects are produced through an online network of remote collaborators interacting with each other and the code repository. An additional OSS example is UpStage, a platform for 'cyberformance' and education that allows remote performers to combine images, animations, audio, webcams, text and drawing in real time for an online audience. The software was developed in 2003 by Douglas Bagnall in collaboration with the performance troupe Avatar Body Collision.

In addition to Open Source Software, Wikis offer customizable, democratic and interactive mediums for digital arts projects. A wiki is a content management platform that enables users to contribute, modify or remove content collaboratively. Developed in 1995 by programmer Ward Cunningham, the first wiki was known as WikiWikiWeb. Between 27 January and 23 February 2010, artist-programmer Lauren McCarthy performed *Script* in which each day of her life was designed by internet followers. Using the wiki-style Tomorrow Script, participants edited the script and provided directions for the artist's behaviours, clothing and environments for the following day. The durational performance blended online and offline environments in which McCarthy attempted to follow the wiki script carefully (McCarthy 2010). In the area of participatory video art, Jared Nielsen's *Chunks of Sensation* is a collaborative cinematic work produced through the distributed authorship model of wikis (Alexenberg 2011: 53). The project makes use of short segments of video or 'chunks', randomly adding another chunk after each ends. The work is comparable to Nielsen's *The Song that Never Ends*, 'a randomly constructed experimental composition composed of audio tracks contributed by musicians internationally' (Nielsen 2008). These examples demonstrate the application of Dadaistic chance operations to social media platforms.

Reflection

In what ways do the artworks described in the previous section exhibit aspects of postdigital art and the broad aim of humanizing technology? How do these projects combine technical experimentation with social concerns to illuminate human behaviour in the digital era?

BACK TO REALITY: ACTIVISM THROUGH DIGITAL ART

How are artists merging technological experimentation and aesthetic innovation with digital activism? In an era of climate change, Peak Oil and burgeoning disparities between the wealthy and the poor worldwide, activism is an evermore vital dimension of digital art. Known variously as internet activism, online activism, cyberactivism and e-campaigning, digital activism is the use of digital communications platforms, such as the internet and social media, for sociopolitical, gender-based and ecological commentaries, awareness and transformation. Ranging from one-off solo performances to extended collective campaigns, digital activism often mobilizes citizen movements and fosters community-building. This section refers to a number of artworks with elements of digital activism that confront the pressing social, political, economic and environmental realities of our era. In particular, we consider issues of surveillance, equity and energy. Continuing the technological theme of the last section, several works exploit relatively new yet commonplace devices, such as Global Positioning Systems (GPS). In concluding the section, we return to Ascott's concept of moistmedia – previously defined as the intermingling of the biological and digital – through a discussion of a seminal artwork, *Interactive Plant Growing* (1993), that uses living plants as interfaces between human users and the virtual world.

PRIVACY AND SURVEILLANCE

From identity theft and account hacking to cyberstalking and email spamming, privacy is a serious concern for internet users. These issues manifest in digital artworks that confront matters of identity and security in online and offline environments. As artist and academic Mary Flanagan observes, 'so many aspects of everyday "digital" have entered the digital arts: popular political, cultural, and personal concerns are both prompted by or reflected within computer-driven art projects' (Flanagan 2011: 94). However, media artists worked with personal privacy as an artistic theme well before the digital revolution of the 1990s. For example, notions of surveillance and counter-surveillance are evident in David Rokeby's computer-based work *Very Nervous System* (*VNS*) (1986) and others created by the artist during the 1980s (see Chapters 2 and 5). Moreover, net artists of the 1990s, such as Mark Napier, explored issues of privacy through software and browser-based works. More recently, Iranian-born artist Wafaa Bilal's performance work *3rdi* (2010–11) used a camera surgically mounted to the back of his head to capture a posterior view of life and transmit one image per minute to the internet (Bilal 2013). These kinds of artworks interrogate both the irreversible loss and possible preservation of individual privacy as hard drives, websites and social media spaces become more susceptible to political surveillance and public abuse.

The interrelated notions of privacy, surveillance and panopticism seen in early video art are unmistakable in Inbar Barak and Ruth Ron's work *Screen-Wall* (2003) conducted at the Liquid Spaces exhibition at Jerusalem's Israel Museum. The work foregrounded the divisions between the public and private areas of museums. By bringing the private areas – archives, offices, storage areas, guard booths – of the institution into public visibility, *Screen-Wall* captured the inherent power structures between the watcher and the watched, the visible and the invisible. Monitors with still images were placed along the gallery walls. In response to a gallery viewer's movements, live video of a private area of the museum replaced the static images and was streamed to the internet (Green n.d.). Other artworks exploit the concept of self-surveillance or 'sousveillance' (Mann et al. 2003). Interrogation by the US Justice Department after September 11 instigated Hasan Elahi's sousveillance project *Tracking Transience*. Combined with a photographic record of his whereabouts, the web-based work utilizes a tracking bracelet affixed to Elahi's ankle to register his locations at all times on a Google map (Elahi 2013). Furthermore, Avi Rosen's *Digital Skin 2* (2008) is an online video bricolage superimposing self-portraits and personal data onto Google Earth and Google Sky images (Alexenberg 2011: 54).

POLITICAL AND SOCIAL EQUITY

Contemporary artist-activists make use of digital technology to expose political and social inequities, to advocate justice and cultivate public awareness. A compelling example is the work of the practitioner collective Futurefarmers, founded in 1995 by media artist Amy Franceschini as a platform for experimenting with the use of new media art for activism projects. Of particular note is *They Rule* (2001), a web-based work by interaction designer Josh On created in conjunction with Futurefarmers and artist Amy Balkin, known for her work *Public Smog* (2004) (an 'atmospheric park' with constantly changing boundaries). As an interactive online project, *They Rule* was developed by On using Flash, PHP (Hypertext Preprocessor) language and the open-source database management software MySQL. Information visualization is used to map corporate interrelationships among the American 'ruling class', focusing on the board members of major companies, notably General Motors, Coca-Cola and Bristol-Myers Squibb. A directory of data about board members, managed by MySQL, allows users to identify the various connections between members, underscoring the alarming fact that a disproportionately low number of CEOs influence the key decisions of an exceedingly high number of American corporations (Lovejoy 2004: 252–3). In 2001, the first version of the project comprised data from the websites of 100 companies. In 2004, the directory grew to 500 companies and, by 2011, it profiled the top 1,000 American corporations (On 2011).

In recontextualizing insider information about corporations, *They Rule* brings to light big business structures that impact people's lives on an everyday basis but could otherwise remain concealed from public knowledge. Users view, create, save and exchange maps that express the embedded relationships between corporate parties, represented by the minimalistic icons of boardroom tables and rotating office chairs. Josh On explains that *They Rule* 'allows users to browse through these interlocking directories and run searches on the boards and companies ... [the work] is a starting point for research about these powerful individuals and corporations' (On 2011). By enabling users to conceptualize the corporate networks graphically, *They Rule* emphasizes the internet's potential to become a democratizing medium rather than a marketing tool (see Chapter 1 for a discussion of democratization as a key concept for the digital arts). The work is politically and ethically comparable to *The File Room* (1994), an internet archive about censorship cases, as presented in Chapter 2.

A further example of politically and socially conscious digital art comes from the performative work of media artist Joseph DeLappe. *Project 929: Mapping the Solar* (2013) was a 460-mile, ten-day ride in which the artist dragged a large piece of chalk attached to the back of his bicycle for the duration of the trip (Figure 9.2). Depending on the viewer's distance, the continuous chalk line could be seen as a faint trace from the air. The environmental sketch resulting from DeLappe's physical movements can be interpreted as broad-scale site-based political art with an ethic of digital activism. The delineated area is expansive enough to accommodate the world's largest solar facility, which would meet the current energy needs of the entire US. DeLappe encircled Federal lands associated with nuclear testing and military exercises, including the infamous Area 51 (the Nevada Test and Training Range and Groom Lake), Yucca Mountain (site of a major nuclear waste storage facility) and Nellis Air Force Base, all within proximity to Las Vegas. The work's title alludes to the 928 nuclear tests that occurred at the Nevada Test Site between 1951 and 1992; DeLappe's 929th test symbolizes the potential for sustainable technologies to satisfy the long-term energy requirements of nations but with few of the side-effects of nuclear or oil-based sources (DeLappe 2013a). In terms of its digital elements,

Figure 9.2 Joseph DeLappe, *Project 929* (2013). Documentation of durational performance, photograph of performance. Image by Laurie A. Macfee.

Project 929 incorporates the MMORPG software Blue Mars Lite in collaboration with Manifest.AR, an artists' collective focused on the application of augmented reality (AR) technologies to public art and activism. The post-performance AR version of the trip will make it possible for viewers to imagine the immense solar farm envisioned by DeLappe and The Union of Concerned Scientists. During the performance, the artist also made continuous use of GPS technology, as well as a bike-mounted digital camera for live streaming video and real-time documentation (DeLappe 2013b).

ENVIRONMENT AND SUSTAINABILITY

DeLappe's site-based performance is conceptual, political and environmental. Other practitioners also embrace themes of environment, sustainability, biology, genetics and interspecies communication in their artworks, especially through the application of ubiquitous GPS and geographical information software. An intriguing example is bioartist Eduardo Kac's *Lagoogleglyph* (2009), a condensation of the words 'lagoglyph' and 'google'. Kac's previous work *Lagoglyphs* entailed a pictographic language he describes as 'rabbitographic'. The series alludes to Kac's earlier project *GFP Bunny* (2000). This well-known project involved the birth, in the year 2000, of an albino rabbit named Alba, a genetically modified creature that glowed fluorescent green when illuminated with blue light and observed through a special filter (Kac 2005: 266). Alba was produced with a variation of the fluorescent gene occurring naturally in the *Aequorea victoria* jellyfish. Kac characterizes *GFP Bunny* not only as the birth of an unusual modified organism but as 'a complex social event that starts with the creation of a chimerical animal that does not exist in nature' (Kac 2005: 264). Through the theme of interspecies communication (indeed, Alba became Kac's loved pet), the work confronted the ethical ramifications of biological engineering and genetically modified organisms. Kac's lagoglyphs are visual symbols consisting of one green and one black component that represent the living rabbit Alba. For instance, *Lagoglyphs: The Bunny Variations* (2007) is a series of twelve silkscreen prints of lagoglyphs. Hence, *Lagoogleglyph* is the outcome of these concepts and experimentations. The work inserts large lagoglyphs into different outdoor settings where they become globally viewable through Google Earth. The 2009 installation of *Lagoogleglyph* included a pixelated lagoglyph (again, representing Alba) placed atop the Oi Futuro building in Brazil. The lagoglyph was customized by Kac for optimal viewing by the Google Earth satellite (Alexenberg 2011: 39). These kinds of works (hybridizing digital and physical spaces) call attention to the forms of writing and inscription that underlie our interactions with the environment and non-human nature (Ryan 2012).

An example of public art with ecological overtones is *Mussel Choir* (2012) by artist-engineer Natalie Jeremijenko. The work enables members of the public to monitor the conditions of aquatic environments through a sonic symphony produced by mussels and their ecosystems. In 2012, a test version of the work premiered at the Venice Biennale, with permanent installations planned for the Hudson River of New York and the Melbourne Docklands. Supported by Carbon Arts and the Australian Network for Art and Technology (ANAT), the Melbourne installation (forthcoming, 2014) uses mussels to amass information about and artistically represent the water quality of the Docklands habitat (Carbon Arts n.d.). The remarkable ability of mussels to filter water is gauged by hall effect sensors, normally used for electronic applications, such as speed gauging. The hall sensors measure the opening and closing of the mussel shells. The data is converted into sound patterns – which become the incantations of the mussels. Thus, evoking Ascott's concept of moistmedia, the behaviours of the creatures correspond to the behaviours of the installation in which the activities of mussels in response to environmental conditions (e.g. seasons, weather and pollution) are translated to sound. The project's audio mappings include sound pitch to water depth, timbre to pollution levels, and tempo to the shells' opening and closing. *Mussel Choir* highlights the fragility and significance of aquatic environments, making audible the elusive biological mechanisms of these irreplaceable aquatic creatures. The work engenders public awareness of ecological issues, connecting the biological to the digital.

MOISTMEDIA AND LIVING INTERFACES

Jeremijenko's *Mussel Choir* is a striking example of moistmedia. As mentioned at the beginning of this chapter, moistmedia comprises the intersection of the digital and the biological. Ascott characterizes 'moistmedia' as the merging of the 'dry' plastic and pixels of the digital realm with the 'wet' molecules and matter of the biological world (Ascott 2000: 2). A play on the term 'multimedia', moistmedia combines inanimate computer hardware and software (disks and bytes) with animate bodies and environments (neurons and genes). In Ascott's vision, moistmedia leads to 'edge-life' or new forms of human identity, social systems and perceptions existing at the crossroads of the virtual and the real. *Mussel Choir* demonstrates how moistmedia can become agents of social and environmental change (Ascott 2000: 4). In particular, Ascott is interested in the possibility of 'cyberbotany' as the intelligent application of botanical architectures and physiologies to the problems of the everyday physical world and to the aesthetic dimensions of creative practices (Ascott 2000: 6).

Moistmedia implies the proposition that art can encompass a dynamic interplay between dry pixels and wet molecules – between the hyperreal world of virtuality and the material world of biology – towards the humanization of technology. An exemplary case of the moistmedia concept is Laurent Mignonneau and Christa Sommerer's *Interactive Plant Growing* (1993), which positioned living plants as the interfaces between participants and the computer. The work consisted of interactions between five plants and five (or more) participants who regulated the growth of digital plants by touching the living ones before them. Coming near to or touching the living plants wired to the computer caused responses in the simulated plant field (Alexenberg 2011: 92). The installation included a screen where the virtual garden was generated and five real plants, each placed on a pedestal at eye level with most of the participants. For example, touching the cactus reset the computerized garden. Measurements of the differences in electrical potentials between the plants and the visitors formed the basis of the physical-to-digital communications (Martins et al. 2008: 123). All in all, the work redefined the notion of an interface as a dynamic site of interaction and exchange rather than a hindrance to communication, as explored in Chapter 7. The use of a 'natural' interface allowed the artwork to become a micro-system capable of spontaneity and complexity.

Reflection

What issues do you think digital art could or should address? In principle, if not in detail, how might artists address these issues? What could be the aim or aims of the digital artist of the future?

FINAL WORD: DIGITAL ARTS COMMUNITIES

As this book has shown, digital art is a complex, dynamic and inclusive field that merges aesthetics, technology and the global issues addressed in the previous section. While hybridizing art and science, digital practitioners cannot exist in isolation and must continuously be energized by online and offline communities of practice. Indeed, the interpersonal, community-based side of digital art extends beyond the use of social media. Multi-nodal networking events known as Dorkbots and PechaKuchas alternate between online and physical environments, providing vibrant venues for collectively pushing the boundaries of arts paradigms in the digital era. Dorkbots are grassroots gatherings of artists, engineers, technicians, designers, scientists, inventors, curators, conservators, appreciators and others involved in electronic art. Begun in 2000 by Douglas Repetto at the Columbia University Computer Music Center and currently with 90 chapters worldwide, Dorkbots are managed by volunteers and have minimal membership structures. Their motto is 'people doing strange things with electricity'. Similarly, Astrid Klein and Mark Dytham founded PechaKucha nights in 2003 to provide venues for young designers to meet informally and exchange ideas. In closing *Digital Arts: An Introduction to New Media*, we suggest that the digital art of the future will be catalyzed by a unprecedented integration of the virtual and the material about which we can now only speculate. Indeed, it is an exciting prospect that we are poised to witness.

ANNOTATED GUIDE TO FURTHER READING

Chapter 2 Key Concepts, Artistic Influences and Technological Origins of the Digital Arts

A number of outstanding introductions to electronic and digital art were published in the 2000s. Christiane Paul's *Digital Art* (2003) explores key themes and discusses in detail the difference between digital technologies as a tool (27–65) and digital technologies as a medium (66–137). Although daunting for beginners at times, Paul's analysis is well-informed and scholarly. Margot Lovejoy's *Digital Currents: Art in the Electronic Age* (2004) presents a comprehensive guide to the field accompanied by generous examples of influential artworks and artists. Her earlier book *Postmodern Currents: Art and Artists in the Age of Electronic Media* (1989) addresses modernist and postmodernist strands of art, as well as computer and video mediums. Her more recent edited work *Context Providers: Conditions of Meaning in Media Arts* (2011) argues that the digital arts should be understood in their multiple artistic, conceptual and historical contexts. Bruce Wands' *Art of the Digital Age* (2006) gives an accessible overview of the digital arts, highlighting imaging, sculpture, installation, performance, music and sound art, alongside software, database, game and net art. The large format of the book and its colour illustrations should make it a requirement for students in the field. Medium-specific books of value include Michael Rush's *Video Art* (2003) with extensive treatment of the historical roots of video-based works. On the theoretical front, Lev Manovich's writings, particularly *The Language of New Media* (2001a) and his essays, are pivotal to conceptualizing new media arts. There are also a few noteworthy introductions to postmodernism and poststructuralism of prime importance to students in the field. Catherine Belsey's *Poststructuralism: A Very Short Introduction* (2002) is an accessible foray into this theoretical area. Understanding the contexts of the digital arts is also about appreciating specific artists and artworks. For critical commentary on Stelarc's work, particularly his investigation of embodiment and the cyborg, see Clarke's *Stelarc: The Monograph* (2005). Nam June Paik's short essay 'Art and Satellite' in *Theories and Documents of*

Contemporary Art: A Sourcebook of Artists' Writings (1996) gives a glimpse into Paik's views of technology and art.

Chapter 3 Dumb Visions and Fabulous Images

Digital photography and visual art are well documented in a number of publications that feature high-quality images and overviews. For a general overview, the Thames and Hudson *World of Art* series is recommended, in particular Rush's *New Media in Late 20th-Century Art* (1999), Michael Rush's *New Media in Art* (2005, new edition) and Christiane Paul's *Digital Art* (2003). These books discuss the many strands of digital art with a strong focus on visual art, photography, virtual realities and installation art. Again, Bruce Wands' *Art of the Digital Age* (2006) offers spectacular images and substantial quotes from the artists themselves. Margot Lovejoy's *Digital Currents: Art in the Electronic Age* (2004) provides an excellent overview of theoretical frameworks around all digital art. Fred Ritchin's *After Photography* (2009) provides a discussion on the cultural impact of digital images, and Sylvia Wolf's *The Digital Eye: Photographic Art in the Electronic Age* (2010) presents a recent historical overview of important contributions to digital photography. The background to computer art and early developments in animation and video art is discussed in Cynthia Goodman's *Digital Visions: Computers and Art* (1987) and, for an engaging and thorough examination of digital video art, Chris Meigh-Andrews' *A History of Video Art: The Development of Form and Function* (2006) is comprehensive and provides a focus on the European traditions. Frank Popper's *Art of the Electronic Age* (1993) provides useful lists of techniques and approaches to video art and photography, while Gene Youngblood's *Expanded Cinema* (1970) outlines precedents to digitization, including a very useful examination of the difference between digital and analogue technologies. Lev Manovich's *The Language of New Media* (2001a) gives an in-depth examination of the nature of the digital, particularly in relation to film and photography.

Chapter 4 Dancing at the Speed of Light

Performance is one of the least documented of the digital arts, and most contributions are written by practising artists. However, the key text is without a doubt Steve Dixon's *Digital Performance: A History of New Media in Theatre, Dance, Performance Art and Installation* (2007). This is an informative and comprehensive overview of many forms of digital performance with many excellent case studies and theoretical underpinnings, including an extensive examination of 'metal performance' from the perspective of queer politics. In addition, Johannes Birringer *Media and Performance: Along the Border* (1998) provides a more poetic and somewhat personalized overview with a welcome focus on dance. Christiane Paul's *Digital Art* (2003) discusses some digital performance, with a focus on the integration of video with performance.

Marvin Carlson's *Performance: A Critical Introduction* (2004) is a good overview to the theory behind performance, and gives an excellent introduction to the genesis of live art. Gabriella Giannachi's *Virtual Theatres: An Introduction* (2004) offers a discussion of the relationships between theatre, performance and digital arts. Brenda Laurel's *Computers as Theatre* (2013) provides an interesting examination of the 'theatre' of computers in our everyday lives, whereas Sue-Ellen Case's *The Domain Matrix: Performing Lesbian at the End of Print Culture* (1997) provides an engaging feminist perspective with a focus on dance. Donna Haraway's essay 'A Cyborg Manifesto: Science, Technology and Socialist-Feminism in the Late Twentieth Century' (1985) is an inspiring socialist-feminist look into the possibilities of technology for social order. Examples of how multiple media have been integrated into theatre and dance since World War II can be found in RoseLee Goldberg's most recent edition of *Performance Art: From Futurism to the Present* (2004). There is much more writing about cyborgs and virtual reality. In addition to Howard Rheingold's seminal text, *Virtual Reality* (1991), a number of other books discuss the cultural impacts of the form, which often includes a discussion about the impact of interactivity in art.

Chapter 5 From Scratchy to Glitchy

Despite a plethora of books on electronic music, there is little literature that focuses on digital sound and music specifically. A wide range of literature on digital tools and techniques is available. However this is a rapidly changing field where many software and hardware developments take place in short time frames. Perhaps the best book currently available is *The Routledge Guide to Music Technology* (Holmes 2006) by Thom Holmes. Christoph Cox and Daniel Warner's edited collection *Audio Culture: Readings in Modern Music* (2006) is an excellent collection of short essays by important practitioners and theorists around many aspects of contemporary electronic music practice. The most recent edition of Thom Holmes' book *Electronic and Experimental Music: Technology, Music and Culture* (third edition, 2008) gives a comprehensive overview of the development of electronic music, as does Joel Chadabe's *Electronic Sound: The Past and Promise of Electronic Music* (1997), which includes discussions of a wide variety of works. The second edition of Peter Manning's *Electronic and Computer Music* (2004) is a comprehensive and detailed exploration of electronic music created with computers. Douglas Kahn's *Noise Water Meat* (2001) is a thorough and creative philosophical study into sound art, music and noise in the twentieth century, whereas Caleb Kelly's *Cracked Media: The Sound of Malfunction* (2009) provides an excellent overview of postdigital concepts as well as other examples of damaged media in the context of music consumerism. Websites such as <http://www.mediaartnet.org> provide a comprehensive overview of digital aesthetics, with copious examples of sound works available to be streamed on the internet. Curtis Roads' *Microsound* (2004) is a detailed investigation into the history of synthesis, with an emphasis on more recent digital developments. Michael Bull and Les Back's edited collection, *The Auditory Culture Reader* (2004) is a collection of articles that examine the challenges to listening in the modern world, brought on by a range of factors from the use of portable digital devices to the implications of traffic noise, presented in a cultural theory context. *The Wire: Adventures in Modern Music* is a monthly English periodical that features reviews of and interviews about contemporary music practices, with considerable coverage on electronic music from around the world. Joanna Demers' *Listening through the Noise: The Aesthetics of Experimental Electronic Music* (2010) is an excellent and accessible book that discusses the evolution and challenges of new digital music, providing some ideas about how electronic music and its performance can be best understood from an aesthetic perspective. Mark Prendergast's *The Ambient Century: From Mahler to Trance: The Evolution of Sound in the Electronic Age* (2001) explores a century of change in music, and provides an excellent bridge between the worlds of classical and rock music. *The Art of Digital Music: 56 Visionary Artists Reveal their Creative Secrets* (2004) edited by David Battino and Kelli Richards is a practical yet brief look at more commercial music makers, and comes with a DVD of audio tracks, interviews and video.

Chapter 6 The Possibilities of a Web

There are several key texts about internet art that you can use to further research this exciting area of the digital arts. Rachel Greene's *Internet Art* (2004) is the first broadly available critical work on net art. Greene had become familiar with net art as the editor of Rhizome.org. Her book offers no firm definition, but rather gives a comprehensive overview of the history, theory, aesthetics and technological foundations of the genre. Josephine Bosma's *Nettitudes: Let's Talk Net Art* (2011) is a well-informed and incisive account of internet art from an author who has been closely involved with the movement and its key artists from the beginning. Eduardo Kac's *Telepresence & Bio Art* (2005) provides fascinating examples of internet-based projects from Kac's extensive body of work. In particular, Chapter 2, 'The Internet and the Future of Art', is worth investigating. Jon Ippolito's writings provide an important theoretical perspective on the position of internet art within the wider art world. In addition to his article 'Ten Myths of Internet Art' (2002), his *At the Edge of Art* (2006) (co-authored by Joline Blais) is a lavishly illustrated book containing numerous excellent examples from the field's leading practitioners. The edited collection *Network Art: Practices and Positions* (Corby, 2006) includes essays by key figures in the study of internet art, such as Bosma, Tilman Baumgärtel, Mark Amerika and 0100101110101101.ORG. Specifically, Charlie Gere's chapter, 'The History of Network Art', gives a useful historical overview, linking net art to technological and artistic developments after the Industrial Revolution. In terms of theoretical positions, Marshall McLuhan's *Understanding Media: The Extensions of Man* (1964) is essential reading for understanding communications technologies. However, in reading McLuhan and other theorists for that matter, it is crucial to consult critical commentaries on their ideas. Works such as S. D. Neill's *Clarifying McLuhan* (1993) can assist you in building the theoretical foundation for understanding internet art.

Chapter 7 I Want it Now

Readings on digital arts distribution are scattered across a number of arts and technology publications. Understanding distribution platforms also requires a willingness to engage with the technical aspects of programming. In terms of theory, Kim Toffoletti's *Baudrillard Reframed: Interpreting Key Thinkers for the Arts* (2011) is an excellent, accessible introduction to the work of Jean Baudrillard. However, it is also best to go to the source and read Baudrillard's writings in translation from French. Baudrillard's key works *Simulacra and Simulation* (1981) and *Symbolic Exchange and Death* (1993) are more accessible when read in tandem with the commentary of Toffoletti and other scholars. Widely regarded as a key text in cultural, literary and art-historical studies, Walter Benjamin's influential essay 'The Work of Art in the Age of Mechanical Reproduction' has itself been reproduced in a myriad of places. Gigi Durham and Douglas Kellner's edited collection *Media and Cultural Studies: Key Works* (2006) provides a complete version of Benjamin's essay, along with other essential resources for students of media studies, cultural studies and communications. For guidance, Robert Hullot-Kentor's essay on Benjamin's notion of mechanical reproduction in the book *Mapping Benjamin: The Work of Art in the Digital Age* (Gumbrecht and Marrinan 2003) is an example of the numerous critical commentaries on Benjamin's oeuvre. Lawrence Lessig's *Free Culture: The Nature and Future of Creativity* (2004) offers a lively yet critical account of copyright, intellectual property and Creative Commons licensing by a key thinker in digital innovation. Bruce Wands' *Art of the Digital Age* (2006) is a copiously illustrated and readable introduction to the digital arts and themes of distribution – surveying sculpture, installation, virtual reality, performance, music, sound, animation, video, software, database, game and internet-based forms. Along with Rachel Greene's *Internet Art* (2004), Wands' coffee table text provides a sound (pardon the pun) overview of the ways in which digital art is found, downloaded and distributed. Jonathan Sterne's *MP3: The Meaning of a Format* (2012) offers an intriguing critical overview of the MP3 file format from a cultural studies perspective. Compression technologies are examined in a number of genre-specific texts, as well as the literature of computer science and programming. Ida Mengyi Pu's *Fundamental Data Compression* (2006) and Khalid Sayood's edited collection *Lossless Compression Handbook* (2003) provide general places to start.

Chapter 8 Ways of Belonging

This chapter has benefitted from a range of resources on the digital arts, spanning the archive, notation systems and information technologies. To begin with, Josephine Bosma's chapter 'The Gap Between Now and Then: On the Conservation of Memory' in her book *Nettitudes* (2011) offers an insider's overview of the challenges facing the conservation of digital artworks. We acknowledge Bosma's valuable chapter in the overall construction of this brief account of preservation. John Barber (2008) provides a pithy but accessible introduction to digital archiving in his chapter 'Digital Archiving and "The New Screen"'. Moreover, Bruce Wands' short chapter 'The Future of Digital Art' in his book *Art of the Digital Age* (2006) provides another brief but important sketch of the challenges facing digital arts conservators. In terms of theory, Boris Groys' *Under Suspicion: A Phenomenology of Media* (2012) is a key work for those interested in the archive as a cultural concept. Additionally, Jussi Parikka and Wolfgang Ernst's *Digital Memory and the Archive* (2013) offers a starting point for understanding Ernst's interesting notion of working memory. Philip Auslander's article 'The Performativity of Performance Documentation' (2006) is a key discussion of the relationship between preservation and performativity. Furthermore, Daren Brabham's *Crowdsourcing* (2013a) is the definitive publication on crowdsourcing as a problem-solving approach applied in digital archiving schemes. Lewis Hyde's *The Gift: Imagination and the Erotic Life of Property* (1999) provides an outstanding entry point for learning about the notion of the gift economy through anthropological perspectives. For specific notation systems, Jon Ippolito's writings on the Variable Media Questionnaire and the particular demands of digital arts preservation are incisive, especially his article 'Accommodating the Unpredictable' in *Permanence Through Change: The Variable Media Approach* (2003a). Finally, there are a number of websites to consult for further reference about issues of archiving, preservation and remembering. UbuWeb (http://www.ubuweb.com) is certainly worth visiting for those interested in analysing an archival project that has outlasted its critics. In fact, most of Kenneth Goldsmith's online articles on archiving and nude media offer a slightly radical activist viewpoint on arts preservation in the public domain and, for this reason, are worth consulting.

EXERCISES AND QUESTIONS

Chapter 2 Key Concepts, Artistic Influences and Technological Origins of the Digital Arts

Exercises

1. Visit Victoria Vesna's internet artwork *Bodies INCorporated* (1996) (http://www. bodiesinc.ucla.edu). With your classmates, write down the ways in which the work allows you to manipulate virtual human bodies.
2. Read through the history of censorship in *The File Room* (http://www.thefileroom. org). Identify a few instances of censorship that are relevant to our discussion of art.
3. Following the example of Marcel Duchamp, design and discuss a 'ready-made' artwork from a found object near you now.
4. Outline an interactive work of your invention using at least three of the following media: television, radio, video, film, music or the internet.
5. Think about a public artwork with which you and your classmates are familiar. Discuss the role the piece plays in the community where it is located.

Questions

1. Should found objects and conceptual works be considered art? Why or why not? If possible, provide examples.
2. What is the distinction between media and a medium?
3. How does a tool differ from a medium, in terms of how artists use technology?
4. What types of technological development have had a bearing upon the development of digital art?
5. How might digital artists use social media in their works today?

Chapter 3 Dumb Visions and Fabulous Images

Exercises

1. Compare an old photograph to a more recent digital image you have made yourself. What elements make the digital image different from the old photograph, and what elements from your digital image could contribute to the idea of the sublime?

2. Make a short video on a mobile device that has no linear narrative, and no editing. Display your film on the mobile device as a site-specific installation. Explain the rationale behind your film to your class.

3. Apply a technique used by digital photographers to manipulate an image of yourself, in a way that you think changes an important aspect of your appearance. You may use cropping, colour changing, perspective distortion, compositing or cut and pasting. There are many free software tools to enable you to do this.

Questions

1. Do you think that the possibility for digital images to distort reality has an impact on our understanding of the world? What are some images that you think misrepresent your own idea of the world?

2. American artist Dara Birnbaum (b. 1946) created an influential series of works entitled *Technology/Transformation: Wonder Woman* (1978) that manipulates images from the 1970s television show *Wonder Woman*. How does this artwork use digital technologies to interact with television and the myth of the superhero?

3. Do you agree with Le Grice's idea that narrative is linked with natural progression of time, and cannot be disrupted? Create an argument for or against this idea of linear narrative as a 'natural' phenomenon in film and animations, and cite examples.

Chapter 4 Dancing at the Speed of Light

Exercises

1. Create numerous short videos on mobile devices that can be used as a 'backdrop' to a poetry reading. Use text as well as effects and sound.

2. Create an 'interactive' theatre script, where audience participation is part of the action. Create it on a computer and use hyperlinks to choose different paths within the story.

3. Enact a performance of any kind over video conferencing to a friend. Give special consideration to your 'sets' using only digital devices in the background.

Questions

1. Do you think Artaud's idea of the double will continue to be relevant as technologies continue to develop?

2. Jeffrey Shaw, discussed in Chapter 3, disputes the term virtual reality, preferring the term augmented reality. Why do you think this is?

3. Discuss the relationship between cinema and virtual reality.

4. Do you believe fiction has been able to predict or shape digital technologies and

our need for them? Discuss this in relation to books or films that you think may have done so.

Chapter 5 From Scratchy to Glitchy

Exercises

1. Try and find an LP record made before 1970, and a turntable to play it on. Or find a cassette, and a cassette player. Search for the same album or track online. Compare the audio quality of each, and discuss the key differences.
2. Make a short audio recording on your mobile device of someone speaking. Search the internet for a free audio editing software program to download. With the aid of the 'magnify' tool, apply the techniques of sampling, cut and paste, fade, cross fade, looping and compressing to the recording, and save it as a format that can be distributed on the internet. Make sure to edit the work in such a way it no longer sounds like spoken words.
3. How many songs do you have on your mobile phone or portable audio player? Add up the total time they would take to listen to, and compare this with the length of a CD, LP or cassette recording.

Questions

1. Consider any genre of electronic music. Describe the characteristics of the genre, and discuss how this relates to the historic precedents of electronic music.
2. Do you agree that enjoying a laptop performance requires the audience to have different expectations of the performance? Discuss this issue with reference to Walter Benjamin's discussion of the aura (see Chapter 3).
3. The term 'postdigital' as used by Kim Cascone describes a music made by errors in digital systems. Discuss ways that this has occurred in other art forms, and any similarity or difference between the disciples.

Chapter 6 The Possibilities of a Web

Exercises

1. Create a 'codework' poem using the source code of one of your favourite websites. In your poem, make use of both 'natural' language and programming language.
2. Devise a narrative email artwork involving a network of users, participants and viewers. The artwork should tell a story, which each participant helps to write. Use text, images, video and other multimedia tools in collectively telling the story.
3. Plan and, where possible, execute a brief internet artwork that uses a video-conferencing platform, such as Skype.
4. Create a conceptual internet artwork employing Twitter or Facebook.

Questions

1. Do you think McLuhan's notion of the 'global village' will continue to be important to the evolution of internet art?
2. Do you agree that internet art fosters the agency of users, participants and viewers? Why or why not?
3. What is the relationship between internet art and conceptual art? What are some of the conceptual underpinnings of the artworks featured as case studies in this chapter?
4. What defines an artist as an 'internet artist'? Might some artists prefer not to be labelled as such? Why or why not?
5. Internet art points to broader relationships between art, science and engineering. What might be some of the difficulties faced by internet artists in crossing between these different areas?

Chapter 7 I Want it Now

Exercises

1. Devise a folksonomy for an archive of digital art based on the examples found in the chapter, such as Flickr. Choose either audio, video or graphic works, and propose a system for user-driven classification through tags and other metadata.
2. Design a new media-based distribution strategy for a digital artwork of your own making. Make sure to outline how the artwork will be found by users and whether or not you will place restrictions on how the public can use the work.
3. Using Google, perform an online search for digital video. Compare and contrast the features of three websites that provide access and decide which website of the three facilitates distribution the best.
4. In a group, upload an audio file to SoundCloud. Over the next week, keep a log of any timed comments you receive. With your group members, outline how the SoundCloud-based social media you participated in during the week increased the visibility of your file.
5. Read Walter Benjamin's essay 'The Work of Art in the Age of Mechanical Reproduction', summarizing in one page the relevance of Benjamin's thinking to digital art today.

Questions

1. What are some of the potential drawbacks of Creative Commons licensing?
2. Do you agree that Lessig's notion of 'free culture' promotes innovation, experimentation and access? How might free culture limit the creativity of digital artists?
3. How is quality control managed in a folksonomy? Can you ensure the accuracy of online information and content when there is no central 'taxonomist'?

4. Does the increased interactivity of social media inherently support creativity? Or does it depend on the artist or project to use social media wisely to his or her benefit?

5. Is the distribution of digital art always based in democratic ideals? How might capitalistic profiteering and private enterprise impact access to digital artworks?

6. What kinds of strategies could be implemented to increase the availability of digital art to disadvantaged populations?

Chapter 8 Ways of Belonging

Exercises

1. Devise a conservation plan for one of the artworks mentioned in this book. Outline which elements of the artwork you would prioritize in producing a score.

2. Enter the URL for Mark Napier's *net.flag* (Case Study 8.1) and produce an internet flag: (http://webart.guggenheim.org/netflag/). With your fellow students, take note of the symbolic dimensions of the flag you create.

3. Watch the online tutorial for the Variable Media Questionnaire (variablemediaquestionnaire.net). Identify the steps involved in signing up a project and adding records to the VMQ.

4. Check out *The Unreliable Archivist* (Case Study 8.4) at its location on the Walker Art Center website. Analyse how the project uses äda'web content to parody the act of archiving and the archivist.

5. Search UbuWeb (http://www.ubuweb.com) for your favourite writers or visual artists. Keep a log of the steps involved in locating information and note any drawbacks or advantages to the minimalistic design of the repository.

Questions

1. To what extent and in what ways have digital practices democratized the archiving of art? In what ways might archiving exclude certain individuals or groups?

2. Critically reflect on the practice of crowdsourcing. For example, how might it actually impede efforts to preserve digital artworks?

3. What are some of the limitations of storing digital artworks? Is Ippolito justified in parodying the archivist in the new media era? Do you think the role of the archivist has changed since *The Unreliable Archivist* (1998)?

4. Do you think that Goldsmith's practice of posting items to UbuWeb without the permission of the creator is ethical? Outline the potential issues involved.

5. How much input should audience members have in the preservation of digital artworks in comparison to the professional opinions of artists, curators and technicians?

6. Do you think that it is right for artists to use archival content to make new work?

7. Why is Bosma concerned about potential 'digital dark ages'? What might cause them, and how might that be negative for society more generally?

BIBLIOGRAPHY

386 DX (1998), '386 DX is For Sale Now! – Buy It in Electroboutique!', http://www.easylife. org/386dx/ (accessed 10 July 2013).

Abelson, H., Adida, B., Linksvayer, M. and Yergler, N. (2012), 'CC REL: The Creative Commons Rights Expression Language', in M. Dulong de Rosnay and J. C. De Martin (eds), *The Digital Public Domain: Foundations for an Open Culture*, Cambridge: Open Book Publishers, pp. 149–88.

ABI Research (2013), 'Wearable Computing Devices, Like Apple's iWatch, Will Exceed 485 Million Annual Shipments by 2018', http://www.abiresearch.com/press/wearable-computing-devices-like-apples-iwatch-will (accessed 16 October 2013).

Alberro, A. (1999), 'Reconsidering Conceptual Art, 1966–1977', in A. Alberro and B. Stimson (eds), *Conceptual Art: A Critical Anthology*, Cambridge, MA: MIT Press, pp. xvi–xxxvii.

—(2003), *Conceptual Art and the Politics of Publicity*, Cambridge, MA: MIT Press.

Alexenberg, M. (2011), *The Future of Art in a Postdigital Age: From Hellenistic to Hebraic Consciousness*, Bristol: Intellect.

Allain, P. (2012), *The Routledge Companion to Theatre and Performance*, Hoboken, NJ: Taylor and Francis.

Allen, G. (2003), *Roland Barthes*, London: Routledge.

Amerika, M. (2011), *Remix the Book*. Minneapolis, MN: University of Minnesota Press.

Anderson, P. (2012), *Web 2.0 and Beyond: Principles and Technologies*, Boca Raton, FL: CRC Press.

Artaud, A. (1958 [1938]), *The Theatre and its Double*, trans. M. C. Richards, New York: Weidenfeld.

Ascott, R. (2000), 'Edge-Life: Technoetic Structures and Moist Media', in R. Ascott (ed.), *Art, Technology, Consciousness: mind@large*, Bristol: Intellect, pp. 2–6.

—(2001), 'Behaviourist Art and the Cybernetic Vision', in R. Packer and K. Jordan (eds), *Multimedia: From Wager to Virtual Reality*, New York: W. W. Norton & Company, pp. 95–103.

—(2003), 'Ten Wings', in E. Shanken (ed.), *Telematic Embrace: Visionary Theories of Art, Technology, and Consciousness*, Berkeley, CA: University of California Press, pp. 184–5.

—(2008), 'Pixels and Particles: The Path to Syncretism', in M. Alexenberg (ed.), *Educating Artists for the Future: Learning at the Intersections of Art, Science, Technology and Culture*, Bristol: Intellect, pp. 47–60.

Auslander, P. (2006), 'The Performativity of Performance Documentation', *PAJ: A Journal of Performance and Art*, 28 (3): 1–10.

—(2008), *Liveness: Performance in a Mediatized Culture* (2nd edn), London: Routledge.

Bainbridge, W. S. (2004), 'Mosaic', in W. S. Bainbridge (ed.), *Berkshire Encyclopedia of*

Human-Computer Interaction: When Science Fiction Becomes Science Fact: Volume 2, Great Barrington, MA: Berkshire Publishing, pp. 454–6.

Balbi, G. (2013), 'Telecommunications', in P. Simonson, J. Peck, R. Craig and J. Jackson (eds), *The Handbook of Communication History*, New York: Routledge, pp. 209–22.

Balsamo, A. (2000), 'The Virtual Body in Cyberspace', in D. Bell and B. M. Kennedy (eds), *Cybercultures Reader*, London: Routledge, pp. 489–503.

Barber, J. (2008), 'Digital Archiving and "The New Screen"', in R. Adams, S. Gibson and S. Arisona (eds), *Transdisciplinary Digital Art: Sound, Vision and the New Screen*, Berlin: Springer, pp. 110–19.

Barthes, R. (1977), *Image, Music, Text*, trans. S. Heath, London: Fontana Press.

—(1981), *Camera Lucida: Reflections on Photography* (1st edn), New York: Hill and Wang.

—(1990), *S/Z*, trans. R. Miller, Oxford: Blackwell Publishing.

Bartlett, M. (2010), '#24hEcho', http://www.manbartlett.com/24hEcho/ (accessed 17 October 2013).

Battino, D and Richards, K. (eds). (2004), *The Art of Digital Music: 56 Visionary Artists and Insiders Reveal Their Creative Secrets*, San Francisco, CA: Backbeat Books.

Baudrillard, J. (1981), *Simulacra and Simulation*, Ann Arbor, MI: University of Michigan Press.

—(1993), *Symbolic Exchange and Death*, trans. I. H. Grant. London: Sage, in association with Theory, Culture and Society, School of Health, Social and Policy Studies, University of Teesside.

Baumgärtel, T. (2001). Net.art 2.0: *New Materials Towards Net Art*, Nürnberg: Verlag für Moderne Kunst.

Bazzichelli, T. (2008), *Networking: The Net as Artwork*, Aarhus: Digital Aesthetics Research Center.

Bell, D. (2000), *An Introduction to Cybercultures*, London: Routledge.

Bell, J. (2010), 'Archiving Experience: The Third Generation Variable Media Questionnaire, v1.1', http://thoughtmesh.net/publish/393.php (accessed 26 July 2013).

Belsey, C. (2002), *Poststructuralism: A Very Short Introduction*, Oxford: Oxford University Press.

Benjamin, W. (1980), 'A Short History of Photography', in A. Trachtenberg (ed.), *Classical Essays in Photography*, New Haven, CT: Leete Island Books, pp. 119–217.

—(2006), 'The Work of Art in the Age of Mechanical Reproduction', in M. G. Durham and D. Kellner (eds), *Media and Cultural Studies: Key Works*, Malden, MA: Blackwell Publishing, pp. 18–40.

Berger, J. (1990), *Ways of Seeing*, London: Penguin.

Bijvoet, M. (1990), 'How Intimate Can Art and Technology Really Be? – A Survey of the Art and Technology Movement of the Sixties', in P. Hayward (ed.), *Culture, Technology & Creativity in the Late Twentieth Century*, London: John Libbey and Company, pp. 15–38.

Bilal, W. (2013), '3rdi', http://3rdi.me/ (accessed 18 October 2013).

Birringer, J. (1998), *Media and Performance: Along the Border*, Baltimore, MD and London: Johns Hopkins University Press.

Bishop, C. (2007), 'Nicolas Bourriaud', in D. Costello and J. Vickery (eds), *Art: Key Contemporary Thinkers*, New York: Berg.

Blais, J. and Ippolito, J. (2006), *At the Edge of Art*, London: Thames & Hudson.

Blecksmith, A. (2011), 'Computer Imaging', in J. Marter (ed.), *The Grove Encyclopedia of American Art*, Oxford and New York: Oxford University Press, pp. 526–7.

Bodies INCorporated. (n.d.), 'Welcome to Bodies INCorporated', http://www.bodiesinc. ucla.edu/welcome.html (accessed 7 September 2013).

Bogost, I. (n.d.), 'A Slow Year: A Chapbook of Game Poems for Atari VCS, PC and Mac', http://www.bogost.com/games/game_poems.shtml (accessed 16 October 2013).

Bolognini, M. (2008), 'From Interactivity to Democracy. Towards a Post-Digital Generative Art', paper presented at the Artmedia X International Symposium, *Ethics, Aesthetics and Techno-Communication: The Future of Meaning*, Bibliothèque Nationale de France, Paris, 12–13 December.

Bolter, J. D. and Grusin, R. (1996), 'Remediation', *Configurations*, 4 (3): 311–58.

—(2000), *Remediation: Understanding New Media*, London and Cambridge, MA: MIT Press.

Bosma, J. (2006), 'Art as Experience: Meet the Active Audience', in T. Corby (ed.), *Network Art: Practices and Positions*, Abingdon: Routledge, pp. 24–39.

—(2011), *Nettitudes: Let's Talk Net Art*, Rotterdam and Amsterdam: Nai Publishers and Institute of Network Cultures.

Bourriaud, N. (2002), *Relational Aesthetics*, trans. S. Pleasance and F. Woods, Dijon: Les Presses du Réel.

Brabham, D. (2013a), *Crowdsourcing*, Cambridge, MA: MIT Press.

—(2013b), 'Crowdsourcing: A Model for Leveraging Online Communities', in A. Delwiche and J. J. Henderson (eds), *The Participatory Cultures Handbook*, Abingdon: Taylor & Francis, pp. 120–9.

Bracken, C. C. and Botta, R. (2010), 'Telepresence and Television', in C. C. Bracken and P. Skalski (eds), *Immersed in Media: Telepresence in Everyday Life*, New York: Routledge, pp. 39–62.

Braester, Y. (2005), 'Feng Mengbo', in E. Davis (ed.), *Encyclopedia of Contemporary Chinese Culture*, Abingdon: Routledge, pp. 202–3.

Breeze, M. (2012), *Human Readable Messages [Mezangelle 2003–2011]*. Vienna, Austria: Traumawien.

Breznican, A. and Strauss, G. (2005). 'Where Have All the Moviegoers Gone?', *USA Today*, 23 June, Section L: 1.

Budd, D. (2005), *The Language of Art Knowledge*, Petaluma, CA: Pomegranate Communications.

Buford, J., Yu, H. and Lua, E. K. (2009), *P2P: Networking and Applications*, Burlington, MA: Elsevier.

Bull, M. and Back, L. (eds) (2004), *The Auditory Culture Reader*, London: Bloomsbury Academic.

Burdea, G. and Coiffet, P. (2003), *Virtual Reality Technology* (2nd edn), Hoboken, NJ: John Wiley & Sons.

Burgess, J. and Green, J. (2009), *YouTube: Online Video and Participatory Culture*, Cambridge: Polity Press.

Busoni, F. (1906[2010]), *A Sketch for a New Aesthetic of Music*, trans. T. Baker, Whitefish, MT: Kessinger Publishing.

Cage, J. (1937[2006]), 'The Future of Music: Credo', in C. Cox and D. Warner (eds), *Audio Culture: Readings in Modern Music*, New York: Continuum, pp. 25–7.

Carani, M. (1999), 'Au-delà de la Photo Positiviste: De la Photo Post-moderne à la Post-photographie', *Visio*, 4 (1): 61–91.

Carbon Arts. (n.d.), 'Melbourne Mussel Choir', http://www.carbonarts.org/projects/melbourne-musselchoir/ (accessed 18 October 2013).

Carlson, M. (2004), *Performance: A Critical Introduction* (2nd edn), London: Routledge.

Carpentier, N. (2011), *Media and Participation: A Site of Ideological-Democratic Struggle*, Bristol: Intellect.

Cascone, K. (2000), 'The Aesthetics of Failure: "Post-Digital" Tendencies in Contemporary Computer Music', *Computer Music Journal*, 24 (4): 12–18.

Case, S-E. (1996), *The Domain-Matrix: Performing Lesbian at the End of Print Culture*, Bloomington, IN: Indiana University Press.

Chadabe, J. (1997), *Electronic Sound: The Past and Promise of Electronic Music*, New Jersey: Prentice Hall.

Cisco Systems (2008), 'Case Study National LambdaRail Project', in C. DeCusatis (ed.), *Handbook of Fiber Optic Data Communication: A Practical Guide to Optical Networking* (3rd edn), Amsterdam: Elsevier, pp. 399–402.

Clarke, J. (2005), 'A Sensorial Act of Replication', in M. Smith (ed.), *Stelarc: The Monograph*, Cambridge, MA: MIT Press, pp. 192–212.

Classitronic (2009), 'Switched on Bach – Where it All Started', http://www.classitronic.net/tag/switched-on-bach/ (accessed 16 January 2013).

Claypoole, T. and Payton, T. (2012), *Protecting Your Internet Identity: Are You Naked Online?*, Plymouth: Rowman & Littlefield.

Clynes, M. and Kline, N. S. (1960), 'Cyborgs and Space', *Astronautics*, 26–7: 4–76.

Collins, N. (2009), *Introduction to Computer Music*, Chichester: John Wiley & Sons.

Colson, R. (2007), *The Fundamentals of Digital Art*, Lausanne: AVA Academia.

Corby, T. (2006), 'Introduction', in T. Corby (ed.), *Network Art: Practices and Positions*, Abingdon: Routledge, pp. 1–10.

Cornish, W. (2004), *Intellectual Property: Omnipresent, Distracting, Irrelevant?*, Oxford: Oxford University Press.

Cox, C. and Warner, D. (eds) (2006), *Audio Culture: Readings in Modern Music*, New York: Continuum.

Cox, M., Tadic, L. and Mulder, E. (2006), *Descriptive Metadata for Television: An End-to-End Introduction*, Burlington, MA: Elsevier.

Creative Commons (2010), 'History', http://creativecommons.org/about/history (accessed 8 July 2013).

Cros, C. (2006), *Marcel Duchamp*, London: Reaktion Books.

Daniel Langlois Foundation (2013), 'DOCAM Documentation Model', http://www.docam.ca/en/documentation-model.html (accessed 25 July 2013).

Davies, C. (1998), 'Osmose: Notes on Being in Immersive Virtual Space', *Digital Creativity*, 9 (2): 65–74.

Davis, J. (2002), *Flash to the Core: An Interactive Sketchbook*, San Franciso, CA: New Riders Publishing.

Debord, G. (1995 [1967]), *The Society of the Spectacle*, trans. D. Nicholson-Smith, Brooklyn, NY: Zone Books.

DeLappe, J. (2013a), 'About the Project', http://www.project929.com/ (accessed 18 October 2013).

—(2013b), 'Project 929: Mapping the Solar', http://rhizome.org/profiles/josephdelappe/ (accessed 17 October 2013).

Deleuze, G. and Guattari, F. (1987), *A Thousand Plateaus*, London: Continuum.

Demers, J. (2010), *Listening Through the Noise: The Aesthetics of Experimental Electronic Music*, New York: Oxford University Press.

Demos, T. J. (2010), 'Globalization and (Contemporary) Art', in J. Elkins, Z. Valiavicharska and A. Kim (eds), *Art and Globalization*, University Park, PA: The Pennsylvania State University Press, pp. 209–13.

Descartes, R. (1960), *The Discourse on Method and Meditations*, trans. L. J. Lafleur, New York: The Liberal Arts Press.

Deseriis, M. (2012), 'Net.Art The Digital Legacies of the Avant-Garde', http://www. booki.cc/the-digital-legacies-of-the-avant-garde/early-internet-art/ (accessed 30 October 2013).

DeviantART (2013), 'deviantART', http://www.deviantart.com (accessed 10 July 2013).

Dewdney, A. and Ride, P. (2006), *The New Media Handbook*, New York: Routledge.

Dietz, S. (1999), 'Archiving with Attitude: *The Unreliable Archivist* and äda'web', http://www. walkerart.org/gallery9/three/dietz_ua.html (accessed 26 July 2013).

—(2005), 'Collecting New-Media Art: Just Like Anything Else, Only Different', in B. Altshuler (ed.), *Collecting the New: Museums and Contemporary Art*, Princeton, NJ: Princeton University Press, pp. 85–102.

Digital Cultures Lab (2005), 'Yacov Sharir', http://www.digitalcultures.org/Symp/Yacov.htm (accessed 16 October 2013).

DiMaggio, P. and Useem, M. (1989), 'Cultural Democracy in a Period of Cultural Expansion: The Social Composition of Arts Audiences in the United States', in A. Foster and J. Blau (eds), *Art and Society: Readings in the Sociology of the Arts*, Albany, NY: State University of New York Press, pp. 141–75.

Dixon, S. (2007), *Digital Performance: A History of New Media in Theatre, Dance, Performance Art and Installation*, Cambridge, MA: MIT Press.

Dodds, S. (2004), *Dance On Screen: Genres and Media from Hollywood to Experimental Art*, Basingstoke: Palgrave Macmillan.

Dougherty, D. (2004), 'What Is Web 2.0: Design Patterns and Business Models for the Next Generation of Software', http://oreilly.com/web2/archive/what-is-web-20.html (accessed 30 October 2013).

Drinkall, J. (2011), 'The Art and Flux of Telepathy 2.0 in Second Life', in N. Zagalo, L. Morgado and A. Boa-Ventura (eds), *Virtual Worlds and Metaverse Platforms: New Communication and Identity Paradigms*, Hershey, PA: IGI Global, pp. 48–50.

Drucker, J. (2009), *SpecLab: Digital Aesthetics and Projects in Speculative Computing*, Chicago, IL: University of Chicago Press.

Durham, M. G. and Kellner, D. (eds) (2006), *Media and Cultural Studies: Key Works*, Malden, MA: Blackwell Publishing.

Elahi, H. (2013), 'Tracking Transience', http://trackingtransience.net/ (accessed 18 October 2013).

Fake, C. (2007), 'The History of Flickr', http://itc.conversationsnetwork.org/shows/ detail1755.html (accessed 10 July 2013).

Falconer, M. (2011), 'Peter Campus', in J. Marter (ed.), *The Grove Encyclopedia of American Art: Volume 1*, Oxford: Oxford University Press, pp. 402–3.

Fauconnier, R. and Frommé, R. (2004), 'Capturing Unstable Media', *Digital Culture and Heritage*, 1–23, http://citeseerx.ist.psu.edu/viewdoc/summary? doi=10.1.1.169.4766 (accessed 30 October 2013).

Feist, R., Beauvais, C. and Shukla, R. (2010), 'Introduction', in R. Feist, C. Beauvais and R. Shukla (eds), *Technology and the Changing Face of Humanity*, Ottawa: University of Ottawa Press, pp. 1–21.

Ferrell, O. C. and Hartline, M. (2008), *Marketing Strategy* (4th edn), Mason, OH: Thomson Higher Education.

Flanagan, M. (2011), 'Play, Participation, and Art: Blurring the Edges', in M. Lovejoy, C. Paul and V. Vesna (eds), *Context Providers: Conditions of Meaning in Media Arts*, Bristol: Intellect, pp. 89–100.

Forging the Future (n.d.), 'Variable Media Questionnaire', http://variablemediaquestionnaire. net/ (accessed 17 July 2013).

Freidberg, A. (2002). 'CD and DVD', in D. Harries (ed.), *The New Media Book*, London: British Film Institute, pp. 30–9.

Fries, B. and Fries, M. (2005), *Digital Audio Essentials: A Comprehensive Guide to Creating, Recording, Editing, and Sharing Music and Other Audio*, Sebastopol, CA: O'Reilly Media.

Funkhouser, C. T. (2007), *Prehistoric Digital Poetry: An Archaeology of Forms, 1959–1995*, Tuscaloosa, AL: University of Alabama Press.

Gagnon, J. (2000), 'Luc Courchesne: Landscape One', http://www.fondation-langlois.org/html/e/page.php?NumPage=127 (accessed 2 September 2013).

Galloway, A. (2004), *Protocol: How Control Exists After Decentralization*, Cambridge, MA: MIT Press.

Gartenfield, A. (2008), 'For the Love of Art: Mark Tribe on Post Digital', *Paper Magazine*, 10 October.

Gere, C. (2002), *Digital Culture*, London: Reaktion Books.

—(2006), 'The History of Network Art', in T. Corby (ed.), *Network Art: Practices and Positions*, Abingdon: Routledge, pp. 11–23.

Giannaci, G. (2004), *Virtual Theatres: An Introduction*, London: Routledge.

Gibson, W. (1984), *Neuromancer*, New York: Ace Books.

Goggin, G. (2006), *Cell Phone Culture: Mobile Technology in Everyday Life*, New York: Routledge.

Goldberg, R. L. (2011), *Performance Art: From Futurism to the Present* (3rd edn), London: Thames and Hudson.

Goldsmith, K. (2001), 'UbuWeb Wants To Be Free', http://epc.buffalo.edu/authors/goldsmith/ubuweb.html (accessed 18 July 2013).

—(2002), 'The Bride Stripped Bare: Nude Media and the Dematerialization of Tony Curtis', http://epc.buffalo.edu/authors/goldsmith/nude.pdf (accessed 17 July 2013).

—(2011a), 'Archiving is the New Folk Art', http://www.poetryfoundation.org/harriet/2011/04/archiving-is-the-new-folk-art/ (accessed 23 July 2013).

—(2011b), 'UbuWeb', http://www.ubu.com/resources/index.html (accessed 30 October 2013).

Golomb, J. (1995), *In Search of Authenticity*, London and New York: Harry N. Abrams.

Goodall, J. (2005), 'The Will to Evolve', in M. Smith (ed.), *Stelarc: The Monograph*, Cambridge, MA: MIT Press, pp. 1–31.

Goodman, C. (1987), *Digital Visions: Computers and Art*, New York: H. N. Abrams.

Graham, B. (2007), 'Redefining Digital Art: Disrupting Borders', in F. Cameron and S. Kenderdine (eds), *Theorizing Digital Cultural Heritage: A Critical Discourse*, Cambridge, MA: MIT Press, pp. 93–112.

—(2010), 'Tools, Methods, Practice, Process ... and Curation', in H. Gardiner and C. Gere (eds), *Art Practice in a Digital Culture*, Farnham: Ashgate, pp. 165–74.

Grau, O. (2003), *Virtual Art: From Illusion to Immersion*, Cambridge, MA: MIT Press.

Gray, S. (2008), 'The Performance Art Documentation Structure', http://www.bristol.ac.uk/nrla/case-study/ (accessed 25 July 2013).

Green, J-A. (n.d.), 'When Bricks Become Pixels', http://turbulence.org/blog/2005/08/30/screen-wall/ (accessed 18 October 2013).

Green, N. and Haddon, L. (2009), *Mobile Communications: An Introduction to New Media*, Oxford: Berg.

Greenberg, I. (2007), *Processing: Creative Coding and Computational Art*, New York: Springer-Verlag.

Greene, R. (2004), *Internet Art*, London: Thames & Hudson.

Groys, B. (2012), *Under Suspicion: A Phenomenology of Media*, New York: Columbia University Press.

Grzinic, M. (2011), 'Identity Operated in New Mode: Context and Body/Space/Time', in M. Lovejoy, C. Paul. and V. Vesna (eds), *Context Providers: Conditions of Meaning in Media Arts*, Bristol: Intellect, pp. 151–74.

Gumbrecht, H. U. and Marrinan, M. (eds) (2003), *Mapping Benjamin: The Work of Art in the Digital Age*, Stanford, CA: Stanford University Press.

Hanhardt, J. (2003), 'Introduction: The Challenge of Variable Media', in C. A. Schaefer, E. Weisberger, Y. Doucet and J. Perron (eds), *Permanence Through Change: The Variable Media Approach*, New York: Guggenheim Museum Publications, pp. 6–9.

Haraway, D. (1991[1985]), 'A Cyborg Manifesto: Science, Technology and Socialist-Feminism in the Late Twentieth Century', in D. Haraway (ed.), *Simians, Cyborgs, and Women: The Reinvention of Nature*, New York: Routledge.

Harvey, R. (2012), *Preserving Digital Materials*, Berlin: Walter de Gruyter.

Hass, J. (2010), 'Digital Audio: Overview and Early History', in *Introduction to Computer Music: Volume One*, http://www.indiana.edu/~emusic/etext/digital_audio/chapter5_digital.shtml (accessed 30 October 2013).

Hecht, J. and Teresi, D. (1998), *Laser: Light of a Million Uses*, Toronto: General Publishing Company.

Heneghan, C. (2013), 'The History, Progression and Future of Digital Music Programming (Part 1)', *SOUNDCTRL*, http://www.soundctrl.com/blog/the-history-progression-future-of-digital-music-programming-part-1/ (accessed 3 September 2013).

Higgins, H. (2002), *Fluxus Experience*, Berkeley, CA: University of California Press.

Holder, J. (2012), 'Digital Baroque', http://www.joeyholder.com/digital-baroque-documentation/ (accessed 2 September 2013).

Holmes, T. (ed.), *The Routledge Guide to Music Technology*, New York: Routledge.

—(2008), *Electronic and Experimental Music: Technology, Music and Culture* (3rd edn), New York: Routledge.

Hope, C. (2006), 'Sound Art: Mobile Art', *Soundscripts: Proceedings of the Inaugural Totally Huge New Music Festival Conference*, 1, pp. 42–8.

Hopkins, D. (2004), *Dada and Surrealism: A Very Short Introduction*, Oxford: Oxford University Press.

Hosken, D. (2011), *An Introduction to Music Technology*, New York: Routledge.

Howard, D. and Angus, J. (2012), *Acoustics and Psychoacoustics* (3rd edn), Hoboken, NJ: Taylor & Francis.

Hughes, T. (2004), *Human-Built World: How To Think About Technology and Culture*, Chicago, IL: The University of Chicago Press.

Hullot-Kentor, R. (2003), 'What is Mechanical Reproduction?', in H. U. Gumbrecht and M. Marrinan (eds), *Mapping Benjamin: The Work of Art in the Digital Age*, Stanford, CA: Stanford University Press, pp. 293–312.

Hyde, L. (1999), *The Gift: Imagination and the Erotic Life of Property*, London: Vintage.

Internet Archive (2013), 'Welcome to the Prelinger Archives', http://archive.org/details/prelinger (accessed 23 July 2013).

Ippolito, J. (2002), 'Ten Myths of Internet Art', *Leonardo*, 35 (5): 485–7.

—(2003a), 'Accommodating the Unpredictable: The Variable Media Questionnaire', in C. A. Schaefer, E. Weisberger, Y. Doucet and J. Perron (eds), *Permanence Through Change: The Variable Media Approach*, New York: Guggenheim Museum Publications, pp. 47–53.

—(2003b), 'Mark Napier, *net.flag*, 2002', in C. A. Schaefer, E. Weisberger, Y. Doucet and

J. Perron (eds), *Permanence Through Change: The Variable Media Approach*, New York: Guggenheim Museum Publications, pp. 109–14.

—(2010), 'Learning from Mario: Crowdsourcing Preservation', http://three.org/ippolito/writing/learning_from_mario/ (accessed 17 July 2013).

Iseminger, D. (2012), 'Works and Expressions in RDA: Problems and Solutions', in P. Lisius and R. Griscom (eds), *Directions in Music Cataloging*, Middleton, WI: A-R Editions, pp. 43–62.

Janson, H. W. (2004), *History of Art: The Western Tradition* (6th edn), Upper Saddle River, NJ: Pearson Education.

Jones, C. and Muller, L. (2008), 'Between Real and Ideal: Documenting Media Art', *Leonardo*, 41 (4): 418–19.

Jones, R. B. (2011), *Postcolonial Representations of Women: Critical Issues for Education*, Dordrecht: Springer.

Juhasz, A. (ed.) (2001), *Women of Vision: Histories in Feminist Film and Video*, Minneapolis, MN: University of Minnesota Press.

Kac, E. (2005), *Telepresence & Bio Art: Networking Humans, Rabbits & Robots*, Ann Arbor, MI: University of Michigan Press.

Kahate, A. (2009), *XML and Related Technologies*, Delhi: Dorling Kindersley.

Kahn, D. (2001), *Noise Water Meat*, Cambridge, MA: MIT Press.

Kaplan, C. (1996), *Questions of Travel: Postmodern Discourses of Displacement*, Durham, NC: Duke University Press.

Kaye, N. (2000), *Site-Specific Art: Performance, Place and Documentation*, London: Routledge.

Kellner, D. (1995), 'Mapping the Present from the Future: From Baudrillard to Cyberpunk', in D. Kellner (ed.) *Media Culture: Cultural Studies, Identity and Politics Between the Modern and the Postmodern*, New York: Routledge, pp. 297–330.

Kellner, D. and Durham, M. G. (2006), 'Adventures in Media and Cultural Studies: Introducing the KeyWorks', in M. G. Durham and D. Kellner (eds), *Media and Cultural Studies: Keyworks*, Malden, MA: Blackwell Publishing, pp. ix–xxxviii.

Kelly, C. (2009), *Cracked Media: The Sound of Malfunction*, Cambridge, MA: MIT Press.

Khosrow-Pour, M. (2007), *Dictionary of Information Science and Technology: Volume 1*, Hershey, PA: Idea Group Reference.

Klein, J. T. (1990), *Interdisciplinarity: History, Theory, and Practice*, Detroit, MI: Wayne State University Press.

Knight, A. (2013), 'Hybridity in New Art: Split Life and Augmented Reality in Six New Art Works', http://www.dazeddigital.com/blog/article/15085/1/hybridity-in-new-art (accessed 1 September 2013).

Knowles, K. (2009), *A Cinematic Artist: The Films of Man Ray*, Bern: Peter Lang.

Kotler, P. (2010), 'The Prosumer Movement: A New Challenge for Marketers', in B. Blättel-Mink and K-U. Hellmann (eds), *Prosumer Revisited*, Wiesbaden: Verlag für Sozialwissenschaften, pp. 51–62.

Kratochvil, M. (2013), *Managing Multimedia and Unstructured Data in the Oracle Database: A Revolutionary Approach to Understanding, Managing, and Delivering Digital Objects, Assets, and All Types of Data*, Birmingham: Packt Publishing.

Kurzweil, E. (1996), *The Age of Structuralism: From Lévi-Strauss to Foucault*, New Brunswick, NJ: Transaction Publishers.

Landau, D. (ed.) (2000), *Gladiator: The Making of the Ridley Scott Epic*, New York: Newmarket.

Laurel, B. (2013), *Computers as Theatre* (2nd edn), Reading, MA: Addison-Wesley.

Le Grice, M. (1997), 'A Non-Linear Tradition: Experimental Film and Digital Cinema', *Katalog 43 Internationale Kurzfilmtage Festival*, Oberhausen, Germany.

Lee, J-A. (2012), *Nonprofit Organizations and the Intellectual Commons*, Cheltenham: Edward Elgar Publishing.

Lee, P. (2012), *Forgetting the Art World*, Cambridge, MA: MIT Press.

Leonardi, P. (2012), 'Materiality, Sociomateriality, and Socio-Technical Systems: What Do These Terms Mean? How Are They Different? Do We Need Them?', in P. Leonardi, B. Nardi and J. Kallinikos (eds), *Materiality and Organizing: Social Interaction in a Technological World*, Oxford and New York: Oxford University Press, pp. 25–48.

Lessig, L. (2004), *Free Culture: The Nature and Future of Creativity*, New York: Penguin.

Levin, G., Gibbons, S., Shakar, G., Sohrawardy, Y., Gruber, J., Lehner, J. and Semlak, E. (2003), '*Dialtones (A Telesymphony)* Final Report', http://www.flong.com/projects/telesymphony/ (accessed 10 September 2013).

Lister, M., Dovey, J., Giddings, S., Grant, I. and Kelly, K. (2003), *New Media: A Critical Introduction*, London: Routledge.

Lopes, D. M. (2010), *A Philosophy of Computer Art*, Abingdon: Routledge.

Lovejoy, M. (1989), 'Postmodern Currents: Art and Artists in the Age of Elecronic Media'. *Technology and Culture*, 32 (1), 138–40.

—(2004), *Digital Currents: Art in the Electronic Age* (3rd edn), New York: Routledge.

Lovejoy, M., Paul, C. and Vesna, V. (2011), 'Introduction', in M. Lovejoy, C. Paul and V. Vesna (eds), *Context Providers: Conditions of Meaning in Media Arts*, Bristol: Intellect, pp. 1–10.

Lovink, G. (2003), *My First Recession: Critical Internet Culture in Transition*, Rotterdam: VP2/NAI Publishing.

Lyotard, J-F. (1994), *Lessons on the Analytic of the Sublime*, trans. E. Rottenberg, Stanford, CA: Stanford University Press.

MacDonald, C. (2009), 'Scoring the Work: Documenting Practice and Performance in Variable Media Art', *Leonardo*, 42 (1): 59–63.

Mann, S. (1998), 'Headmounted Wireless Video: Computer-Supported Collaboration for Photojournalism and Everyday Use', *IEEE Communications Magazine*, June: 144–51.

Mann, S., Nolan, J. and Wellman, B. (2003), 'Sousveillance: Inventing and Using Wearable Computing Devices for Data Collection in Surveillance Environments', *Surveillance & Society*, 1 (3): 331–55.

Manning, P. (2004), *Electronic and Computer Music* (2nd edn), London: Oxford University Press.

Manovich, L. (1995), 'The Paradox of Digital Photography', in H. Von Amelunxen and F. Rotzer (eds), *Photography After Photography: Memory and Representation in the Digital Age*, pp. 240–9, http://manovich.net/TEXT/digital_photo.html (accessed 30 October 2013).

—(1996), 'The Death of Computer Art', http://www.manovich.net/TEXT/death.html (accessed 28 August 2013).

—(2001a), *The Language of New Media*, Cambridge, MA: MIT Press.

—(2001b), 'Post-Media Aesthetics', http://www.manovich.net/TEXTS_07.HTM (accessed 26 September 2013).

—(2003). '"Metadating" the Image"', in L. Manovich (ed.), *Making Art of Databases*. Rotterdam: V2_Publishing/NAi Publishers, pp. 12–27.

—(2005), *Soft Cinema: Navigating the Database*, Cambridge, MA: MIT Press.

Marinetti, F. T. (1960 [1909]), 'The Futurist Manifesto', in G. Joll (ed.) *Three Intellectuals in Politics*, New York: Pantheon Books, pp. 179–84.

Martins, T., Correia, N., Sommerer, C. and Mignonneau, L. (2008), 'Ubiquitous Gaming Interaction: Engaging Play Anywhere', in C. Sommerer, L. Jain and L. Mignonneau (eds), *The Art and Science of Interface and Interaction Design*, Berlin: Springer-Verlag, pp. 115–30.

Massumi, B. (2005), 'The Evolutionary Alchemy of Reason', in M. Smith (ed.), *Stelarc: The Monograph*, Cambridge, MA: MIT Press, pp. 124–90.

McCarthy, L. (2010), 'Script 2010', http://lauren-mccarthy.com/script/ (accessed 17 October 2013).

McHaney, R. (2011), *The New Digital Shoreline: How Web 2.0 and Millennials are Revolutionizing Higher Education*, Sterling, VA: Stylus Publishing.

McLuhan, M. (1964), *Understanding Media: The Extensions of Man*, London: Routledge & Kegan Paul.

Meigh-Andrews, C. (2006), *A History of Video Art: The Development of Form and Function*, London: Berg.

Mey, K. (2007), *Art and Obscenity*, London: I.B. Tauris.

Mina, A. X. (2010), 'Always Social: Right Now (2010–), Part Three', *Hyperallergic: Senstive to Art & its Discontents*, http://hyperallergic.com/6648/social-media-art-pt-3/ (accessed 30 October 2013).

Mitra, P. and Bokil, H. (2008), *Observed Brain Dynamics*, Oxford: Oxford University Press.

Monoskop (2013), 'Textz.com', http://monoskop.org/Textz.com (accessed 25 June 2013).

Moran, J. (2010), *Interdisciplinarity* (2nd edn), Abington: Routledge.

Morley, D. (2007), *Media, Modernity and Technology: The Geography of the New*, Abingdon: Routledge.

—(2009), *Understanding Computers in a Changing Society* (3rd edn), Boston, MA: Course Technology.

Munster, A. (2006), *Materializing New Media: Embodiment in Information Aesthetics*, Lebanon, NH: Dartmouth College Press.

Muntadas, A. (n.d.), 'The File Room', http://www.thefileroom.org (accessed 13 September 2013).

Museum of Modern Art (2006), *Still Moving: The Film and Media Collections of The Museum of Modern Art*, New York: Museum of Modern Art.

Napier, M. (n.d.), 'About *net.flag*', http://webart.guggenheim.org/netflag/about.html (accessed 27 July 2013).

Neill, S. D. (1993), *Clarifying McLuhan: As Assessment of Process and Product*, Westport, CT: Greenwood Press.

New Museum of Contemporary Art (2009), 'Guthrie Lonergan', http://www.gclass.org/artists/gutherie-lonergan (accessed 17 October 2013).

Nicolescu, B. (2002), *Manifesto of Transdisciplinarity*, trans. K-C. Voss, Albany, NY: State University of New York Press.

Nielsen, J. (2008), 'The Song That Never Ends', http://www.jarednielsen.com/song.html (accessed 17 October 2013).

Nonini, D. (2007), 'Introduction', in D. Nonini (ed.), *The Global Idea of 'The Commons'*, New York: Berghahn Books, pp. 1–25.

Nora, S. and Minc, A. (1981), *The Computerization of Society*, Cambridge, MA: MIT Press.

O'Hagan, S. (2011), 'Analogue Artists Defying the Digital Age', *Observer*, http://www.theguardian.com/culture/2011/apr/24/mavericks-defying-digital-age (accessed 29 August 2013).

On, J. (2011), '*They Rule*: Overview', http://www.theyrule.net/about (accessed 18 October 2013).

Osthoff, S. (2005), 'From Mail Art to Telepresence: Communication at a Distance in the Works of Paulo Bruscky and Eduardo Kac', in A. Chandler and N. Neumark (eds), *At a Distance: Precursors to Art and Activism on the Internet*, Cambridge, MA: MIT Press, pp. 260–80.

Paik, N. J. (1996), 'Art and Satellite', in K. Stiles and P. Selz (eds), *Theories and Documents of Contemporary Art: A Sourcebook of Artists' Writings*, Berkeley, CA: University of California Press, pp. 434–6.

Parikka, J. and Ernst, W. (2013), *Digital Memory and the Archive*, Minneapolis, MN: University of Minnesota Press.

Paul, C. (2003), *Digital Art*, London: Thames & Hudson.

—(2008), 'Digital Art/Public Art: Governance and Agency in the Networked Commons', in C. Sommerer, L. Jain and L. Mignonneau (eds), *The Art and Science of Interface and Interaction Design*, Berlin: Springer, pp. 163–85.

—(2011), 'Contextual Networks: Data, Identity, and Collective Production', in M. Lovejoy, C. Paul and V. Vesna (eds), *Context Providers: Conditions of Meaning in Media Arts*, Bristol: Intellect, pp. 103–22.

Paz, O. (2002), 'The Ready-Made', in J. Masheck (ed., *Marcel Duchamp in Perspective: Writings on Duchamp by Jasper Johns, Donald Judd, Clement Greenberg, John Cage, Octavio Paz, & Others*, Cambridge, MA: Da Capo Press, pp. 84–9.

Pelizzari, E. (2012), 'Harvesting for Disseminating: Open Archives and the Role of Academic Libraries', in A. Fenner (ed.), *Managing Digital Resources in Libraries*, New York: Routledge, pp. 35–52.

Petrović-Šteger, M. (2011), 'Spools, Loops and Traces: On *etoy* Encapsulation and Three Portraits of Marilyn Strathern', in J. Edwards and M. Petrović-Šteger (eds), *Recasting Anthropological Knowledge: Inspiration and Social Science*, Cambridge: Cambridge University Press, pp. 145–64.

Pfaffenberger, B. (2003), '"A Standing Wave in the Web of Our Communications": Usenet and the Socio-Technical Construction of Cyberspace Values', in C. Lueg and D. Fisher (eds), *From Usenet to CoWebs: Interacting with Social Information Spaces*, London: Springer, pp. 20–44.

Piana, B. (2009), 'Ellsworth Kelly Hacked My Twitter', http://rhizome.org/artbase/artwork/49315/ (accessed 17 October 2013).

Poole, D. and Le-Phat Ho, S. (2011), *Digital Transitions and the Impact of New Technology on the Arts*, Ottawa: Canadian Public Arts Funders.

Poole, H. (2005), *The Internet: A Historical Encyclopedia*, New York: MTM Publishing.

Popper, F. (1993), *Art of the Electronic Age*, trans. B. Hemmingway, London: Thames & Hudson.

Poslad, S. (2009), *Ubiquitous Computing: Smart Devices, Environments and Interactions*, Chichester: John Wiley & Sons.

Preece, J. (2000), *Online Communities: Designing Usability, Supporting Sociability*, New York: John Wiley.

Prelinger, R. (2009), 'Points of Origin: Discovering Ourselves Through Access', *The Moving Image*, 9 (2), 164–75.

Prendergast, M. (2001), *The Ambient Century: From Mahler to Trance: The Evolution of Sound in the Electronic Age*, New York: Bloomsbury.

Pu, I. M. (2006), *Fundamental Data Compression*, Oxford: Butterworth-Heinemann.

Ramey, C. D. (2003), 'Napster', in J. Shepherd (ed.), *Continuum Encyclopedia of Popular Music of the World: Performance and Production: Volume 2*, London: Continuum, pp. 251–4.

Ran, F. (2009), *A History of Installation Art and the Development of New Art Forms: Technology and the Hermeneutics of Time and Space in Modern and Postmodern Art from Cubism to Installation*, New York: Peter Lang.

Randell, C. (2008), 'Wearable Computing Applications and Challenges', in P. Kourouthanassis and G. Giaglis (eds), *Pervasive Information Systems*, Armonk, NY: M. E. Sharpe, pp. 165–79.

Ratliff, C. (2009), '"Some Rights Reserved": Weblogs with Creative Commons Licenses', in S. Westbrook (ed.), *Composition and Copyright: Perspectives on Teaching, Text-making, and Fair Use*, Albany, NY: State University of New York, pp. 50–67.

Reas, C. and Fry, B. (2007), *Processing: A Programming Handbook for Visual Designers and Artists*, Cambridge, MA: MIT Press.

Reed, S. A. (2013), *Assimilate: A Critical History of Industrial Music*, Oxford: Oxford University Press.

Repko, A. (2008), *Interdisciplinary Research: Process and Theory*, Los Angeles, CA: Sage.

Rheingold, H. (1991), *Virtual Reality*, London: Secker & Warburg.

Rhizome.org (2013), 'Rhizome', http://rhizome.org/ (accessed 13 June 2013).

Richmond, A. (2012), *Conservation*, Hoboken, NJ: Taylor & Francis.

Rinehart, R. (2004a), 'Appendices to a System of Formal Notation for Scoring Works of Digital and Variable Media Art', *Archiving the Avant-Garde: Project Documents and Papers*, pp. 1–23, http://www.bampfa.berkeley.edu/about/formalnotation_apndx.pdf (accessed 30 October 2013).

—(2004b), 'A System of Formal Notation for Scoring Works of Digital and Variable Media Art', *Archiving the Avant-Garde: Documenting and Preserving Digital/Variable Media Art: Project Documents and Papers*, pp. 1–25, http://www.bampfa.berkeley.edu/about/formalnotation.pdf (accessed 30 October 2013).

—(2007), 'The Media Art Notation System: Documenting and Preserving Digital/Media Art', *Leonardo*, 40 (2): 181–7.

Ritchin, F. (2009), *After Photography*, New York: W. W. Norton.

Roads, C. (2004), *Microsound*, Cambridge, MA: MIT Press.

Rogers, H. (2013), *Sounding the Gallery: Video and the Rise of Art-Music*, Oxford: Oxford University Press.

Rosler, M. (2004), *Decoys and Disruptions: Selected Writings, 1975–2001*, Cambridge, MA: MIT Press.

Rucker, R. (2013), 'What is Wetware?', http://www.rudyrucker.com/blog/2007/08/25/what-is-wetware (accessed 2 February 2014).

Ruff, T. (2009), *jpegs*, New York: Aperture Foundation.

Rush, M. (1999), *New Media in Late 20th-Century Art*, London: Thames & Hudson.

—(2003), *Video Art*, London: Thames & Hudson.

Russolo, L. (1913[1987]), *The Art of Noises*, New York: Pendragon Press.

Ryan, J. (2012), *Green Sense: The Aesthetics of Plants, Place and Language*, Oxford: TrueHeart Press.

Salavon, J and Hill, J. (2004), *Jason Salavon: Brainstorm Still Life*, Bloomington, IN: School of Fine Arts Gallery, Indiana University.

Salomoni, P. and Mirri, S. (2011), 'Adaptation Technologies in Mobile Learning', in L. Chao (ed.), *Open Source Mobile Learning: Mobile Linux Applications*, Hershey, PA: Information Science Reference, pp. 18–34.

Salter, C. (2010), *Entangled: Technology and the Transformation of Performance*, Cambridge, MA: MIT Press.

Santos, P. G. (2012), *European Founders at Work*, New York: Apress.

Sayood, K. (2003), 'Preface', in K. Sayood (ed.), *Lossless Compression Handbook*, San Diego, CA: Academic Press, pp. xix–xx.

Schaffer, K. (1999), 'The Game Girls of VNS Matrix: Challenging Gendered

Identities in Cyberspace', in M. A. O'Farrell and L. Vallone (eds), *Virtual Gender: Fantasies of Subjectivity and Embodiment*, Ann Arbor, MI: University of Michigan Press.

Scholte, J. A. (2005), *Globalization: A Critical Introduction* (2nd edn), Basingstoke: Palgrave Macmillan.

Scott, J. and Bisig, D. (2011), 'Art and Science Research: Active Contexts and Discourses', in M. Lovejoy, C. Paul and V. Vesna (eds), *Context Providers: Conditions of Meaning in Media Arts*, Bristol: Intellect, pp. 299–328.

Scott, T. (2001), *Glitch Art Visualisation*, http://www.beflix.com/tech.html (accessed 13 September 2012).

Sexton, J. (2008), 'Digital Music: Production, Distribution and Consumption', in G. Creeber and R. Matin (eds), *Digital Cultures: Understanding New Media*, Maidenhead: McGraw-Hill, pp. 92–103.

Seymour, S. (2008), *Fashionable Technology: The Intersection of Design, Fashion, Science and Technology*, Vienna: Springer.

Shanken, E. (2002), 'Cybernetics and Art: Cultural Convergence in the 1960s', in B. Clarke and L. D. Henderson (eds), *From Energy to Information: Representation in Science and Technology, Art, and Literature*, Stanford, CA: Stanford University Press, pp. 255–77.

—(2003), 'From Cybernetics to Telematics: The Art, Pedagogy, and Theory of Roy Ascott', in E. Shanken (ed.), *Telematic Embrace: Visionary Theories of Art, Technology, and Consciousness*, Berkeley, CA: University of California Press, pp. 1–94.

Shanken, E. (ed.) (2009), *Art and Electronic Media*, London: Phaidon Press.

Sharir, Y. (2008), 'Learning through the Re-embodiment of the Digital Self', in M. Alexenberg (ed.), *Educating Artists for the Future: Learning at the Intersections of Art, Science, Technology and Culture*, Bristol: Intellect, pp. 217–28.

Shaw, J. and Weibel, P. (eds) (2003), *Future Cinema: The Cinematic Imaginary After Film*, Cambridge, MA: MIT Press.

Simanowski, R. (2011), *Digital Art and Meaning: Reading Kinetic Poetry, Text Machines, Mapping Art, and Interactive Installations*, Minneapolis, MN: University of Minnesota Press.

Sito, T. (2013), *Moving Innovation: A History of Computer Animation*, Cambridge, MA: MIT Press.

Slack, D. and Wise, J. W. (2005), *Culture and Technology: A Primer*, New York: Peter Lang.

Small, J. S. (2001), *The Analogue Alternative: The Electronic Analogue Computer in Britain and the USA, 1930–1975*, London: Routledge.

Smith, O. (2005), 'Fluxus Praxis: An Exploration of Connections, Creativity, and Community', in A. Chandler and N. Neumark (eds), *At a Distance: Precursors to Art and Activism on the Internet*, Cambridge, MA: Massachusetts Institute of Technology, pp. 116–38.

Soulé, M. and Press, D. (1998), 'What is Environmental Studies?', *BioScience*, 48 (5), 397–405.

Speigel, L. (1980), *The Expanding Universe*, Philo Records, Cat. 9003, LP Record Liner Notes.

St Laurent, A. (2004), *Understanding Open Source and Free Software Licensing*, Sebastopol, CA: O'Reilly Media.

STARS (2013), 'Search: Richard Layzell', http://stars.ilrt.bris.ac.uk/StarsWeb/stars?keywords =Richard Layzell&action=search (accessed 25 July 2013).

Steciw, K. (2012). 'Popular Options (Yellow Diamonds in the Light)', http://www.katesteciw. com/index.php?/popular-options-2012/ (accessed 2 September 2013).

Stelarc, and Smith, M. (2005), 'Animating Bodies, Mobilizing Technologies: Stelarc in Conversation', in M. Smith (ed.), *Stelarc: The Monograph*, Cambridge, MA: MIT Press, pp. 214–41.

Sterne, J. (2006), 'The MP3 as Cultural Artifact', *New Media & Society,* 8 (5): 825–42.

—(2012), *MP3: The Meaning of a Format*, Durham, NC: Duke University Press.

Stiles, K. and Shanken, E. (2011), 'Missing in Action: Agency and Meaning in Interactive Art', in M. Lovejoy, C. Paul and V. Vesna (eds), *Context Providers: Conditions of Meaning in Media Arts*, Bristol: Intellect, pp. 31–54.

Stringari, C. (2003), 'Beyond "Conservative": The Conservator's Role in Variable Media Preservation', in C. A. Schaefer, E. Weisberger, Y. Doucet and J. Perron (eds), *Permanence Through Change: The Variable Media Approach*, New York: Guggenheim Museum Publications, pp. 54–9.

Stuart, C. (2002), 'Yasunao Tone's Wounded and Skipping Compact Discs: From Improvisation and Indeterminate Composition to Glitching CDs', *Leonardo Electronic Almanac,* 10 (9): 2–11.

—(2003), 'The Object of Performance: Aural Performativity in Contemporary Laptop Music', *Contemporary Music Review,* 22 (4): 59–65.

Stuckenschmidt, H. H. (1995), 'The Third Stage: Some Observations of the Aesthetics of Electronic Music', *Die Rheihe,* 1 (1): 11–13.

Swanwick, M. (1987), *Vacuum Flowers*, New York: Penguin.

Swedin, E. and Ferro, D. (2005), *Computers: The Life of a Technology*, Baltimore, MD: Johns Hopkins University Press.

Taylor, I. (2005), *From P2P to Web Services and Grids: Peers in a Client/Server World*, London: Springer-Verlag.

TED (2009), 'Golan Levin Makes Art That Looks Back at You', http://www.ted.com/talks/golan_levin_ted2009.html (accessed 13 June 2013).

Telegraph Media Group (2013), 'Flickr: The World's Photo Album', *Telegraph,* http://www.telegraph.co.uk/finance/newsbysector/mediatechnologyandtelecoms/digital-media/8500577/Flickr-the-worlds-photo-album.html (accessed 10 July 2013).

Terras, M. (2008), *Digital Images for the Information Professional*. Aldershot and Burlington, VT: Ashgate Publishing.

The Solomon R. Guggenheim Foundation (2013), 'The Variable Media Initiative', http://www.guggenheim.org/new-york/collections/conservation/conservation-projects/variable-media (accessed 13 June 2013).

Thill, S. (2009), 'March 17, 1948: William Gibson, Father of Cyberspace', *WIRED,* http://www.wired.com/science/discoveries/news/2009/03/dayintech_0317 (accessed 30 October 2013).

Toffoletti, K. (2011), *Baudrillard Reframed: Interpreting Key Thinkers for the Arts*, London: I.B. Tauris.

Tofts, D. (2005), *Interzone: Media Arts in Australia*, Fishermans Bend, VIC: Craftsman House.

Tribe, M. and Jana, R. (2006), *New Media Art* [wiki version], https://wiki.brown.edu/confluence/display/MarkTribe/New+Media+Art (accessed 30 October 2013).

Tsiavos, P. (2011), 'Extracting Value from Open Licensing Arrangements', in W. Leister and N. Christophersen (eds), *Open Source, Open Collaboration and Innovation*, Oslo: Norwegian Computing Center, pp. 119–62.

Tsunoda, T. (2007), 'Toshiya Tsunoda Interview' http://www.inpartmaint.com/pdis/pdis_e/plop_e_feature/toshiya_tsunoda.html (accessed 26 June 2008).

UNESCO (2003), *Guidelines for the Preservation of Digital Heritage*, Paris: United Nations Education, Scientific and Cultural Organization.

Valéry, P. (1964), *Aesthetics*, trans. R. Manheim, New York: Bollingen Foundation.

Van Dijck, J. (2013),*The Culture of Connectivity: A Critical History of Social Media*, Oxford: Oxford University Press.

Van Saaze, V. (2009), 'Doing Artworks: An Ethnographic Account of the Acquisition and Conservation of *No Ghost Just a Shell*', *Krisis: Journal for Contemporary Philosophy*, 1: 20–33, http://www.krisis.eu/content/2009-1/2009-1-03-saaze.pdf (accessed 30 October 2013).

Varèse, E. (1975), Interview with Gunther Schuller, in R.Erickson (ed.) *Sound Structure in Music*, Los Angeles, CA: University of California Press, p. 34.

Vickery, L., Hope, C. and James, S. (2012), 'Digital Adaptations of the Scores for Cage Variations I, II and III', paper presented at the International Computer Music Conference, Ljubljana, Slovenia, 9–15 September.

Video Data Bank (2013), 'Surveying the First Decade: Video Art and Alternative Media in the US 1968–1980', http://www.vdb.org/titles/surveying-first-decade-video-art-and-alternative-media-us-1968-1980 (accessed 14 July 2013).

Virillio, P. (1977 [1986]), *Speed and Politics: An Essay on Dromology*. New York: Semiotext(e).

Voyce, S. (2013), *Poetic Community: Avant-Garde Activism and Cold War Culture*, Toronto: University of Toronto Press.

Walker Art Center (1998), 'The Unreliable Archivist' http://www.walkerart.org/collections/artworks/the-unreliable-archivist (accessed 11 August 2013).

—(n.d.), 'life_sharing', http://www.walkerart.org/gallery9/lifesharing/ (accessed 2 July 2013).

Walls, L. D. (1995), *Seeing New Worlds: Henry David Thoreau and Nineteenth-Century Natural Science*, Madison, WI: University of Wisconsin Press.

Wands, B. (2006), *Art of the Digital Age*, New York: Thames & Hudson.

Watkinson, J. (2001), *The Art of Digital Audio* (3rd edn), Oxford: Focal Press.

Weibel, P. and Shaw, J. (eds) (2003), *Future Cinema: The Cinematic Imaginary After Film*, Cambridge, MA and London: MIT Press.

Weidenbaum, M. (2006), 'Serial Port: A Brief History of Laptop Music', *New Music Box*, http://www.newmusicbox.org/articles/Serial-Port-A-Brief-History-of-Laptop-Music (accessed 20 September 2012).

Weinbren, G. (n.d.), 'Navigating the Ocean of Streams of Story', http://www.guggenheim.org/images/content/pdf/new_york/ocean of streams.pdf (accessed 22 July 2013).

Welch, C. (1995), *Eternal Network: A Mail Art Anthology*, Calgary: University of Calgary.

Werbach, K. (2008), 'The Implications of Video Peer-to-Peer on Network Usage', in E. Noam and L. M. Pupillo (eds), *Peer-to-Peer Video: The Economics, Policy, and Culture of Today's New Mass Medium*, New York: Springer Science + Business Media.

Wiener, N. (1961 [1948]), *Cybernetics, or, Control and Communication in the Animal and the Machine* (2nd edn), Cambridge, MA: MIT Press.

Wilson, E. O. (1998), *Consilience: The Unity of Knowledge*, New York: Alfred A. Knopf.

Wilson, S. (1993), 'The Aesthetics and Practice of Designing Interactive Computer Events', *SIGGRAPH 93 Visual Proceedings Art Show Catalog*, http://userwww.sfsu.edu/swilson/papers/interactive2.html (accessed 30 October 2013).

—(2002), *Information Arts: Intersections of Art, Science, and Technology*, Cambridge, MA: MIT Press.

Wolf, S. (2010), *The Digital Eye: Photographic Art in the Electronic Age*, Munich: Prestel.

Yi, K. (2008), 'Mining a Web2.0 Service for the Discovery of Semantically Similar Terms: A Case Study with Del.icio.us', in G. Buchanan, M. Masoodian and S. J. Cunningham (eds), *Digital Libraries: Universal and Ubiquitous Access to Information*, Heidelberg: Springer-Verlag.

Youngblood, G. (1970), *Expanded Cinema* (1st edn), New York: E. P. Dutton & Co.

Zolberg, V. (2003), '"An Elite Experience for Everyone": Art Museums, the Public, and Cultural Literacy', in D. Sherman and I. Rogoff (eds), *Museum Culture: Histories, Discourses, Spectacles*, London: Taylor & Francis, pp. 49–65.

INDEX